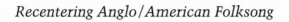

Recentering Anglo/American Folksong

Recentering Anglo/American Folksong

SEA CRABS AND WICKED YOUTHS

Roger deV. Renwick

University Press of Mississippi   *Jackson*

www.upress.state.ms.us

Publication of this book made possible in part by a University Cooperative Society Subvention Grant awarded by The University of Texas at Austin.

09 08 07 06 05 04 03 02 01   4 3 2 1

⊗

Library of Congress Cataloging-in-Publication Data

Renwick, Roger deV., 1941–

    Recentering Anglo/American folksong : sea crabs and wicked youths / Roger deV. Renwick.

      p. cm.

    Includes bibliographical references and index.

    ISBN 1-57806-393-0 (cloth : alk. paper)

    1. Folk songs, English—Great Britain—History and criticism. 2. Folk songs, English—United States—History and criticism.

ML3545 .R46   2001

782.42'1622—dc21   2001022618

British Library Cataloging-in-Publication Data available

CONTENTS

FOREWORD

This book explores a topic that not too many years ago was favored in folklore scholarship but that has now declined significantly from its privileged position: Anglo/American folksong.[1] To my mind the most lamentable corollary of this decline has been a waste of the huge data banks of anglophone folksong texts and tunes that serious field-collecting built up in the British Isles over the two hundred or so years before 1950, in North America over the first fifty years of the last century. Because these data could not easily be fit into the "new directions" that post-1970 theoretical models demanded, we turned our backs on them, with the result that thousands of texts now lie neglected in archives, books, even sound recordings.

I hope the essays that follow can stimulate folklorists to rediscover this extraordinarily rich body of material. I do not propose yet another "new direction," nor do I advocate that we "reinvent" ourselves. Indeed, I have no particular theoretical axe to grind; I urge only that we take as our mission the task of explaining, not "expressive enactments," not "cultural processes," but *folksong*. To do so in an effective, convincing, and collective way we must "recenter" our studies in the materials that once gave us great strength but that we self-defeatingly abandoned in an obsessive search for new ideas at the expense of seeking truly to understand our subject matter.

While many—perhaps all—of the people who helped me in one way or another might disclaim loyalty to the particular points of view, attitudes, values, axioms, and so forth advanced in the following pages, most I think share my love of the material and, probably, the hope that, as a subject of study and writing, its popularity will increase. My thanks, then, to C. J. Bearman, Vic Gammon, Joseph C. Hickerson, Roger Janelli, John Minton, Elliott Oring, Bob and Jacqueline Patten, Peter Robson, Steve

Roud, Hugh Shields, Gary Smith, and Yvette Staelens. Special thanks go to Chris Heppa, who took an unusually keen interest in my work and who supplied me both with needed song texts and with critical ideas.

For translations of non-English material, I'm indebted to Jeffrey Barnouw, Moyra Byrne, John Sotter Kolsti, and Mrs. Elis Uka Suhartini. Institutions that were of immense help were, first and foremost, the Vaughan Williams Memorial Library of the English Folk Dance and Song Society in London, through its librarian, Malcolm Taylor; the University of Virginia's Alderman Library through its head of public services, Heather Moore; and the University of North Carolina at Chapel Hill's Archives of Folklore through its archivist Michael Taft. For permission to reprint song texts I'm extremely grateful to Lance Bertelsen for allowing reproduction of "The Crab" from his *The Nonsense Club: Literature and Popular Culture, 1749–1764* (London: Oxford University Press, 1986); to Robin Morton for "Roll Me from the Wall" from his copyrighted book, *Folksongs Sung in Ulster* (Cork: Mercier Press, 1970—soon to be reprinted); to the Canadian Museum of Civilization for "The Bonavist Line," "Grandfather Bryan," and "Olden Days" from Kenneth Peacock's *Songs of the Newfoundland Outports* (3 vols. Ottawa: National Museum of Man, 1965); to Roy Palmer for "The Lobster" from *Everyman's Book of British Ballads* (London: J. M. Dent, 1981; reprinted in 1998 as *A Book of British Ballads* by Llanerch Publishers of Felinfach); to Charles L. Perdue, archivist of the Virginia Folklore Society, for "William, William, I love you well . . ."; to Andy Rouse for "A crabbefishe was ther . . ."; and to the University of Texas at Austin's Center for American History for "The Rambling Boy" from John A. Lomax's papers.

INTRODUCTION

"I have yet to find an approach to folksong from which I have not learned something," D. K. Wilgus first wrote over thirty-five years ago (1964: 39). Only someone who found folksong deeply absorbing would have made that claim, and Wilgus indeed was such a person: he possessed a huge collection of field tapes and sound recordings of Anglo/American folksong that he seemed to know intimately and exhibited just as much detailed familiarity with published collections. He also labored for years constructing two thorough, wide-ranging databases, one of anglophone Irish ballads, the other of ballads from the whole British/North American English-speaking continuum. Believing folksongs to be worthy in their own right, therefore, he was naturally drawn to any analytical perspective that revealed something of serious interest about them, whether the insight was to their history, to their form, to their significance, or to their purpose. He illustrated majestically the depth and breadth of his attachment as well as commitment to the subject with his definitive intellectual history of *Anglo-American Folksong Scholarship Since 1898* (Wilgus 1959).

Wilgus wasn't the only scholar deeply loyal to the study of Anglo/American folksong when he wrote the above words. At the University of California at Berkeley, Bertrand Harris Bronson was bringing together in a four-volume work, decades in the making, a huge number of English-language texts-with-tunes of a Pan-European genre we call the "Child ballad" (Child [1882–98] 1963; Bronson 1959–72). Tristram Potter Coffin had just updated his *British Traditional Ballad in North America* delineating patterns in story-change that New World singers of traditional songs made in *their* versions of the self-same Child ballads, as indicated mostly by the published record (Coffin 1963). G. Malcolm Laws Jr. had just revised his *Native American Balladry*, which along with its companion *American Balladry from British Broadsides*, codified the Anglo-North American repertoire of folksongs exhibiting a different set of compositional conventions, those characterizing a newer "broadside ballad" type (Laws 1957; [1964] 1975).

Wilgus and his mid-twentieth-century contemporaries like Bronson, Coffin, and Laws exhibited a common purpose in constructing their folksong reference works: they expected their publications to facilitate a host of detailed, focused, analytically rich case studies, comparable to what, beginning more than half a century earlier, Child's own volumes had stimulated. To that end each tried to encompass the whole population of his subject matter and so canvased an enormous number of song texts, eventually bringing them—or at least synopses of them, or references to them—together in a single, accessible location, saving future scholars much time in simple example-gathering. More than that, though, each tried to systematize the vast, scattered, even piecemeal data by constructing categories, templates, paradigms, unique code letters and numbers, all of which would constitute a common frame of reference for folksong scholars. Such an apparatus was considered essential for the continued growth of a shared, corporate, ongoing, accumulative, disciplined enterprise, the study of Anglo/American folksong.

The effect of all this devoted work was the legacy now at folklorists' command. Today we not only have huge inventories of Anglo/American folksongs, published and unpublished, that even earlier generations of data-gatherers produced over a roughly two-hundred year span—at first in the British Isles (starting as early as the first half of the eighteenth century but gaining real momentum after the publication of Bishop Percy's *Reliques of Ancient English Poetry* in 1765), later in North America as well (starting in the early twentieth century)—but we also possess systematic frames of reference organizing those data banks into databases for serious, coordinated analysis and interpretation.

But those folksong data banks and databases, which by 1970 were set to enable a flood of productive scholarship similar to that let loose by Child's work in an earlier generation, instead found themselves very quickly cold-shouldered and unused. Certainly, some fine case studies that probably couldn't have been completed without them have appeared—for example, David Buchan's *Ballad and the Folk* (1972), Flemming G. Andersen's *Commonplace and Creativity* (1985), William

Bernard McCarthy's *The Ballad Matrix* (1990)—while Britain's *Folk Music Journal* continues to publish shorter, essay-length analyses grounded in the classic Anglo/American traditional song repertory. Moreover, a few scholars have maintained strong dedication to the traditional textual resources and continued to produce work of high quality— Barre Toelken in the United States (for example, Toelken 1995), David Atkinson in Britain (for example, Atkinson 1995; 1999). And indeed new databases consistent with the models of Child, Laws, and their kin continue to be constructed (Preston n.d.; Roud 1974a–present; 1974b– present; Waltz and Engle n.d.–present).

Still, within the context of the supra-discipline, folklore, the number of analytical and interpretive studies of Anglo/American folksong, book-length as well as article-length, is small, and their wider intellectual impact, minor in Great Britain, is minute in the United States. Meanwhile, the great published song collections of England, Scotland, Ireland, Canada, and the United States, as well as the basic reference works of Bronson, Coffin, Laws, and their kind, not only are long out of print but languish unborrowed in library stacks, while probably just as much unpublished data lies unsought-out in archives. Judging from the paucity of their citing in current scholarship, even the newer electronic databases are severely underused.

It's no mystery why folklorists, even many dedicated folksong specialists, apparently lost long-held interest—or in the case of younger scholars, failed to develop new interest—in all that material, especially in North America: their loyalty was captured by novel epistemologies and intellectual imperatives into whose requirements the existing Anglo/ American folksong data could not readily be configured. Differences between the pre-1970 and post-1970 ways of thinking, multifaceted but interrelated, are too well-known to bear detailed discussion here. They include such aspects as pre-1970 emphasis on the normalized, even canonized "ideal type" that scholars somewhat arbitrarily determined constituted folksong vs. post-1970 "realist" emphasis on what people actually sang and listened to—which was often not the same material at all (Porter 1993); pre-1970 elevation in the analyst's hierarchy of values of song words and music in and of themselves vs. post-1970 elevation of the people—their experiences, circumstances, thoughts, attitudes—who supplied those artifacts (Boyes 1986); a "textual" sensibility that assumes songs constitute a (somewhat) self-contained system with its own internal rules of form and meaning vs. an "ethnographic" sensibility that puts great causal emphasis on songs' historically-determined contexts; an orientation toward reifying folksongs into tangible "products" vs. a preference for conceptualizing one's subject matter as a fluid, amorphous practice—"singing activity"; a tendency to conceive of songs as the collective, normative possession of a community of people (hence to privilege the similarity among and reproduction of traditional material) as opposed to conceiving of them as expressions of specifically situated individuals (hence privileging difference among, emergence in, even uniqueness of traditional materials); a bias toward seeking cultural homogeneity among the people whose songs one chooses to study (for example, "Anglo-American") as opposed to a sensitivity to and understanding of diversity (Greenhill 1997); a tendency to romanticize (the past, "tradition," "the folk," even "folksong" itself) that effects an imaginary *construction* of the object of study rather than *representing* it with critical self-awareness; a concomitant pre-1970 belief that a folklorist can be "objective" in describing and explaining what is actually "out there" vs. a post-1970 assumption that the observer is inevitably subjective and so actively participates in creating the object of study; a pre-1970 supposed insensitivity to what is, when all's said and done, the folklorist's reactionary undermining of the well-being of the people whose songs he or she studies as opposed to a post-1970 "progressive" urge to aid their empowerment and greater human fulfillment.

The list could easily be extended. But for our purposes, the result is obvious: folklorists today have on their hands a huge mass of both raw and organized data, gathered under the pre-1970 way of thinking, going to waste because it's incompatible with the post-1970 way of thinking. The study of Anglo/American folksong, especially in this country, has been more or less "erased," the raison d'être of few papers and virtually no panels at American Folklore Society annual meetings; internationally, it's become at the very least "ghettoized," found for instance only in small, cutoff, uninfluential communities like the International Ballad Commission. Increasingly it seems that the same fate may very well be in store for the supra-discipline, folklore itself.

*   *   *

While many onetime as well as might-have-been folksong scholars responded to the intellectual demands of the post-1970 mentality by abandoning the traditional Anglo/American folksong databases in favor of more personally rewarding subject matter, some have stuck with the material but brought to it new perspectives. For example, some students of folksong have shifted to a "meta" level of analysis and turned intellectual historian: their topics then become the ideologies, premises, theories, and methods of the ancestors who produced the data banks and databases we have in such profusion today. Typically, however, practitioners of such studies stigmatize the work of earlier folksong scholars (for example, Boyes 1993; Harker 1985; Palmer 1996; Webb 1992); consequently, they ultimately differ little from the cease-and-desist proponents just mentioned, since they essentially sanction the jettisoning of our inherited folksong resources.

Other folksong analysts have turned to hitherto untried theoretical perspectives consistent with "new directions." As this strategy customarily works, one selects a theory informed by post-1970 epistemology and, in deductive fashion, shows just how some set of data from the existing folksong resources fits that theory. In Britain, for example, Marxist-historicism has been particularly popular with folksong scholars (see Porter 1991), while in North America models of deconstructive "defamiliarization"—gender studies, for example—have been more enticing sources of inspiration (for example, Greenhill 1995). But like the first strategy of ancestor bashing, this strategy of theory borrowing, however promising in appearance, in effect hasn't reinvigorated Anglo/American folksong study as a scholarly specialty either.

One prominent reason for this lack of success is, I think, a common weakness in the particular style of theory borrowing and the deductive brand of reasoning that follows: such studies tend to be totalitarian rather than selective or integrative. Folklorists too often force their data into the preformed molds of the borrowed theory rather than, as in the ideal of deduction, looking for data that would falsify the theory's major premises (for example, Preston 1992). Such practices I call "hypertheorizing" when the act of theorizing rather than the illuminating of some body of data becomes the investigation's chief rationale.

An example of such an instance is, indeed, the stimulus for chapter 1 of this work, where I try to show that a particular folksong study began by taking for granted what in fact had to be proved: that a theory of creoli-zation explained a certain body of anglophone folksong materials. I mus-ter quite a bit of evidence to show that it does no such thing. In short, just like other responses of abandonment and repudiation, retheorizing—and especially hypertheorizing—has not proved the best model for restoring folksong study to what I think is its deserved position in our pantheon of valued enterprises.

While some of these newer analytical strategies may on the surface seem to be consistent with D. K. Wilgus's eclectic claim that all approaches to folksong teach us something worthwhile, the fact remains that neither ancestor bashing nor hypertheorizing has worked—or shows any signs of working—to the advantage of Anglo/American folksong study. A better, qualitatively distinct strategy, one in more perfect har-mony with the Wilgus sensibility, requires us first of all to recenter our attention in the remarkable folksong data that once we found so fruitful and that provided us with a heightened sense of mission; from that criti-cal beginning we can pursue any direction in which the material leads us in our attempt to understand it. Of course, many of us will first need to accomplish some attitude engineering: for example, repress our thirst for the status consequent upon being thought au courant and cutting edge, or resist market-based impulses to go with what sells, or transcend our late-twentieth-century infatuation with newness for its own sake, since all of these drives, I suspect, have contributed to the severe devaluation of our Anglo/American folksong data banks, perhaps just as much as has our craving for intellectual gratification. What I envisage is the revitaliza-tion of an Anglo/American folksong community of scholars who, like their forebears, will *like* folksong and take pride in the texts our predeces-sors so cherished and left in legacy to us (rather than be ashamed of them), who will recognize what an enormous asset they do in fact repre-sent, and who will dedicate themselves to finding out whatever it is of interest that *the songs* have to say rather than using them as convenient, however ill-suited, vehicles for what *we* want to say.

It is in the D. K. Wilgus spirit, then, that the essays to follow were written. Each starts out with some set of Anglo/American folksong mate-rial and tries to see how it fits into larger contexts that *directly* inform or are informed by it. I draw upon any epistemological, theoretical, or methodological principles that can aid me in this task of gestalt-building, whether idealist or realist, pre-postmodern or postmodern, text-centered or performance-centered. The first essay addresses what I consider a paradigmatic instance of how we Anglo/American folksong scholars lost our way in the post-1970s era: it demonstrates that even the best of folklorists can produce an unconvincing, invalid study when he's insensitive to the wealth of our folksong data banks, to the benefits of comparative textual analysis, and to the circularity inherent in "hypertheorizing"—that is, the valorizing of theory making that willy-nilly denigrates the importance, even integrity, of textual data. The remaining essays are all informed by a similar sensibility and set of procedures. In each case, I try to hear the folksong materials' own "voice" rather than using them as a convenient mouthpiece for a dogma I've learned in some other context or find personally compelling: we can liberate that voice only by engaging in comparative analysis of *large* samples and by reasoning *both* inductively and deductively.

Thus the second essay tries to reconstruct the traditional varieties of a single Anglo/American ballad by looking at practically all of its published and many of its unpublished versions; the most interesting patterns emerge in the difference between a British and British diasporic eighteenth-century form of the song on the one hand and a Southern American post–Civil War oikotype (a regionally distinctive form of a more widely distributed item) on the other. Hence both the old folkloristics concern with *variation* and the "new directions" concern with multicultural diversity gain expression. The third study, again highly inductive in approach, sees so many recurring patterns in a large number of Anglo/American folksongs that it proposes we recognize the existence of a very old, extremely widespread, perhaps tacitly felt but certainly never before formalized trans-Atlantic (probably even transcultural) genre, the *catalogue*. Once again, however, sensitivity to realist need for some reference to behavioral, "native" awareness of what an "idealist" approach has reified is not lacking.

If we're to recenter our studies in a canon of Anglo/American song, then it's important that canonical items be recognized accurately, and chapter 4 addresses this matter by also treating a topic previously unrecognized: not a genre this time, but more modestly a particular ballad that I call "Oh, Willie." Though often collected from Anglo-American tradition bearers, the song has not been identified as a distinct composition in any of our databases. The final chapter takes us beyond the boundaries of Anglo/American songs like "The Rambling Boy" of chapter 2 and "Oh, Willie" of chapter 4 into certain relationships the genre bears to international tale tradition, examining the global appearance of a naughty story that, recorded as a prose piece as early as the fourteenth century, first appeared in mid-seventeenth-century England as a song that's still sung in Britain and America today. I end the case study of this "Crabfish" ditty with the most context-sensitive attention I'm capable of: I look at an event that took place in the summer of 1904, when a working-class rural mother and housewife from Somerset in the West of England sang the song to her country's most eminent folksong collector. Once again, however, the continuities, both in the data and in the informing analytical apparatus the folklorist employs, are of paramount interest, and I end by discussing the links this single performance bears both to the story's regionally distinctive manifestations and to its globally common tradition.

Recentering Anglo/American Folksong

I

On Theorizing Folksong

Child Ballads in the West Indies

As folklorists increasingly attempt to address their current crisis of identity by, for example, adopting the terminology of other disciplines (we seldom seem to "collect folklore" any more, for instance, but instead "do ethnography") and by striving mightily to be considered progressive (so that insistent "theorizing" of every aspect of our discipline is all the rage), we find ourselves paradoxically becoming less respected rather than more. It doesn't make sense. After all, if we're employing the same terminology ("discourse," "representation," "site[s] of contestation"), addressing the same issues ("authenticity," "sexuality," "power"), and drawing upon the same sources of intellectual inspiration (Foucault, Bakhtin, Bourdieu), why can't we enjoy the same prestige as colleagues who align themselves with, say, the suddenly cachet-laden "cultural studies"? Folklore's malaise seems particularly intense in its subfield of Anglo/American folksong, which was once a highly favored child in the discipline's family but now seems to enjoy little prestige—indeed, not even much presence.

The cause of Anglo/American folksong study's semi-"erasure" is almost certainly multifaceted and complex, and I couldn't hope to answer it myself, but I do think that I have some insight into one aspect of it: we've abandoned the comparative sensibility that, while not unique to our discipline of course, was one of our greatest strengths. This strength—and the accompanying identity and, yes, even respect we gained from it—not only flowed organically from what is a truly defining feature of our folksong subject matter, its variability, but also was rooted in our fortunate possession of, first, large data banks of material available-for-study and, second, incomparable reference works like *The English and Scottish Popular Ballads* (Child [1882–98] 1963), *Native American Balladry* (Laws [1964] 1975), and more recently, the *Folksong Index* and the *Broadside Index* (Roud 1994b–present; 1994a–present) organizing, codifying, and making accessible those huge stores of data with which we're so blessed.

When we neglect the necessity for comparative awareness, ignore our magnificent data banks of folksong that not only evidence its wide dissemination and variability but also provide factual checks on fanciful speculation, and disproportionately valorize the act of "theorizing" to the point of what I've called "hypertheorizing," we run the risk both of being false to our subject matter and, concomitantly, of yet further distancing ourselves from a common identity. In my opinion, even one of America's very best and deservedly renowned folklorists, Roger D. Abrahams, produced these very results in his work on Child ballads in West Indian singing tradition: he proved so eager to theorize folksong that he privileged explanatory concepts to the extent of virtually ignoring comparative data (Abrahams 1987: 101–34). Over the past four decades Abrahams's contributions to a vast range of folkloristic knowledge, including Anglo/American folksong, have been enormous, but in this case hypertheorizing effected a study exhibiting neither much validity nor much heuristic value.

The study's general goal was to explain the special nature of ballad performances by Afro-Caribbean singers in the once colonial territory known as the British West Indies, especially in the islands of St. Vincent (in the Windward Islands group) and Nevis (in the Leeward Islands). The author concentrated on three aspects of such performances: the kinds of social occasions most congenial to ballad singing (these were primarily events at which several competing voices vied for the spotlight, such as tea meetings—which are like amateur concerts—and burial wakes); the interpersonal attitudes and postures evinced by ballad-performance participants (chiefly—no surprise—"contestative"); and the form and content of ballad texts. As was and continues to be true in Anglo/American folksong scholarship, it was on this third aspect of folklore performance, ballad textualization, that the essay spent most of its analytical resources.

As for the study's theoretical underpinnings, two constructs provided the main explanatory principles: one was the importance of what the author called (à la Bakhtin, though more figuratively than literally) the *marketplace* locale of Caribbean ballad performances. As a social setting, the *marketplace* is characterized as more heterogeneous, permeable, and fluid than settings typical in the "folk community" of conventional depiction; the expressive productions of its habitues are more open to nonindigenous influences as well as more "polyphonic" in that several distinct voices and agendas might vie simultaneously for audience attention.

The second, far more important explanatory construct for the textual form Child ballads attained in the British West Indies was creolization, signifying very simply the merging of at least two distinctive cultural systems (Abrahams 1983: 26). So, for example, a West Indian *cante-fable*, "Matty Glow and Garoleen"—in which a talking parrot, carrying news of a wife's infidelity to her absent husband, loudly broadcasts the scandalous events to all and sundry along its route—was a local adaptation of the three-hundred-plus-year-old British ballad "Little Musgrave and Lady Barnard" (Child 81; Roud 52) that illustrated a "creole" merging of African Caribbean cultural preferences and an Old World content: British Isles culture had provided the basic plot of unfaithful wife and vengeful husband, while Afro-Caribbean culture had substituted an animal messenger for the British human one and made what in the British form was a private family matter into a loudly public one. A similar analysis was made of three other Child ballad texts collected from Afro-Caribbean singers in 1960s St. Vincent and Nevis: "The Maid Freed from the Gallows" (Child 95; Roud 144), "Bonny Barbara Allan" (Child 84; Roud 54), and "Our Goodman" (Child 274; Roud 114).

I strongly suspect that, in thinking through his material for this essay, Abrahams worked deductively: he began with the theory of creolization and, confining himself to his collected West Indian material, mapped onto his preformulated theory whatever features of that material seemed to "fit." Here, I'll approach the subject differently: I adopt a comparative awareness in employing the sizable body of Anglo/American folksong data that previous generations of folklorists have made available to us and eschew the urge to privilege theorizing. I'll look at all four of the West Indian items, compare them with their related anglophone cognates, and eventually argue that many Anglo-British and Anglo-North American versions of the same or closely related Child ballads—

occasionally, even Continental European versions—evince the *very same kinds of textual adaptations* that occur in Afro-Caribbean culture. I think the result will cast great doubt on the usefulness of "creolization" as an explanatory construct—at least for ballad study.

I'll start with "Maid Freed from the Gallows," which was collected from Nora Bristol of Richland Park, St. Vincent, some time in the early 1960s and which like so many West Indian renditions of traditional narratives (not only ballads but also legends, fairy tales, fables, and others) is in *cante-fable* form (Abrahams 1987: 127–9). Much of Nora Bristol's story parallels that of "Maid's" normative anglophone tradition, common in both Old World and New: the relatives to whom the condemned narrator appeals sequentially for ransom money, and hence for deliverance from the gallows, are mother, sister, brother, and sweetheart. Of course, in Anglo versions the father usually participates in this "climax of relatives," as the trope is sometimes called, but the creolization analysis does not consider his absence from the Vincentian text significant, possibly because he is also absent from several Anglo versions (#20 from Dorset, #32 and #58 from Appalachia, in Bronson 1959–72: 2: 456, 460, 471). Other somewhat distinctive features of this West Indian "Maid" are (1) that none of the relatives, not even the sweetheart, has brought ransom money and (2) that the condemned narrator is male rather than female, but these traits too are not considered "creole," probably because, once again, they appear often in the ballad's wider singing tradition, particularly in Anglo-American versions—often enough, in fact, to gain recognition in *The British Traditional Ballad in North America* as markers of distinct story types: Type C (male protagonist) and Type D (no ransom from sweetheart; see Coffin 1977: 92).

What the creolization analysis *does* consider significant in Nora Bristol's version is a motif that is indeed quite striking and unusual: the appearance of a *second* sweetheart, one who had been earlier discarded for a new lover. The current lover brings no ransom, while the former one does. But the author's explanation for this unusual motif is that the singer herself introduced it as reflective of her own circumstances: Nora Bristol was an older woman, for the moment unattached romantically and in fact seeking a mate. Thus, in her version of Child 95 she assigned to a fictional counterpart of herself a heroine's role as the young man's savior.

Apparently, then, the substitution of content from personal experience for a received, older content is a "creole" practice.[1] But this phenomenon is so common in Anglo ballad singing, especially among more creative or in some way individualistic bearers of tradition, that Eleanor Long has coined for its perpetrators a special name, "confabulators" (Long 1973). Phillips Barry made a similar generalization about Anglo singing conventions: "Back of the ballad," he wrote, "is always the ballad-singer, who constantly intrudes his critical personality" (Barry 1936: 16). Indeed, Barry characterized one such confabulation of the selfsame "Maid Freed from the Gallows" as a "regressed infantile type recovered . . . from tradition in Maine. . . . The array of relatives who pass in succession through the drama includes parental siblings and grandparents, four of the last. . . . [I]t is 'the other grandmother' who finally saves the little heroine from hanging" (Barry 1961: 64). In fact, even Nora Bristol's two-lovers motif may not be as idiosyncratic as it seems: an African American prose version of the story from Missouri also features two lovers, a current beau who won't save the heroine and a former suitor who will (Barry, Eckstorm, and Smyth 1929: 211).[2]

Creolization theory also considers the Caribbean attraction to multigeneric forms to be important evidence in its favor—in particular, the attraction to composite or hybrid genres, as in the intermingling of prose and poetry, or of verbal and kinesic codes, or of recitation and music, all of which are presumably syncretisms that parallel the convergence of the macro-culture's African and European influences. Hence Nora Bristol's "Maid Freed from the Gallows" is of interest as a creole product not only because of its content but also because it's in *cante-fable* form, as indeed are several other West Indian versions (for example, Jekyll [1907] 1966: 58–9). But a *cante-fable* version of "Maid" is also common in Anglo British and North American traditions, usually cited by folklorists as "the golden ball" type (Coffin 1977: 92–4; 243–4). In fact, Anglo tradition has brought yet a third genre, drama, into the "Maid's" fold: "A few years ago," wrote Lucy E. Broadwood in 1915, "I noted down from old Mrs. Thompson, a cottager at Churchtown, in the old part of Southport, a description of 'The Golden Ball' as acted by herself when a young girl, with her companions, in her uncle's cart-house, and also by grown-up people in the schoolroom at Blowick . . . when she was about eleven" (*Journal of the Folk-Song Society* 1915: 5: 233). While we have no reports of British West Indians dramatizing "Maid Freed from the Gallows," we do know that African Americans acted out the ballad in the southern United States, a merging which could possibly be used to support ballad creolization theory (Scarborough 1925: 39). But the fact remains that those two examples, the African American one and the English Mersey-side one, are clearly similar composites, indicating that the British were just as capable of blending genres as were West Indians.

A second British West Indian version of a Child ballad analyzed from a creolization perspective is "Bonny Barbara Allan" (Abrahams 1987: 115). The text, as sung by Maybelle Simmonds of Nevis, a bit north of St. Vincent but in the Leeward Islands group, is five stanzas long. It begins with Barbara's "going along the road," hearing the church bells, and meeting the funeral cortege. In stanza 2, she asks that the coffin be laid down and she be allowed to view the corpse. In stanza 3, she addresses the (apparently) dead suitor, saying that although her kiss may yet save him, she still won't grant one. In stanza 4, Barbara asserts that a young man died for her today, she herself may die tomorrow. Stanza 5 repeats 3: no kiss, no saving.

There's nothing obvious in those five stanzas that's not found throughout the anglophone tradition of "Barbara Allan," but the analysis specifies two attributes of Maybelle Simmonds's rendition that exemplify "creolization": first, much of the usual "Barbara Allan" narrative—the summons to the dying swain's sickbed, for instance, or the face-to-face dialogue between the one-time sweethearts—has disappeared, resulting in a song that's more lyric than ballad; and second, what little story appears is told in first person. But again, both kinds of variation (if that's what they are; my own analysis obviously implies that they could just as easily have been already present in the received British version) are so common in Anglo traditions of both Old and New Worlds that they're virtually ballad-theory cliches. The movement from more narrative to more lyric certainly is, as Abrahams himself acknowledges: it's the thesis of one of the more famous scholarly essays on the genre, Tristram Potter Coffin's " 'Mary Hamilton' and the Anglo-American Ballad as an Art Form," which employed the phrase that has become a staple analytical construct in ballad study, "emotional core" (Coffin 1957). Indeed, "lyricization" has been canonized in Tom Burns's list of textual variations typical of Anglo/American folksong tradition, as in fact has been "personification," a second feature the essay under discussion associates with "creolization," as exemplified by the Nevitian text's apparent switch to a first-person *participant* narrator, Barbara herself, which contrasts with the more usual third-person and first-person *nonparticipant* narrators.

At least three Anglo texts of "Barbara Allan" in Bronson's *Traditional Tunes of the Child Ballads* seem to me fully as lyrical as the Nevis one, however. Moreover, these come from both sides of the Atlantic and from both printed and oral tradition, suggesting that the feature is not peculiar to one facet of song transmission but is pervasive. The printed texts are from a Manchester broadside of the late eighteenth century and from a nineteenth-century American songster (Bronson 1959–72: 2: 326 [#3]; 329–30 [#15]). Most lyrical is perhaps the oral version, sung by a Mr. Rew of Sidbury, Devonshire, in the 1950s (Bronson 1959–72: 2: 327 [#6]). As for personification, we find all possible permutations of voice in presumably noncreole Anglo cultures. After third person, most common is first person nonparticipant narrator; but we find first-person participant narrators—as in the Caribbean text—as well, even the dying lover (though these texts do switch to third person once he's expired!). The Manchester broadside mentioned above as highly lyrical possesses this further supposedly creole feature of Barbara as first-person narrator, similar to Maybelle Simmonds's West Indian rendition. There's even a version told from *two* first-person participant-narrator points-of-view, Barbara *and* her spurned suitor; it was sung for Cecil Sharp by Lula McCoy of Chicopee County, Georgia, in 1914 (Bronson 1959–72: 2: 353 [#88]).[3] We even find for "Barbara Allan" examples of the generic hybridization that's so strongly associated with the creole concept: "In the first quarter of this century," wrote William Wells Newell in 1888, "this celebrated ballad was still used in New England as a children's game or dance at evening parties" (Newell [1903] 1963: 79). In short, the descendants of British settlers in Massachusetts, Vermont, New Hampshire, and their fellow states could evidently "creolize" with the best, combining the ballad of "Barbara Allan" with at least two other genres.[4]

"Our Goodman" is a third British ballad given in the essay under discussion (Abrahams 1987: 116–8). It's perhaps the most popular of the few Child ballads that entered Caribbean repertoires, but it's also one that's varied the least textually. In the version used to support the creolization hypothesis (collected from Ruth Hanley of Nevis), the wife mocks her husband in the most British of terms: he is a "blind bat" and a "silly billy." The objects this West Indian husband finds in his home are a walking stick, a man in his chamber, a horse, and a watch, which the wife explains away as a candlestick, a counterpane, a chambermaid, and a frying pan. Most of these objects have their analogues in white versions, and none is in any meaningful sense Caribbean or even tropical, for that matter. The analysis is not specific on what's particularly creole-like about the Nevitian text, only characterizing the song as generally "embodying contention" in its depiction of the husband/wife dialogue; but since "contention" literally defines the story of "Our Goodman" in *all* its manifestations, regardless of the local culture's ethnic particularities, it cannot be considered oikotypal. Indeed, A. L. Lloyd might have said that this feature defines the very type *ballad* itself (1967: 147).

While the text of "Our Goodman" may not vary significantly in Caribbean tradition, its generic form certainly does: like most anglophone versions, Ruth Hanley's is all song, but in Elsie Clews Parsons's Bahamian collection we find a *cante-fable* rendition and even an all-prose one (Parsons 1918: 162–3). Once again, though, while this general plasticity of form is certainly more common in Afro-Caribbean and even African American cultures than in Anglo-based ones, as we've seen, those more "creolized" cultures haven't had a monopoly on the phenomenon, and they don't in the case of "Our Goodman" either: "The lace-makers of Vorey," Child writes in his headnote on the Continental French tradition of 274, "are wont to recite or sing this ballad winter evenings as a little drama. . . . So do the young girls in Lorraine during carnival . . . and the young fellows in Provence" (Child [1882–98] 1963: 5: 90). In fact, the Scottish Child A, from David Herd's manuscript and published in his *Ancient and Modern Scottish Songs* (1776) is in *cante-fable* form!

The fourth item, which Abrahams identifies as a version of Child 81 (Roud 52), "Little Musgrave and Lady Barnard," is the chief beneficiary of the essay's analytical attention. Three versions, all collected in St. Vincent, are given, all in *cante-fable* form and all telling a similar tale: while her husband is living and working away from home, a wife forms a sexual liaison with another man. The household pet, a parrot, makes a lengthy journey to inform the husband of the wife's infidelity. Accompanied by the parrot, the husband returns home, surprises the adulterers in bed together, and kills them both. The discussion of this *cante-fable* contains the most detailed and explicit depictions of West Indian "creolization": on one hand, the Caribbean *cante-fables* downplay (1) the act of adultery itself, (2) the confrontation between husband and lovers caught in flagrante delicto, and (3) the punishment administered to both wife and lover; on the other hand, they play up the messenger's publicizing of the private (however illicit) affair and substitute an animal—the parrot—for the very human tale-bearer in British and Anglo North American versions of Child 81/Roud 52, usually a servant or pageboy (Abrahams 1987: 120–6).

A comparative foray into our extensive Child ballad data banks, however, reveals that this analysis is a bit too facile. We're fortunate in having three other British West Indian versions of "Little Musgrave" ready to hand (all from Jamaica), and the first thing we see is that even though they come from an island with a culture very similar to that of both St. Vincent and Nevis, to none of them is this creole characterization applicable. In fact, all three emphasize exactly what presumably Anglocentric texts from Britain, Canada, and the United States do: the making of the love tryst and the angry husband's confronting of the lovers (Beckwith 1924a: 470–3; Leach 1963: 190–1). Moreover, the messenger in all three is a boy rather than a bird. And none spends any more time than do Anglo versions in dramatizing that messenger's journey and his repeated trumpeting of the adultery to everyone within earshot. In fact, the Jamaican singer William Forbes's versions (he performed "Musgrave" twice for Martha Warren Beckwith around 1920) don't even have the message-bearer as a character or the bearing of the message as an episode: the tattletale pageboy is mentioned in a single line, when Lady Barnard tells Musgrave that her husband may be approaching ("Fo' I t'ink I heah Lord Barnaby horn was blowin' so loud an' clear / Fo' I understan' dat little Footspeed can very well see an' can heah"). In other words, three of the six Caribbean texts are *less* creole-like than the majority of British and North American texts! Moreover, on the other side of the coin, we find that supposedly creole features are a staple in British versions of many other Child ballads: for example, we find talking birds in "Lady Isabel and the Elf-Knight" (Child 4; Roud 21), "Child Waters" (Child 63[C]; Roud 43), "Young Hunting" (Child 68; Roud 47), and "Johnie Cock" (Child 114 [F, H]; Roud 69), among others. In fact, many of these British ballad-birds (in

"Lady Isabel" and "Young Hunting," for example) are very much like the Vincentian *cante-fable* bird in that their ability and willingness to drag private family concerns into public view are integral to their characters and to their ballads' plots.[5]

All three of Abrahams's Vincentian versions and one of Martha Warren Beckwith's two Jamaican renditions were *cante-fables,* a generic hybridization that the published record does not reveal to have been associated with "Musgrave" in Anglo-American tradition and which, hence, could conceivably exemplify "creolization." But I'll argue by analogy in drawing attention to a remarkable version of the ballad that Ned Odell of Pinware, Labrador, sang for MacEdward Leach in the summer of 1960 that was about as proselike as a piece could be while remaining metrical and strophic. In Leach's transcription, ten stanzas have five lines, two have eight lines, two have three lines, one has seven, and one has six. The remaining seven stanzas are in the familiar ballad quatrain form (Leach 1965: 32–5). But in performance the text was in no way fragmented, incoherent, or discontinuous. "It is much better heard than read," the collector wrote. "The singer compensates for lack of rhyme, for uneven metre, and so builds the song as an unbroken continuity. Perhaps, it would be better to transcribe it without stanzaic breaks to try for the effect of the epic lay, really achieved by the singing." Leach went to say that "This ballad bears study as a mutation, for it suggests a possible method by which new narrative patterns or forms develop" (Leach 1965: 35). He might instead have said "creole patterns and forms develop," it seems to me, though I don't see how such a characterization would have heightened our understanding.

I think we can say with confidence, then, that when we look comparatively at the larger picture of a ballad's wider traditional manifestations, there is great similarity between, on the one hand, texts from Caribbean singers who are steeped in diverse cultural influences and whose ballads are said to reflect that diverseness and, on the other hand, texts from supposedly monocultural Scottish, English, and Anglo-North American singers. Recognition of this more solid empirical context must inevitably lead the creolist to some additional "theorizing," or perhaps "untheorizing": the creolist has no choice but to deduce either that (1) *all* cultures are in fact creole cultures, or that (2) neither a song's generic vehicle nor the tale it tells is terribly dependent on cultural influences. If the first conclusion is valid, then for ballad studies the creolization construct has no explanatory value at all and only a weak sort of descriptive value— "weak" because all it can do is very generally characterize the entire body of Child ballads; it cannot differentiate an eighteenth-century north of England version from a twentieth-century Eastern Caribbean one. If the second conclusion is valid, then the creolization construct has *neither* descriptive *nor* explanatory value, since the existence of cultural creolization itself has no necessarily distinctive effect on song texts.[6]

The urge to abandon folksong scholarship's traditional strength, comparative employment of its large data banks, and to valorize the act of theorizing for reasons that, to my mind, are often extrinsic to theory's true duty (explaining the subject matter) may promote still further errors in judgment and resulting weak arguments. One such is misidentification of the folklore item under discussion. By definition, creolization theory requires accurate identification of genetic ancestry, since it posits that inherited materials have been merged with, adapted to, and transformed by distinctive cultural systems. If the analyst assumes that a text under consideration has been creolized from a source item with which it in fact had minimal contact, then obviously his or her conclusions will be faulty, since the facts from which such conclusions were drawn are faulty. The chances are strong that Abrahams made that very error in identifying his three Vincentian "Matty Glow and Garoleen" *cantefables* as versions of "Little Musgrave and Lady Barnard."

When in 1986 I first read the "Child Ballads in the West Indies" essay I was immediately uneasy about the identification of the Vincentian song-story as a direct descendant of Child 81. Why? Initially, because I knew that "Little Musgrave" had been collected from British West Indian tradition before and that those three earlier Jamaican versions—the Beckwith and Leach versions mentioned above—were textually quite close to British forms. The Vincentian *cante-fable,* in contrast, displayed little textual resonance with those other Caribbean renditions of "Musgrave," and such great variation in a ballad's tradition within the same culture area and in the same general time period is rare. A better candidate for kinship, I felt, was the related but distinct Child 82/Roud 3972, "The Bonny Birdy," in which a talking bird journeys from home to tell a knight that his lady lies in another man's arms. Husband and bird return home together, where the lovers are discovered in bed and the male adulterer killed.

At the most concrete level of comparison, the actual language of the texts, the Vincentian "Matty Glow and Garoleen" exhibits no stronger, nor weaker, links with "Bonny Birdy" than it does with "Little Musgrave," but this is understandable, since the West Indian product is a *cante-fable*: most of its text is in prose, only a small portion of it in the more stable, less varying form of poetry. And even so the verse parts have all the appearance of ballad formulas and so can't be used convincingly as evidence of close genetic relationship: for example, the master, on receiving the bird's initial report, reacts with a variant of the "You lie, you lie" ballad formula found not only in both "Bonny Birdy" and "Little Musgrave" but also elsewhere (for example, Child 63C, "Child Waters" [Roud 43]; Child 86A, "Young Benjie" [Roud 3911]; Child 106A, "The Famous Flower of Serving-Men" [Roud 199]; Child 192E, "The Lochmaben Harper" [Roud 85]). And the West Indian *cante-fable*'s most striking portion, the sung verse containing the bird's warning, made as it approaches the house with the returning husband, that "If any man, if any man / In another man's home / It is time, it is time / For to rise and go home" (Abrahams 1987: 125), is matched equally by "Bonny Birdy's" " 'For he that's in bed wi anither man's wife / Has never long time to stay' " and "Little Musgrave's" "He that's in bed wi anither man's wife / 'Tis time he was awa" (Child 81G).

What about a second level of comparison, that of story told? In this aspect the *cante-fable*'s similarity with "Bonny Birdy" becomes sharper, as does its difference from "Little Musgrave." Most obvious is the matter of *dramatis personae*: the witness/messenger is a talking bird both in "Bonny Birdy" and in the Caribbean piece, but a human pageboy in all versions of "Musgrave." Of course, talking birds are common in both British Isles and British Caribbean folklore (see note 5), so to this similarity of motif we must add the further likeness that two characters, parrot and husband, dominate both the Vincentian "Matty Glow" and the Scottish "Bonny Birdy," while in "Musgrave" four characters possess extensive speaking and acting roles: not only the husband and the messenger, but also the two lovers. A similar parallel exists in setting: two settings— away from home, where the bird seeks and eventually meets his master, and at home, where the lovers sport, where the bird warns the man to leave, and where the husband commits his murder—dominate in "Matty Glow" and "Bonny Birdy," while "Musgrave" is more complex, featuring prominently the playhouse or church where the lovers plan their assignation in addition to the other locales.

Even more striking is a parallel in narrative technique: the Vincentian *cante-fable* and the Scottish ballad share a distinct economy of action— for example, developing the journey episodes while only alluding to the lovers' initiating their liaison—while "Musgrave" *habitually* draws out its many scenes, of Lady Barnard's initial seduction of Little Musgrave, of the confrontation between husband and lover, later between husband and wife. David Buchan, among others, sees these two techniques as distinct ways of telling a story. "Bonny Birdy" exemplifies what Buchan calls the "dramatic ballad" type, which "tend[s] to have a small number of tightly integrated scenes including one pronounced climactic scene, while the long narrative ballads tend to be in three Acts with some Acts incorporating a number of scenes, and to maintain a general balance among these scenes and Acts. . . . In short, the dramatic ballads tend to have a simple climbing construction, while the narrative ballads tend to have a more level, complicated construction" (Buchan 1972: 135). Both the West Indian *cante-fable* and "Bonny Birdy" quite clearly are of the "dramatic" type, "Little Musgrave" just as clearly of the "narrative" type.

As for the more abstract aspect of informing idea, or theme, here the Caribbean song-tale moves yet closer to "Bonny Birdy" and still further from "Little Musgrave." "Musgrave's" theme is clearly one of gender-and-marriage politics: who is empowered to control a woman's behavior, it asks, her husband or the woman herself? Lord Barnard seems to consider his wife just another material possession (even at times just a means of production), as evidenced both by his words to the pageboy-messenger—

"Is my castle burnt," he said,
"Or is my tower tane?
Or is my lady lighter yet,
Of a daughter or son?"
    (Child 81H)

—and, later, by his question to Musgrave:

"How do you love my soft pillow?
Or how do you love my sheets?
Or how do you love my fair lady,
That lies in your arms and sleeps?"
   (Child 81I)

Lady Barnard, on the other hand, displays her independence not only by taking the initiative in bringing a lover to bed in the first place but by responding to the lord's question to *her* that parallels his just-quoted question to Musgrave; although perfectly aware that her life depends on her answer, having just witnessed her lover chopped up for giving the wrong reply, she is uncowed and unpersuaded:

"Full well I love your cherry cheeks,
Full well I love your chin
But better I love little Sir Grove, where he lies,
Than you and all your kin."
   (Child 81I)

The West Indian *cante-fable*'s theme is quite different: the song-story is centered in the related concepts of sacrifice, obligation, and betrayal, all mirroring real life. Employment is scarce in rural Caribbean villages, and many working-class West Indian husbands must leave home to find work (often overseas), as is the case in "Matty Glow." Such a sacrifice on the part of a husband creates an obligation on the part of his wife to be faithful, among other things, but the wife in the *cante-fable* betrays that trust. The very same triad of themes informs "Bonny Birdy": the knight-husband has been forced to leave home on his quest (he couches this sac-rifice in strangely modern sentiments: "O what needs I toil night and day / My fair body to kill"), thus creating an obligation on his wife's part to suffer her own version of his ordeal by refusing lovers, an obligation she, like the Vincentian wife, fails to fulfill.

In sum, conclusions drawn about Vincentian variations of a British "Little Musgrave" stemming from creolization, marketization, and the imposition of an Afro-Caribbean worldview are highly suspect, since "Musgrave" and "Matty Glow" are very probably not the "same" item. Once "Matty Glow's" source is accurately identified, we see yet again that the supposed creolizations of the song-tale, such as the absence of husbands because of labor conditions, the animal messenger, that figure's elevation to main protagonist, the deemphasizing of both the confrontation between husband and adulterers and the subsequent revenge, the publicizing of private matters, and so on, were *already* prominent in the British source-ballad and so aren't even particularly West Indian! To repeat, failure to consult comparative data led to the mistake.

In fact, the author compounded that mistake by refusing to take comparative data seriously even after this deficiency in his study was pointed out. I myself did the pointing, in my capacity as one of the specialist readers who agreed to evaluate the essay in manuscript form when it was submitted to the *Journal of Folklore Research*. Abrahams did address my concerns in an endnote to his essay's eventual published version, where he wrote very graciously that "a reader of this paper . . . suggested that . . . the stories here are closer to the very rare 'Bonny Birdy' than to 'Little Musgrave.' " But he went on to reject the legitimacy of the parallel on the sole grounds that "the use of the name 'Matty Glow' in the Vincentian texts for the interloping male seems to argue against such an attribution" (Abrahams 1987: 133).

Those grounds, however, exhibit both theoretical and empirical weakness. First of all, change of names, whether of people or places, is just about the most pervasive kind of textual variation in the anglophone oral tradition of folksong. For instance, in North American tradition, "Lady Isabel and the Elf-Knight," "Earl Brand" (Child 7; Roud 23), "Lord Randal" (Child 12; Roud 10), "Fair Margaret and Sweet William" (Child 74; Roud 253), "The Famous Flower of Serving-Men," and "James Harris" (Child 243; Roud 14) all in one version or another identify their protagonist as "Sweet William," while "Sweet William's Ghost" (Child 77; Roud 50) and "Knight and the Shepherd's Daughter" (Child 110; Roud 67) call him "Sweet Willie"; the central figures of both "The Death of Queen Jane" (Child 170; Roud 77) and "The Brown Girl" (Child 295; Roud 180) are called "Queen Sally" (Coffin 1977). Indeed, two British versions of "Child Maurice" (Child 83E, F; Roud 53) call the husband of the woman our hero supposedly fancies (he's actually her son) "Lord Barnard," while in "Johnny Armstrong" (Child 169B; Roud 76) the footpage who carries news of her husband's death to the wife is called "Little Musgrave." I doubt most folklorists—Abrahams included—would really consider these shared names evidence of a close genetic link among the several ballads. As for empirical weakness in the name-similarity rationale, in his endnote the author errs in identifying the Vincentian *cante-fable* lover as "Matty Glow" and thus implicitly analogizing him with the lover of many American Lady Barnard-equivalents, "Matty Groves," for in all three Vincentian texts "Matty Glow" is actually the *wife's* name; the lover's name is "Garoleen." So even if the phonetic similarity between "Matty Groves" and "Matty Glow" had indicated a genetic link of wider scope than the sharing of a single ballad-motif, the significance of that connection would have been weakened considerably by the fact that the characters are quite different.[7]

It is, of course, possible that a devotee of creolization theory might consider my demonstration that many non-African influenced versions of Child ballads reveal characteristics much the same as the Caribbean ones to be proof of creolization theory's *strength* rather than, as I think it is, weakness. My comparative analysis, such a devotee might say, shows only how all-pervasive—and hence how compelling—is the process of creolization. It is, the creolist might say approvingly, a "transnational" theory, appropriate for an age of "globalization." He or she might point out that "Bonny Birdy," which has been collected only once from oral tradition (in Scotland, by Robert Jamieson from Mrs. Brown of Falkland in 1783), more than likely postdates "Little Musgrave," which was evidently well-known in England as early as 1611 or so (when it was quoted in Beaumont and Fletcher's *Knight of the Burning Pestle*) and which since then has been quite popular with both broadside printers and bearers of oral tradition; consequently—the creolist might continue—the similarity between the two British ballads suggests that the English "Little Musgrave" was remade in Scotland as "Bonny Birdy," just as it was, according to Abrahams, remade in St. Vincent as the *cante-fable* "Matty Glow and Garoleen." In short, the theory's adherents might explain "Bonny Birdy" as being "Little Musgrave" creolized in the syncretic Anglo-Celtic culture of eighteenth-century northeast Scotland. Put another way, creolization theory might claim that, at least as far as the Child ballad is concerned, Scotland is to England as St. Vincent is to Great Britain (I say Great Britain rather than England because such ballads could have come to the Caribbean from Scotland, England, or even Ireland).

At first encounter, this is an intriguing homology; let's pursue some logical extensions of it by looking at another—and far more widely known—talking parrot-witness ballad, "Lady Isabel and the Elf-Knight," one of the handful of British ballads of the Child type that, like "Maid Freed from the Gallows," "Bonny Barbara Allan," "Our Goodman," and "Little Musgrave and Lady Barnard," has been found in British West Indian oral tradition. Recall, first, that in its British and British North American tradition, "Lady Isabel" tells a fairly uniform story: the heroine steals her father's horses and money to run off with a lover who turns out to have murder, not romance, on his mind. She escapes by throwing the false lover into the sea, where he drowns. Isabel then mounts her horse to sneak home before her absence can be discovered, only to be confronted by the household's pet bird, a parrot, which threatens to tell the father about her escapade. She bribes the creature to keep silent.

As we know from Holger Olof Nygard's "Heer Halewijn" study, however, this concluding parrot episode is, in the European traditions of Child 4/Roud 21, peculiar to Britain, traveling from there to become normative in diasporic North American singing tradition; evidently an English bearer of tradition *added* it to a version crossing the Channel from France, a version that, as European renditions generally do, ended with the chastened girl's return home (Nygard 1958). It seems to me that creolization theory's reading of "Matty Glow's" *Afro-Caribbean* variation from its supposed *British* ancestor, "Little Musgrave," is strikingly like the *British* "Lady Isabel's" variation from its *French* ancestor: the role "of the message carrier is greatly expanded," the parrot "enters into the action only to stir things up," the creature "makes embarrassing private matters public by singing about them" (or threatens to until bribed into silence), and "in the main, his messages are unmotivated" (Abrahams 1987: 120). So this similarity leads us to a logical extension of our earlier homology: just as St. Vincent is to Great Britain, so Scotland is to England, and so England is to France. Once again a somewhat intriguing notion—that, as far as the Child ballad is concerned, British-Caribbean, Anglo-Celtic, and Anglo-Norman syncretisms may have something in common—though my own opinion, as I've already stated, is that if the "creolization" concept can be stretched so far, then its analytical and explanatory power is considerably weakened, since any Caribbean specificity represented in the "Matty Glow and Garoleen" song-tale is by now just about lost.

This weakness will become one not just of blandness but of illogic if we take a British West Indian version of "Lady Isabel" that Abrahams himself collected in Nevis in the 1960s and follow *its* logical ramifications for our growing homology (Abrahams 1968: 94–5). Since this text hasn't been analyzed from a specifically creolization perspective, I'm not sure exactly what the results might look like; but extrapolating from Abrahams's comments on "Matty Glow and Garoleen," which stressed the parrot-messenger as a particularly Caribbean interpolation, along with its move in the plot to center stage and its accompanying highlighted role as a public broadcaster of private matters, I would expect "Lady Isabel's" final scene (which, in the British "outlandish knight" strain of the ballad that was clearly the West Indian version's source, invariably consists of a talking parrot threatening to tell Isabel's father the secret of her near-disastrous rendezvous with the Elf-Knight) to be lengthened and developed in more detail. But no; instead, the formative mind behind this West Indian version (perhaps the mind of Charles Walters, whom local singers credited with the song's actual *making*) saw fit to drop the parrot episode in the British source-version entirely and to substitute something quite different: after arriving home safely, Lady Isabel drops to her knees and thanks God for her narrow escape. In other words, here we have happening textually exactly the reverse of what supposedly occurred in the case of "Matty Glow": a British ballad, which in its *British* tradition prominently featured a "tale-telling parrot" seeking to "make private matters public" by tattling in an unmotivated "stirring up" of "things," was altered in West Indian tradition to expurgate all those features and to add a moralistic conclusion that one usually associates with a pious, bourgeois, Anglo worldview. In this Nevitian version, in other words—as was the case with the Jamaican "Little Musgrave"—we have a text that is in fact *less* creole-like than the majority of Anglo texts.[8] And once again logic leads us to extend our homology yet another step: just as St. Vincent is to Great Britain, and Scotland is to England, and England is to France, so is Great Britain to Nevis! Unfortunately for creolization theory, that logical extension brings us to the point of circular reasoning, of the tautology that the Caribbean is to Great Britain as Great Britain is to the Caribbean.

*   *   *

Whether one is an ardent creolist or not, "hypertheorizing"—excessive devotion to theorizing at the expense of close attention to the wide array of folklore data that bear on the topic at hand—may have even further detrimental effects on our field of study. In the case of Abrahams's essay, I'm willing to suggest that the allure of theorizing Child ballads in the West Indies so consumed the analyst's attention, so propelled his mind-set along certain pathways, that other patterns in the data, however ubiquitous, may have remained simply unseen, if not intentionally disregarded. For example, there's a feature that appears too often in Caribbean versions of the few Child ballads that have diffused into West Indian tradition to be coincidental: marked affinities with significantly *older* versions of their progenitors. For instance, in Maybelle Simmonds's version of "Barbara Allan," discussed earlier, the heroine is inexplicably hardhearted, refusing even to grant the kiss that would revive her dead lover. Here's what Bronson has to say about this feature: "tradition has gradually but surely transformed the character of the heroine. In the earliest of our texts . . . unexplained obduracy was her characterizing trait. . . . It has been the main effect of tradition to rationalize and minimize this quality. The popular sensibility has been unable to stomach her stonyheartedness, and has gone to work on motivation" (Bronson 1959–72: 2: 321). Not in the Caribbean tradition Maybelle Simmonds's version represents, though, where Barbara remains like her earlier British ancestor. Another example can be found in Nora Bristol's rendition of "Maid Freed from the Gallows": the condemned lover is male, which according to Eleanor Long is an older trait. In more modern British tradition, the supplicant is female (Long 1971: 38, 42). And this phenomenon of British West Indian archaism is not peculiar to the Eastern Caribbean or to small islands like Nevis. In an early-twentieth-century Jamaican version of "Riddles Wisely Expounded" (Child 1; Roud 161), the Devil is the riddle-posing protagonist, as he is in the oldest layer of British tradition, according to both Child and Bronson; more recent tradition makes him a nonsupernatural wooer whose suit is successful (Child [1882–98] 1963: 5: 283; Bronson 1959–72: 1: 3). Indeed, this Jamaican "Riddles Wisely Expounded" is rife with supernatural elements, including a biblical snake/Devil pairing (Jekyll [1907] 1966: 26–7).

Even more unexpected—hence more requiring of explanation—are

Caribbean similarities to even older *non*-British European features. For example, in a Jamaican "Maid Freed from the Gallows" text, the girl must be rescued from a sailor (Jekyll [1907] 1966: 58). This parallels the common motif in many European traditions—older than the British, in which it doesn't appear—of the maid's capture by seafaring pirates or corsairs, from whom she must then be ransomed (Child [1882–98] 1963: 2: 346–8). And as we've already discovered, "Lady Isabel and the Elf-Knight's" final scene of the parrot/maid interchange, found in almost all British and British diasporic versions, is absent from the Nevitian text: Isabel reaches home safely after her "near-death experience" and thanks the Lord for her lucky escape. In this, to repeat, the West Indian story again resembles older European versions, none of which contains the parrot episode, since that episode was added in Britain, where the ballad arrived late in its traditional history (Nygard 1958). And what about that apparently creolelike hybrid, the *cante-fable* form itself, so much more popular with twentieth-century Caribbean village singers than with singers from any other contemporary anglophone tradition of Child ballad performance? Child quotes Robert Jamieson as saying about "Lady Isabel and the Elf-Knight" that "a tale to the same effect, intermixed with scraps of verse, was familiar to him when a boy, and that he afterwards found it 'in much the same state, in the Highlands, in Lochaber and Ardnamurchan' " (Child [1882–98] 1963: 1: 24). Indeed, while we usually assume that West Indians inherited a predilection for *cante-fable* directly from their African ancestors, the form itself may be the oldest European vehicle for stories of the Child type. This at least was Martha Warren Beckwith's hypothesis, very tentative to be sure, in her pioneering essay on "The English Ballad in Jamaica": that the European medieval ballad *derived* from *cante-fable* (Beckwith 1924a: 469–70).

In short, the archaic nature of the West Indian oikotypes constitutes a palpable, recurring, and distinctive pattern in the data, while, as we've seen, the cited "creolizations" do not. And even though this phenomenon can easily be accommodated within the terms of creolization theory in general (which comes chiefly from linguistics [Abrahams 1983: 26]), I must assume that Abrahams ignored it—indeed, didn't even award it an endnote—because it's incompatible with his theoretical partialities toward synchronic study, contextualism, performance, and the like, which are commonly (and in my view mistakenly) regarded as incompatible with comparative textual analysis. In other words, he may have wished—quite understandably—to provide a consistent, unified perspective on his material. But if so, then there's yet another potential weakness inherent in theorizing folksong: the analyst may, in avoiding certain aspects of the data that may not neatly fit the informing paradigm, willy-nilly contradict some of that paradigm's own premises.

I can see only one obvious example of inconsistency in "Child Ballads in the West Indies," though to my mind the seductiveness of hypertheorizing renders it a continual threat. The example to which I refer is the breaking of a principle highly valued in the context-sensitive perspective that characterizes Abrahams's scholarly agenda: the observer should attend to the "native voice"—that is, the perceptions, definitions, terminology, and explanations that the people whose folklore you're studying themselves employ. The inconsistency to which I refer is as follows: in one of the three versions of the "Matty Glow and Garoleen" *cante-fable* subjected to creolization analysis, the informant, Sephus Jobe, provided an unequivocal gloss on the story's meaning. After returning home to verify the parrot's report that his wife's in bed with a lover, the husband kills both adulterers with a single pistol shot, at which point Sephus Jobe ends his song-tale thus: "Is that so you see now, 'oman cause man death, still today" (Abrahams 1987: 123). Not only is this "moral" remarkably like one that seems implicit in most Anglo versions of both "Little Musgrave" and "Bonny Birdy" (in "Musgrave," Lady Barnard usually initiates the tryst, often having to cajole the reluctant lover into bed; moreover, in both ballads she insists he stay put when, hearing a distant horn, he suspects the husband's coming and so wants to leave), but it is also typically Vincentian, for Abrahams himself calls it a "conventional" sentiment. In fact, it may have been British West Indian in general: in a Jamaican version of "Riddles Wisely Expounded" only one of the several riddles usually found in Anglo-American tradition as posed by the man to the maid is retained, and it's not "what's louder than a horn," "what's greener than grass," "what's heavier than lead" and their ilk, but "what is roguer than a woman-kind," to which the answer is "the Devil" (Jekyll [1907] 1966: 27). In his discussion of "Matty Glow's" native significance, however, the folklorist makes no room for Sephus Jobe's "emic" interpretation, dwelling instead on such purported significations as the undesirability of private domestic affairs leaking out into the public gossip mart. Perhaps the informant's assertion was set aside because it provided little support for the creolization hypothesis—perhaps even because to enlightened North American academics it's unattractively misogynistic and hence best shrugged off. But in either case, cannot the ballad scholar's avoidance in this example be said to have *silenced* the native voice? *Appropriated* the expressive culture of *subaltern* peoples for the scholar's own *ideological* ends? Been inconsistent, in short, with the principles of the creolist's very own *discourse?*

I've italicized certain words in the preceding paragraph for emphasis because they suggest to me one reason behind the current rage for theorizing in the study of folklore, despite its capacity to produce—even from the very best folklorists, a category to which Abrahams indisputably belongs—an offspring like the creolization hypothesis that exhibits innumerable weaknesses and possesses little potency for ballad study, as I think I've shown. The reason is that we wish to be considered one of *them*—those scholars who have transcended the parochialism of specific "fields," like "literary criticism" and "history," in order to align themselves with a far more modish community, the community of "social thinkers," "public intellectuals," and "cultural theorists." Although such a desire may be understandable and even intellectually praiseworthy, the fact remains that it's not working for us: folklorists—and especially folksong scholars—continue to be marginalized and to suffer low self-esteem and a weak sense of identity.

If any theorizing—preferably not of the "hyper" sort, the motives underlying which are suspect, the results it produces even more so—is to bring (back) to folksong scholars some recognition and respect, that theorizing will have to rediscover both the discipline's greatest strength, its vast systematized data banks, and the will to consult them comparatively. It will also, unlike creolization theory, have to do a better job of fitting the evidence, of offering logical arguments, and of being true to its own premises.

2

From Newry Town to Columbus City

A Robber's Journey

This chapter offers a study which avoids weaknesses that arise when we draw too restricted a set of boundaries around folksong's textual subject matter. It accepts the premise that a song's whole tradition—its life history, so to speak—is an important context within which one must see any single version. To say that is not to deny the obvious individuality of each singer, the uniqueness of each performance event, the special nature of an oikotype; it is simply to assert that enough continuity in any song's life-history exists that drawing boundaries that are too parochial or too arbitrary often leads to conclusions whose validity will be more-than-usually doubtful (see Dundes 1971: 296).

In addition, the investigation here is primarily inductive: that is to say, I gather as many examples of the subject song as I can and look for patterns among them. I try to let my material speak to me about itself rather than, as it were, shouting it down, forcing upon it a dogma I personally find compelling. In the process, I hope to present a more accurate picture of textual reconfiguration and its enabling conditions than creolization theorizing reveals about Child ballads in West Indian tradition. To accomplish this goal, I'll pay particular attention to the data's distinctively American guise.

This guise is couched in a recurring *form* folklorists call the "blues ballad," a genre which, while well discussed as a type, has not been exemplified with many case studies (see Minton 1993; Wilgus 1960; Wilgus and Long 1985; Wilgus and Montell 1968). The dearth is especially unfortunate because the genre was nurtured principally in the American South, which means that a better understanding of a blues ballad provides us with a better understanding of a regional taste and, hence, of a cultural *identity*, a concept of strong intellectual interest to present-day folklorists. Also of much current interest is another blues ballad trait, *hybridity*: the genre fuses elements of both Anglo-and Afro-American song aesthetics into a distinctive style, with the result that many of its representatives, such as "Wild Bill Jones" (Laws E10; Roud 2246) and "John Hardy" (Laws I2; Roud 3262), have been found in both Black and White performance repertoires (see Laws [1964] 1975; Roud 1994b– present).

Although the blues ballad is a compositional model employed by both Black and White southerners, the particular song this chapter investigates has been found only in White tradition: it is a narrative song, or ballad, that folklorists identify for comparative purposes as Laws L12 (Roud 490) and call by its American title, "The Rambling Boy" (see Laws 1957). The song evinces yet further manifestations of hybridity because it's a New World revoicing of an originally British song. Of course, hundreds of British folksongs diffused to North America and entered oral tradition here, but far more often than not such imported songs could be better called reproductions rather than revoicings: they retained most of their Old World characteristics, even such wildly non-American elements as aristocratic *dramatic personae*—the King in "Willie o Winsbury" (Child 100; Roud 64), for instance, or Lady Margaret in "Sweet William's Ghost" (Child 77; Roud 50 [Child (1882–98) 1963; Coffin 1977]). The kinds of changes to which British songs *were* customarily subjected as they diffused over the North American English-speaking landscape were microtextual ones, such as localization of place names, or modernization of cultural artifacts—the sorts of variations in surface text that occur everywhere when oral traditions diffuse over time and space. Indeed, even when the variations were of a more structural kind, we find that the same transformations occurred within Great Britain itself and hence were not particularly American (see Hyman 1957; Wilgus 1958). What's unusual about "The Rambling Boy" is that it *dramatically* transformed its British ancestor: not only did it undergo typical surface-textual changes like localization of place names, but it also experienced more deep-seated macrotransformations, both in how it constructed an imagined world (its *poetics*) and in what human values it seemed to espouse (its *semantics*), that were distinctly American, even more distinctly Southern Upland American.

"The Rambling Boy's" British progenitor, which I'll call "The Wild and Wicked Youth" (its most common title in broadsheet printings), was probably composed in the eighteenth century.[1] I make that inference on three grounds. First, the British ballad evinces a compositional style folklorists identify as the "broadside ballad" type that became prevalent in popular street literature after 1700: the story is told in a reportorial, unadorned, and linearly chronological way that contrasts with the pre-1700 narrative style of the Child ballad, which customarily made heavy use of dialogue, of hyperbolic imagery and formulaic word use, and of highly parallel structures (Andersen 1985; Buchan 1972: 74–165; Gerould 1932: 84–130; Moreira 1997; Pettitt 1997; Renwick 1996). Second, broadsheet versions of "Wild and Wicked Youth" reflect eighteenth-century conditions. For example, the protagonist does not consider his decision to turn highwayman out of the ordinary; moreover, his success as a thief in London suggests a somewhat primitive peacekeeping system, one that predates the establishment of the Metropolitan Police Force in 1828.[2] Third, and perhaps most compelling, is the British ballad's frequent mention of the lawbreaking protagonist's eventual capture by "Fielding's gang" or "crew," an apparent reference to London's proto-police force of Bow Street Runners formed and led by Sir John Fielding, who was a magistrate for the borough of Westminster and the County of Middlesex from 1754 (taking over the office upon the death of its previous holder, Sir John's stepbrother, the novelist Henry Fielding) until his death in 1780.

The earliest texts we have of the British "Wild and Wicked Youth" are on broadsheets, a commercial form in which the ballad probably (but not necessarily) originated, from there entering oral tradition, no doubt many times. A measure of its popularity with the broadsheet-buying public is that, as of July 1998, the Roud *Broadside Index* (Roud 1994a–present) listed seventeen broadsheets in Cambridge University's Madden Collection containing "Wild and Wicked Youth." All were probably printed in the nineteenth century, but eighteenth-century versions would have differed little from those later ones we *do* have, since with few exceptions the surviving nineteenth-century slips are very much alike in their surface texts and even more so in the story they tell, even though the twenty-four I have at my command come from the presses of twelve different printers, situated not only in London but also in the English Midlands (Birmingham), in the Northeast (Newcastle and Durham), in Ireland (Dublin), and even in the United States (Boston; see Laws 1957: 172).

Here is a very typical English broadsheet text of this British ballad, "The Wild and Wicked Youth," direct ancestor of Laws L12:

WILD AND WICKED YOUTH

J. Catnach, Printer, 2, Monmouth-court 7 Dials

[1] In Newry town I was bred and born
In Steven's Green I died with scorn,
I served my time in the saddling trade,
And always was a roving blade.

[2] At seventeen I took a wife,
I loved her dear as I loved my life,
And to maintain her fine and gay,
A robbing went on the highway.

[3] But my money did grow low,
On the highway I was forced to go,
Where I robbed both lords & ladies bright
Brought home the gold to my heart's delight.

[4] I robbed Lord Golding I do declare,
Lady Mansfield in Grosvenor Square,
I shut the shutters, bid 'em good night,
And went away to my heart's delight.

[5] To Covent Garden I took my way,
With my blooming to see the play,
Till Fielding's gang did me pursue,
Taken I was by the cursed crew.

[6] My father cries I am undone,
My mother cries for her darling son,
My wife she tears her golden hair,
What shall I do for I'm in despair.

[7] But when I am dead, and in my grave,
A decent funeral let me have,
Six highwaymen to carry me,
Give them broad swords and liberty.

[8] Six blooming girls to bear my pall,
Give them gloves and ribbons all,
When I am dead, they'll tell the truth,
He was a wild and wicked youth.[3]

"The Wild and Wicked Youth" also became popular in British oral tradition, though chiefly among male singers. A representative oral text is the Norfolk singer Harry Cox's rendition:

NEWLYN TOWN

[1] In Newlyn town I was bred and born
At Stephen's Green where I died of scorn
I served my time at the saddler trade
And I always was a roving blade.

[2] At seventeen I took a wife
And I loved her dearly as I loved my life
All for to keep her both fine and gay
A-robbing I went on the King's highway.

[3] I robbed Lord Golden I do declare
And Lady Mansfield in Grosvenor Square
I robbed them of the gold so bright
And I took it home to my heart's delight.

[4] To Covent Gardens we went straightway
Me and my wife we went to the play
Ned Fielding's gang there did me pursue
Taken I was by that cursed crew.

[5] My father cried "I am undone"
My mother cried for her darling son
My pretty damsel she tore her hair
Said "What shall I do for I am in despair?"

[6] Now when I'm dead and go to my grave
A decent funeral let me have
Six highwaymen for to carry me
Give them broadswords and sweet liberty.

[7] Six highwaymen for to bear my pall
Give them white gloves and sweet ribbons all

And when I'm gone they will tell the truth
Here lies a wild and a wicked youth.
  (Cox 1947)

Obviously, Harry Cox's oral text is quite close to the broadsheet one;
while there are minor verbal differences, the link between each distinctive episode and the stanza depicting it is consistent. The only substantive differences are (1) that the Cox version *twice* asks for "six highwaymen" pallbearers, whereas the broadsheet version requests six
highwaymen the first time, for "six pretty maids" the second, and (2) the
episode portrayed in the broadsheet's third stanza—the youthful protagonist turns to highway robbery because his "money did grow low"—is
absent from Cox's oral version. The forty oral texts at my disposal suggest that traditional singers in general did not agree with Harry Cox on
the first matter but did agreed with him on the second: overwhelmingly
oral texts, like the broadsheet, ask for six highwaymen in one stanza, for
six pretty maids in the next, while unlike the broadsheet they devote
only one stanza to the young man's turn to crime. (Since the preceding
stanza had already introduced and explained his becoming a thief—he
wished to support his wife in style—this additional stanza seems to us
confusingly ambiguous, and apparently household and village singers
like Harry Cox felt the same way; while the two stanzas appear together
in fully seventeen of the twenty-four broadsheets in my sample, they do
so in only four of the forty oral versions consulted for this study).[4]

Did "Wild and Wicked Youth" originally treat a historical event?
While the narrator's criminal career fits a standardized plot found in
other traditional Anglo/American songs and hence may be purely conventional fiction, the broadside ballad genre's strongly journalistic
nature—its propensity for close links to real life—makes it possible that
an actual instance stimulated a songmaker to adapt historical facts to the
well-known narrative template (cf. Cohen 1973; Dugaw 1989). Indeed,
the presence of such nonformulaic details as the young man's apprenticeship in "the saddlery trade"; the place names Newry Town, Stephen's
Green, Grosvenor Square, and Covent Garden (as opposed to, say, the
more formulaic Dublin or London—though both places also appear in
many versions of the song); and especially the role of "Fielding's gang" in
the robber's capture encourage this supposition of a historical wild-and-

wicked-youth.[5] However, not only has no folklorist yet turned up a case from the court records of John Fielding's tenure as magistrate (or for that matter, Henry's) convincingly matching the content of "Wild and Wicked Youth,"[6] but in any event, domestic singers like Harry Cox had little reason for concern about the ballad protagonist's empirical status. The story probably seemed plausible to them. In fact, more important was undoubtedly the attractiveness of the worldview and values the song expressed.[7]

This attraction also held for traditional singers in English-speaking North America, for "The Wild and Wicked Youth" was brought to this continent—not only in the performance repertoires of immigrants, one suspects, but almost certainly in printed form as well (see Laws 1957: 172; UCLA Special Collections, Box 605)—where it continued to thrive. In both the United States and Canada, this broadside-influenced form was sung in everyday settings, little changed from its Old World manifestations either in text or, in the three cases where North American folksong collectors have supplied us with the music, in tune. I know of seven such versions from North American oral tradition: from Ontario (Fowke 1965: 44–5), Massachusetts (Huntington 1958), North Carolina (Warner 1982: 249–50), Virginia (University of Virginia Special Collections, Box 29, Folder 1547; Rosenberg 1969: 106), Missouri (Belden 1940: 136–7), Utah (Hubbard 1961: 262), and California (Gordon 1924).[7]

At some time, however—probably in the later years of the nineteenth century, when the blues ballad most likely jelled in general popular consciousness as a distinctive, pleasing, and usable compositional model—some more creative New World singer varied the song enough to originate the American oikotype, "The Rambling Boy." Here is a traditional version collected by Bristol Taylor of Berea, Kentucky, from the singing of William Francis around 1911:

THE RAMBLING BOY

[1] I once was a rich but a rambling boy
Through many a city I did go
Columbus City I paid my way
And I spent my money in golden play.

[2] And then I married me a pretty little wife
I loved her as I loved my life

And she was grand both young and gay
And she caused me to rob in the road highway.

[3] I robbed them all I will declare
I robbed them all in deep despair
I robbed them of one thousand pounds
One night when I was rambling round.

[4] I had dry goods for to carry me through
Two glittering watches and a pistol too
And a pretty fair maiden for to pay my toll
In her pretty pink silk and silver and gold.

[5] And now I am compelled to die
A many a pretty girl for me will cry
But all their crying won't set me free
For I am bound for the gallos [sic] tree.

[6] And my old mother she sits and mourns
My sister says she is all alone
My true love sits in deep despair
In her pretty pink silk and her curly black hair.

[7] The roses are red and the stems are green
These days to come and they may be seen
They may be many and they may be few
But I hope to spend them all with you.

[8] I'll buy me a ticket in Greenville town
I'll get on the train and I'll sit down
The train will whistle and the car wheels roll
Just a few more days and I'll land at home.

(Lomax [John Avery] Family Papers, box 3D179, folder 6)

While some folksong editors are ambivalent or unsure about the genetic relationship between "Wild and Wicked Youth" and "Rambling Boy,"[9] the narrative and verbal similarities are too great to allow serious doubt that the two pieces are direct relatives, not just more or less independent songs sharing several themes and verbal commonplaces popular in the cultural repertoire. They are, in short, the "same song."

*   *   *

The sample texts of "The Wild and Wicked Youth" and "The Rambling Boy" exhibit the narrative conventions of two related but distinct ways of articulating images in sung verse (see Renwick 1996). "The Wild and Wicked Youth" exemplifies the broadside ballad, a type found throughout European and Euro-diasporic cultures, including North America, that favors a relatively detailed, objective, linearly plotted way of telling a story. "The Rambling Boy," on the other hand, exhibits the compositional style of the blues ballad, a genre informed by a more distinctly bicultural, southern U.S.-nurtured song poetics that prefers an impressionistic, semilinear, highly lyrical storytelling style. Note, for example, how much more expository is the geography of the British highwayman's world as mapped in Harry Cox's broadside-styled text: he was born in Newry, went robbing in Grosvenor Square, was captured in Covent Garden, and died, evidently back in Ireland again, in Stephen's Green. The American robber's blues-ballad geography is both more limited and more sketchy: in the Kentucky text above he sports in Cumberland City, later buys a train ticket in Greenville, and that's it. As is also typical of the two strains, more personnel appear in the Norfolk broadside-ballad version of the song than in the Kentucky blues-ballad one: the two share the presence of nuclear family members, but "Wild and Wicked Youth" also includes a large cast of victims, lawmen, and funeral participants not found in "Rambling Boy." Moreover, many of these characters are *named* in the British version—Lord Golden, Lady Mansfield, and the law officers' leader, Ned Fielding—while personnel in "Rambling Boy" are rarely subject to such specification.

Another typical difference is that, in virtually all "Wild and Wicked Youth" versions, the story unfolds linearly, following a sequence of causally and/or chronologically related events, while "Rambling Boy" arranges episodes in an order that's as much associational as empirical. For example, in the Kentucky text above the robber's inventory of personal assets in stanza 4 (dry goods, watches, pistol) comes *before* his capture, but even more often it comes *after* (for example, Randolph 1946-50: 2: 84–5; Belden and Hudson 1952a: 355). Or again, his train ride (stanza 8) ends the song in five of the eleven texts that contain this episode, which implies that the rambling boy was freed; but in another four versions it comes *before* the two mourning stanzas (5 and 6), which suggests that he was going home for one last farewell before his execution (Lomax

1960: 193). There's even a version sung by Effie Cormack of Kentucky which fuses the train ride and the robbery (stanza 3) so that the rambling boy robs the train on his way home (Cormack 1949; in Darling 1983, 109–10, he robs the train right *after* it brings him home). As for the blues ballad's urge toward lyricism, this aspect will soon be discussed in some detail; for now, it may be illustrated by a consistent preference in "Rambling Boy" for *two* motifs of lament, a general mourning (stanza 5) and a family mourning (stanza 6), twice as many as "The Wild and Wicked Youth"—in which only family members mourn—typically contains.

Much of "Rambling Boy's" distinctiveness exemplifies the blues ballad's cultural eclecticism: that is, its employment of both Black and White American content. Take for example the robber's inventory of assets, which appears in thirteen of our twenty-three versions:

> I had dry goods to carry me through,
> A bright new sword and a pistol too,
> A forty-four that never did fail,
> When my true love come for to go my bail.
>   (Henry 1938: 327)

The imagery of the highly effective pistol and the importance of access (or lack of access) to bail money are blues ballad staples; indeed, their New World-ness so struck the English folksong scholar Anne G. Gilchrist that she was moved to denigrate "the American doggerel of murderers and gangsters, bristling with pearl-handled '44' guns" (1940: 157). Laws ([1964] 1975: 89–91) points to the repeated appearance of both the pistol and bail motifs in some ballads that were primarily African American, like "Delia" (Laws I5; Roud 3264) and "Bad Lee Brown" (Laws I8; Roud 780); and in others that were of principally Anglo currency, like "Wild Bill Jones" (Laws E10; Roud 2246) and "Talt Hall" (Laws dE42; Roud 4102); and in still others that were shared by both Black and White singers, like "John Hardy," "Frankie and Albert" (Laws I3; Roud 254), and "Railroad Bill" (Laws I13; Roud 4181).

Imagery in the train journey stanza is also common in other blues ballads of law breaking that probably originated in African American culture (Laws [1964] 1975: 91–2), like "The Coon-Can Game" (Laws I4; Roud 6378) and "Ida Red" (Roud 3429; see Lomax and Lomax [1934] 1994: 111).

Once again, though, variants are found in blues ballads of chiefly White currency, like "Talt Hall" and "Twenty-One Years" (Laws E16; Roud 2248). Indeed, the "Rambling Boy's" train trip at times seems to be there for generic convention's sake rather than for realism or even dramatic effect, since the robber may be depicted as buying his own train ticket home—hence, is presumably a free man—but then in the very next stanza declaiming his imminent execution (for example, Combs 1967: 184–5. The train journey may, of course, be metaphorical; see Cohen 1981: 596–644).

Cultural sharing also characterizes two other typical stanzas found in several "Rambling Boy" texts: a request for clemency from the authorities and a distinctive (though commonplace) form of burial instructions. The former, which appears in five of our "Rambling Boy" versions, may be illustrated by Justus Begley's rendition:

> So I'll get me some paper and it's I'll sit down,
> Drop a few lines to my Governor Brown,
> And every word shall be the truth,
> O pray for the governor to turn me loose.
>   (Lomax 1960: 193)

Like the train journey and the list of personal assets, this plea-for-clemency motif is peculiarly American: the wild and wicked youth never comes close to petitioning the Crown for a pardon! Accordingly, we find the theme in other southern U.S. traditional songs, both Black (e.g. "Goin' Home" [Roud 15035; see Lomax and Lomax (1934) 1994: 84–6]) and White ("Twenty-One Years"). Also indigenous to America is a distinctive set of burial instructions that appears in three of the twenty-three texts and is carried by a more or less fixed-form commonplace stanza:

> When I am dead, don't bury me at all;
> Just put me away in alcohol.
> Place a gallon jug at my head and feet
> And tell those girls I am just asleep.
>   (Bush n.d.: 57)

The editor of *The Frank C. Brown Collection of North Carolina Folklore*'s fourth volume makes the point about biculturalism for us: the stanza "seems to have a special appeal for negroes [sic], though it is not confined to them nor is it, probably, of Negro origin" (Schinan 1957: 69).

In short, "The Rambling Boy" exhibits hybridity on two interfacing levels. At one level, it synthesizes the British-derived taste for a chronologically ordered, expository, reasonably self-contained recounting of events with the American preference for elliptical narration and emotionally-associative ordering. On a second level, the U.S. contribution is not simply an Anglo-North American variant of an Anglo-British ancestor but is itself significantly bicultural and emergent, a product of two distinctive but integrated sets of stylistic elements, Anglo/American on the one hand and African American on the other.

In order to talk about either the broadside or the blues ballad *tradition* as a cultural phenomenon rather than as an assortment of individual renditions, one has to accept the commonsense premise that a statistically derived normative form composed of a song's most frequently sung episodes or, better, *narrative themes* (following Wilgus 1970: 161–77) represents what bearers of tradition regard as the most compelling and memorable points in the robber's life story. Within the population of twenty-three available "Rambling Boy" traditional texts, we find that seven narrative themes compose such a normative form. All seven (and their associated stanza-vehicles) appear in the eight-stanza Kentucky version given above; only stanza 7, the lyric "roses are red and the stems are green" verse, is untypical, as it's found in only six versions. Similarly, Harry Cox's rendition given earlier is about as close as we can get to a normative form of "Wild and Wicked Youth" oral manifestations, the only significant difference being in the aforementioned burial-instructions stanzas, where Cox has highway*men* both bearing the dead robber's pall and being given "white gloves and sweet ribbons"; overwhelmingly, *women* perform this task in broadside-ballad versions.

A total of seven narrative themes, then, appear in more than half of both the forty "Wild and Wicked Youth's" oral versions (three were collected in Scotland, one in Canada, six in the United States, and the remaining thirty in England) and the twenty-three "Rambling Boy" versions (all collected from southern U.S. singers). As is typical of Anglo/American folk poetry, each narrative theme is commonly linked to a single stanza, a sign/referent relationship that's quite stable throughout the population.[10] Here, letter-coded and juxtaposed for ease of comparison, are schemas of both the broadside-ballad-influenced and blues-ballad-influenced normative forms we shall consider typical of the two song-strains' respective traditions:

The Wild and Wicked Youth	The Rambling Boy
(A) *robber's-early-life-and-character*	(A) *robber's-early-life-and-character*
(B) *marriage-and-resulting-criminality*	(B) *marriage-and-resulting-criminality*
(C)	(C) *inventory-of-robber's-resources*
(D) *description-of-a-particular-robbery*	(D) *description-of-a-particular-robbery*
(E) *robber's-pursuit-and-capture*	(E)
(F)	(F) *general-mourning-and-resignation-to-fate*
(G) *family-reaction-to-robber's-fate*	(G) *family-reaction-to-robber's-fate*
(H)	(H) *robber's-train-journey*
(I) *burial-instruction-for-male-participants*	(I)
(J) *burial-instructions-for-female-participants*	(J)

Broadside and blues ballad strains share four narrative themes: (A) *robber's-early-life-and-character* (of the four shared themes, this one evinces the greatest verbal differences between broadsheet and blues ballad renditions), (B) *marriage-and-resulting-criminality*, (D) *description-of-a-particular-robbery*, and (G) *family-reaction-to-robber's-fate*. The three narrative themes specific to the broadside-ballad type—(E) *robber's-pursuit-and-capture*, (I) *burial-instructions-for-male-participants*, and (J) *burial-instructions-for-female participants*—never appear in "Rambling Boy" (burial instructions *in general* do, but they are both textually and thematically too distinct from the British form to be regarded as the "same"). As for the narrative themes that are part of "Rambling Boy's" normal form but not of "Wild and Wicked Youth's," two—(C) *inventory-of-robber's-resources* and (H) *robber's-train-journey*—are native to American folk tradition, while the third—(F) *general-mourning-and-resignation-to-fate*—originated in Britain but was evidently not popular with singers, since it's found in only five of the forty oral versions of "Wild and Wicked Youth" and three of the twenty-four broadsheets.[11] Theme (F) *is* popular with U.S. singers, however, and hence can be regarded as more typical rather than less typical, appearing in twelve of the twenty-three "Rambling Boy" oral versions.

The question of variation is inevitably central to much folklore study, especially when texts compose most of the available record we have of singing as a social activity. Since variation is, for competent bearers of tradition, motivated and purposeful, it signifies what is particularly meaningful in the songs relative to the human contexts in which they are sung. What kinds of meaningful changes has our blues ballad's normative form wrought in its ancestral British broadside ballad? First, and most strikingly, "The Rambling Boy" has *personalized* its "Wild and Wicked Youth" progenitor considerably so that the narrator becomes a much more prominent focus of attention. Although *all* versions of *both* strains of the song (as is true of most Anglo/American ballads of crime and criminals) are told in first person, the broadside-ballad strain's narrator is constantly interacting with a host of very specific Others. Many of these are Significant Others like the wife, the father, and the mother, who, through ties both socially structural and affective, are close to the protagonist-Self. Many personnel, however, are more removed from Self: these are General Others, like the bold highwaymen and pretty maiden soulmates who will be the chief participants in his burial ritual. But there are even several Others more distant whom we might call Institutional Others, like the wealth-holding members of the aristocracy, Lord Golden and Lady Mansfield, and the representatives of the law enforcement system, Ned Fielding and his gang.[12]

The blues ballad normative form, on the other hand, is much more ego-centered because, by rejecting the three narrative themes (E) *robber's-pursuit-and-capture,* (I) *burial-instructions-for-male-participants,* and (J) *burial-instructions-for-female-participants,* it has reduced the cast of characters considerably, eliminating General and Institutional Others and retaining only the Significant Others of the immediate family. Any General Others in the blues ballad normative form are typically vague collectives, like the "Many a poor girl [who] for me will cry" of (F) *general-mourning-and-resignation-to-fate.* Similarly, the particularized vic-

ˉtims in the broadside ballad's (D) *description-of-an-actual-robbery* stanza, Lord Golden and Lady Mansfield, become severely adumbrated, as the American robber preys only on "them all." Indeed, even in the closest analogue of the two broadside-styled burial stanzas we can find among our twenty-three blues ballad versions, only the robber himself is personified: there are no bold highwaymen and no pretty maidens, just completely offstage, entirely unembodied preachers of orations and players of tunes:

> When I am dead, laid in my grave,
> The final funeral preached over my head,
> All round my grave play tunes of joy,
> Away goes the reek an' ramblin' boy.
>
> (Randolph 1946-50: 2: 85; see also Lomax and Lomax [1934] 1994: 314–5)

Such blues ballad personnel are even more remote from Self than are General and Institutional Others: at best, they might be called Abstract Others.

Reinforcing this *personalization* is a U.S. emphasis on possessions as indices of the protagonist's identity, most prominently in the narrative theme (C) *inventory-of-robber's-resources* that the blues ballad added to its inherited story. In a typical stanza, the rambling boy has "dry goods" (clothing), weapons (pistol, sword), and a partner (often beautiful and well-dressed, presumably his wife) who can provide him with money:

> Many dry goods for to carry me through
> My pistol, sword, my money too
> My forty-four it never did fail
> My true love came for to go my bail.
>
> (Ramsey 1958)

In contrast, similar goods in broadside-strain versions are not depicted as possessions of the narrator but as items to be bestowed upon the participants at his funeral: bright swords for six highwaymen in narrative theme (I) *burial-instructions-for-male-participants*, white gloves and pink ribbons for six maids in (J) *burial-instructions-for-female-participants*. In fact, in most broadside-ballad versions the narrator distances himself from any strong personal attachment to material possessions by, for

example, robbing unequivocally for his wife's gain, not his own: "And for
to maintain her fine and gay / I went a-robbing on the king's highway"
(Karpeles 1974: 2: 162).[13] Indeed, several "Wild and Wicked Youth" versions go so far in negating the link between material possessions and the
Self as to contain a Robin Hood motif, the robber stealing from the rich
and giving to the poor:

> For neither have I robbed a poor man yet
> Nor caused the tradesman for to fret,
> From the rich I took, to the poor I gave,
> And it brought me unto my untimely grave.
>   (Hubbard 1961: 262)

In short, material goods in "Rambling Boy" have much more self-enhanc-
ing, individuating value than outwardly directed use value or even
exchange value, reinforcing the American narrator-robber's relative
detachment from a range of social Others—especially those outside his
nuclear family—and heightened concern with his own particular situation.

A second major difference between broadside-ballad and blues-ballad
normative forms emerges most strikingly in the way each strain handles
the robber's death. "The Rambling Boy" *emotionalizes* his fate considerably. In virtually every broadside-influenced text I've seen, the robber's
death is communicated in the two funeral stanzas, (I) *burial-instructions-
for-male-participants* and (J) *burial-instructions-for-female-participants*,
that make the occasion an opportunity for what is practically a revolu-
tionary statement: empower the underclass by giving highwaymen both
arms ("good broadswords") and "sweet liberty," and by giving "pretty
maidens" both trappings of finery ("white gloves and pink ribbons") and
a forum—and license—to "speak the truth." At the very least, these
instructions celebrate and affirm support for a lifestyle that is, if not
criminal, distinctly subcultural. Blues-ballad versions, on the other hand,
overwhelmingly view the robber's fate from the vantage point of his feel-
ings. For example, "The Rambling Boy" consistently treats the robber's
death only in the two stanzas of lament which carry the (G) *family-reaction-to-robber's-fate* and the (F) *general-mourning-and-resignation-to-
punishment* narrative themes. Quite in contrast to the broadside-strain's

burial instructions, both of these lament stanzas are purely affective in their appeal, charged with the language of sorrow: the mother "mourns," the wife "sits in deep despair," and many a pretty girl weeps "tears of grief." Mother and wife grieve in broadside-influenced versions as well, but that grief is countered by the two celebratory burial stanzas, with whose participants the wild and wicked youth identifies far more than he does with his immediate family.

The already emotionally laden tone is intensified in most of the twenty-three blues-ballad texts by the addition of lyric stanzas, none of which constitutes a majority (hence doesn't appear in the plot schema), but all of which reinforce the normative form. For example, six versions contain a letter-writing motif that appears in two guises, both of which evoke pity and add to the emotional resonance of the narrator's plight. In one form, the condemned robber writes a letter soliciting from the civic authorities a pardon for his crimes:

> I'll take a chair and I'll sit down;
> I'll write a letter to old Frankfort town;
> In every word I'll write the truth,
> And I'll beg the Lord to turn me loose.
> (Henry 1938: 327)

In the other, the letter's recipient is the robber's wife, as in this stanza written down by Corrie Hammontree of Burnt Mountain, Georgia, for the E. C. Perrow collection: "O love O love come and read these lines. for it may be the last you read of mine for some those time you hear tell no more of the Ramblry Boy" (UCLA Folklore Archives). To the rural southerners who sang and heard "The Rambling Boy," these stanzas almost certainly resonated with the Anglo/American lyric song genre in which heightened feeling is taken for granted and in which letter writing is a commonplace (see Belden and Hudson 1952b: 270–377); thus they reinforced the blues ballad's conversion of the British robber's attitude from defying authority to invoking pity.

A couple of blues-ballad versions go so far in their *emotionalizing* appeal to pity as to actually free the rambling boy, thus completely inverting their broadside-ballad narrative parent. This freedom may be encapsulated in the added narrative segment (H) *robber's-train-journey,* as a locomotive brings the rambling boy home to wife and family (see stanza 8 of the Lomax Kentucky version given above), or even assimilated into the letter-writing stanza, as another Kentucky version illustrates:

> Oh, bring me a chair and I'll sit down,
> And I'll write me a letter to London Town;
> I'll write it to let my true love know
> I'm an innocent boy and free once more.
>
> (Fuson 1931: 63)

And in fact some versions raise the emotional level even higher by suggesting a spiritual experience: they make the train ride home only one leg of the condemned man's longer journey to heaven, as the execution-bound rambling boy tells his mourners in narrative theme (F) *general-mourning-and-resignation-to-fate* that he "hope[s] to meet [them] by and by" (Lomax 1960: 193; see also Henry 1938: 327; Cambiare 1934: 43; Ritchie 1962).[14]

A third significant transformation "Rambling Boy" brought about on its "Wild and Wicked Youth" progenitor is a magnifying of the female presence in and quality of the world portrayed, a change we can call *feminization*. For example, in the broadside-ballad tradition, narrative theme (G) *family-reaction-to-robber's-fate* invariably lists father, mother, and wife as the distraught kin, and usually in that order. In contrast, only five of the seventeen blues-ballad versions containing this narrative theme depict father as a lamenting family member, while twelve substitute for him a family member who is *never* found in the broadside versions, the robber's sister. For instance:

> Now my mother sits and weeps and moans,
> My sister says she's left alone,
> My true love cries in deep despair
> With her dark brown eyes and her long curly hair.
>
> (Lomax 1960: 193)

At the same time, the *nature* of the family members' reactions are more predictably affecting in the blues ballad. In some "Wild and Wicked Youth" texts, for example, the father's reaction is a patriarchal one of revulsion at the shame his son has brought upon him, as he cries to the robber, "What have you done?" or "I am undone" (see Beckett 1952; Cox 1947; *Journal of the Folk-Song Society* 1901: 1: 115; Kennedy 1975: 712; Shuldham-Shaw et al. 1981–97: 2: 265. Virtually all broadsheet versions have "I am undone"). Sometimes even the mother's response is implacably judgmental: she expresses the wish that "in the cradle he should have died" (O'Lochlainn 1965: see also Brightwell 1975: Hall 1994). In contrast, the southern American sister's reaction, as well as wife's and mother's, is to lament the suffering their kinsman's death will cause his family.

Another example of *feminization* may be found in a narrative theme-cum-stanza that appears in well over half of the blues-ballad versions but in only four of the forty broadside-ballad-influenced oral versions: (F) *general-mourning-and-resignation-to-fate*. Here, a common line brings in additional mourners—*not* family members—who are all women: "For me many a poor girl will cry." These female mourners are perhaps functional analogues of the six pretty maids in the broadside strain's narrative segment (J) *burial-instructions-for-female-participants* (which does not appear in blues ballad tradition), but the difference between the two is huge: the broadside female burial participants, with their various combinations of gloves, gaily colored ribbons, and flowers, are "making a statement" defying conventionality, whereas the blues ballad's women mourners seem purely emotive.

And while the blues ballad increases the feminine presence, it decreases the masculine—by deleting the burial instructions of narrative segment (I), for example, which eliminates an unusually macho set of male personnel, the funeral's bold highwaymen, and by dropping episode (E) *robber's-pursuit-and-capture*, in which law officers arrest the robber. Indeed, these British representatives of government authority could be contrasted with their U.S. counterpart that three "Rambling Boy" texts *add* to the song: this is the state governor, who appears in all three versions as the recipient of the robber's letter pleading for a pardon, as discussed above (Lomax 1960: 193; Ritchie 1962: 193; Roberts 1974: 106). But unlike the "Fielding's gang" of Bow Street Runners or the funeral's bold highwaymen, this figure is in no sense a forbidding, authoritarian, or adversarial male; indeed, in one version he even goes so far as to empathize with the condemned man:

It's I'll buy me a paper and I'll sit down
To write a few lines to my Governor Brown
He received that letter and he read it a while
He began to think on his woman and child.
(Ritchie 1962)

In other words, the governor's reaction to the robber is not at all unlike those of the condemned man's female relatives, or of the crowd of female mourners, or even indeed of the robber's wife herself, since in two of the eight examples of letter writing that appear in the population of twenty-three blues ballad texts consulted for this study the recipient is not some governmental representative but the narrator's wife, which suggests a semantic equivalence between letter receivers.[15]

Feminization does not necessarily mean that "The Rambling Boy" represents women only in a favorable, sympathetic light, however; just that they are portrayed in a more causal, infrastructural light, as both sentient and active beings. The most striking example of this idea is the depiction of the robber's wife and her role in the husband's criminality. The broadside-ballad wife possesses elevated tastes and must be "maintained" in the style to which she's accustomed, but the husband chooses his particular method of acquiring the means to support her. Indeed, he seems to take pride in his wife's ability to exercise her exalted tastes: after robbing the Grosvenor Square aristocrats, "[I] carried the gold to my love straightway" (Karpeles 1974: 2: 163). The blues-ballad wife, on the other hand, is invariably said to "cause" her husband to rob, and he is not portrayed as having any choice in the matter. One result of this southern American tendency to demonize the wife is that the occasional version will add a moral in order to make her guilt explicit, as in a North Carolina version (from Belden and Hudson 1952a: 355; see also Ritchie 1962):

Come all young men, take warning by this,
Never to marry a ficety turst [sic].
She'll cause you to rob, to murder and to steal,
She'll cause you to hang on the gallows tree.

Indeed, a virtually ironbound distinction between the British broadside strain's consistent specification of the robber's age (as young as fifteen, as old as nineteen, but most commonly seventeen) and the American blues ballad's equally consistent silence on the matter (his cognomen "boy" has, in southern usage, far wider denotations than just age-in-years) reinforces this aspect of fixing blame on the wife: in other words, it can't be claimed that his youthfulness and not the wife's influence was at fault in the rambling boy's fall into crime.

To summarize what we've learned so far about the ballad: what apparently happened to the British "Wild and Wicked Youth" is that it originated on an English broadsheet in the later eighteenth century, from where it entered oral tradition throughout England and Scotland. Later it diffused with immigrants and/or with imported broadsheets to the New World, where heavily Anglo-influenced tradition-bearers—especially in northern and western parts of the continent—considered it to be more or less already compatible with their tastes, values, and beliefs, so that they wrought only very minor variation upon the received text (and tune) in adapting it to their New World contexts of song performance. On the other hand, in the southern U.S., the song was not only reconstituted into a distinctive generic format but textually varied to southern tastes. Most prominent in the textual transformation were three kinds of variations. First, there was *personalization*, which removed most of the robber's social Others, such as representatives of the wealth-holding class (Lord Golden, Lady Mansfield), the law-enforcement authorities (Ned Fielding's gang), and members of resistant subcultures (bold highwaymen, six pretty maidens) in order to concentrate on the robber himself. Intimately a part of this *personalization* was the bringing in of such markers of self-identity as the robber's weapons, his money, and someone "to go his bail." This foregrounding of the individual did not stop at the outer self, however: a second kind of revoicing was achieved by also interiorizing the robber's depiction so that he became a much more *emotionalized* figure, both as recipient of others' grief and as a source of strong feeling himself. A major index of this feature was the blues ballad's version of the robber's fate, which seldom constituted a cause for celebration, much less for defiance, but more often one for the display of sorrow and a sense of loss—occasionally, for joy, when he was freed. Third was what I've called *feminization*, a marked increase in the number and importance of females and concomitant decrease in males: more often than not all men found in the broadside ballad tradition other than the narrator himself were removed from the cast of characters, even the narrator's father, while a sister was added, a group of grieving women (who originated in Britain but who drop out in the song's Old World forms) consistently retained, and the wife's role in the robber's fate intensified.

In its New World reconfiguration, "The Rambling Boy" apparently both reflects and reinforces a particularly southern American mentality that privileges the individual's experience over his or her effect on the social order, that foregrounds what it considers to be female sensibilities and influence, and—especially—that prefers the expression of feeling to the expression of ideology. Clearly, these three attitudes are so inter-twined that they constitute a unified value-system that, in the British and British diasporic case, we can characterize as "outer-directed," in the southern U.S. case, as "inner-directed."

In the broadside strain of our ballad, this outer-directedness has a number of ramifications for our understanding of its supporting value system. The British robber is consistently depicted as representative of a social category, such as "youth" (he is only a teenager when he marries), or "the apprentice class" (he is a saddler's apprentice), or even "the crimi-nal class" (see especially Barrett 1891: 36; Reeves 1960: 152), and each of these socially constructed identities significantly affects his life's course. Moreover, his career *stands for* some more or less objectified, socially rooted principle. Most often, the principle is a fairly muted one and is a function of his membership in the class, "youth": that there's a certain charm in reckless, even anti-establishment behavior. The youthful rob-ber is "bold," "undaunted," "wild," "wicked," even "flash," all of which epithets have in varying degrees undertones of attractive rebelliousness, an image climaxed with dying words from the condemned protagonist that display little sense of shame, guilt, regret, or hope for redemption that native Anglo-North American ballads of crime and criminals so often do (see Laws [1964] 1975: 175–89).[16]

Another aspect of his "youth" persona is a generation gap between himself on the one hand and his father and mother on the other, and the song is not unsympathetic toward the youth's failure to embrace conser-vative parental values. The disjunction is expressed most poignantly in versions where the father makes his impassioned "What have you done?" or "I am undone" cry, apparently most grieved by his loss of social face in having a criminal son, and where the mother disavows her child ("My mother she tore her white locks and cried: / I wish that in his cradle he had died" [Karpeles 1974: 2: 160]), rejecting her deviant offspring in her support of social norms.[17] In two oral and two broadside texts, adversarial intergenerational relationships are rendered unequivocal with some variant or other of the following stanza:

> My parents oft times told me I should rue
> If such wicked ways I did pursue;
> I never minded what they did say,
> But still kept on in my wicked way.[18]

The son's refusal to compromise on his chosen style of life, however, and the triumphal denouement of that life—the song's ending line is invariably the spirited, ringing cry, "There goes a wild and a wicked youth"— clearly win the admiration of the ballad's narrative voice, and thus almost certainly its singer's.

Those defiant burial instructions communicate an even more pronounced social ideology: they seem clearly political in advocating a counterhegemonic enfranchising of the underclass, consisting of both criminals ("bold highwaymen") and what are evidently their street-people companions/accomplices ("Dublin ladies," the Ontario singer O. J. Abbott called them; see Fowke 1965: 45). An equally pronounced class consciousness, though of a more conventional kind, is also present in the broadside strain's habit of specifying, on the one hand, the robber's place in the social hierarchy as a saddler's apprentice and, on the other, the titles his victims possess (Lord Golden, Lady Mansfield), as well as their posh West End addresses (Grosvenor Square). Even representatives of such social institutions as law-enforcement may be depicted in class-conscious terms, suggesting not just class-based antagonism but perhaps even oppression, as when the captors' leader is assigned to the nobility (he is Lord Fielding in Karpeles 1974: 2: 163, Lord Mansfield in Hall 1994, Lord Patrick in more than one broadsheet from the Madden Collection in Vaughan Williams Memorial Library Microfilm Collection, reel no. 88. In Shuldham-Shaw et al. 1981-97: 2: 264, the judge is Sir John Bregswell). The notion of endemic inequity is made most explicit of all in ten of the sixty-four broadside-influenced texts that contain a stanza-cum-narrative theme elevating the wild and wicked youth to the status of "social bandit," even class hero:

> I never robbed a poor man yet,
> Or caused a tradesman for to fret,
> I robbed the rich, but I served the poor,
> Which brings me to this dismal door.
> (Kidson and Moffat 1926: 96)

In fact, the presence of a socially relevant ideological stance may be so integral to the Old World value system underlying "Wild and Wicked Youth" that apparently *any* stance will do! I say this because while most broadside-styled versions align their narrator's point of view with the Left, some seem to do just the opposite. Thus the occasional text will decry the robber's transgressing of the dominant culture's standards of behavior (though I should note that these more conservative ideologies tend to come from idiosyncratic versions). For example, H. E. D. Hammond collected "Wild and Wicked Youth" in 1906 from a Mrs. Webb of King's Norton near Birmingham that clearly rejects the robber as a role model: "Bad company did me entice," asserts the protagonist, so that "I left off work—took bad advice" (*Journal of the Folk-Song Society* 1930: 8: 190–1). In one of Baring-Gould's versions, the judge exhibits Christian clemency to our hero on his first offense, but the young man proves to be an incorrigible repeat offender:

> The judge his mercy he did extend
> He pardoned my crime, bade me amend
> But still I pursued a thriving trade.
> (Reeves 1960: 152)

Perhaps the most uncompromising conservative point of view appears in an unattributed version from W. A. Barrett's *English Folk-Songs* in which the robber and his accomplices cold-bloodedly kill one of their victims for no evident reason. "When you hear my death-bell toll," he says later, "Pray God for mercy on my soul" (Barrett 1891: 20; see also Goldie Hamilton's "Dublin City" in University of Virginia Special Collections, box 29, folder 1192, accession no. 1547).[19] Whether the values espoused are radical or conservative, however, they are both objectified and relevant to a social collective.

In contrast, the inner-directed blues ballad ethos is reluctant to make value judgments on the robber's life story and to draw from it any point of general social application, moral or political. If the occasional version does make a point it's invariably about interpersonal matters rather than social ones—about, say, relationships of trust, betrayal, and even victimization between man and woman, along the lines of Kentuckian Justus Begley's 1937 version:

> So my pretty little miss now fare you well
> I love you so well no one can tell
> Your face never more on earth I'll see
> Oh I wouldn't serve you as you served me.
>   (Lomax 1960: 192)

Indicative of its turn away from more externalized social concerns is "The Rambling Boy's" expunging of most male figures, apparently because they typify a patriarchal society, which is to say a society both deeply institutionalized and constructed on hierarchical principles. Instead, the blues ballad gives more weight to female figures whose identities are representative of not the social order but the familial one, or whose functions are in no way political or moralistic, only expressive. In short, in its *personalization, emotionalization,* and *feminization* the blues ballad projects a subjective sensibility that's much more interested in the personally tragic aspects of a picaresque lifestyle, of the sorrowful consequences that follow a man's poor judgment or even bad luck in love and marriage, of the pain and suffering that attend the rending apart of a nuclear family, of a doomed man's heartfelt desire to live, of human yearning for home and freedom.

Of the many varieties of context causally and reciprocally interfacing with ballad texts, the one folklorists can treat most competently is "generic context" (Toelken 1995: 61). This construct is rooted in the assumption that folksong constitutes a distinct language, or perhaps "dialect," even indeed a "discourse," since it manifests not only a characteristic vocabulary and syntax but also a characteristic worldview. What a folklorist should be able to do better than anyone is situate any text not only in relation to its many examples (versions) but also in relation to the traditional song corpus with whose members it shares motifs, themes, and commonplaces. By immersing oneself in the habitual language, imagery, and ideas a culture's folksong repertoire exhibits, the analyst will much better understand single items (Andersen 1985: 102–296).

If we follow this "intertextual" strategy in understanding the ballad of the wild and wicked rambling boy, we will see still more striking consistencies within each of our two ballad strains, the British and British diasporic folksong community's broadside-ballad strain on the one hand and the southern American folksong community's blues-ballad strain on the other. For example, in imagery and tone, "Wild and Wicked Youth's" burial instructions projecting narrative themes (I) and (J) are very similar to the burial instructions in "rake" songs that treat "alternative life-styles" like "The Tarpaulin Jacket" (Roud 829), "Rosin the Beau" (Roud 1192), and "The Sailor Cut Down in His Prime" (Laws Q26; Roud 2 [see Karpeles 1974: 2: 119–25]). While the phraseology of these related songs is distinctive and while they do not share "Wild and Wicked Youth's" political implications of arming the underclass, they certainly do share, in addition to content, the celebratory tone and attitude toward death and funeral rites—as well as the concomitant attitude of resistance toward conventionally mournful, lugubrious, maudlin, often self-incriminating dying words. The blues ballad "Rambling Boy," however, as we've seen rejects these two burial stanzas.

The most overt index to semantic equivalence between different songs is actual phraseology, or what are often called ballad "commonplaces" or "clichés," and when we examine such formulaic usage, we find a clear pattern: "Wild and Wicked Youth" tends to share verbal commonplaces with other British broadside ballads of what Laws (1957; 1964) calls Crime and Criminals. For example, the couplet mentioned above as implying a "generation gap" between parents and children ("My mother she tore her white locks and cried: / I wish that in his cradle he had died") appears in another popular British highwayman ballad, "Brennan on the Moor" (Laws L7; Roud 476), which like "Wild and Wicked Youth" seems to take the point of view of lawbreaker-as-sympathetic-figure (Palmer 1983: 25–6). Verbal equivalencies are also found with "Jack Williams" (Laws L17; Roud 1906) and "Salisbury Plain" (Roud 1487), both of whose male protagonists, like the wild and wicked youth, "went a-robbing on the highway." Their motives to do so are also textually very close to the wild and wicked youth's: "to maintain you as some lady so gay" in "Salisbury Plain" (Karpeles 1974: 2: 155), "to keep Ena fine and gay" in "Jack Williams" (Karpeles 1974: 2: 152). In "The Irish Mail Robber" (Laws L15; Roud 1905), the protagonist says "Then I married a fair one and to dress her up gay / I then took to driving along the highway" (Creighton 1962: 161). In "The Croppy Boy" (Laws J14; Roud 1030), an Irish political prisoner, executed by British authorities, gives almost the same burial instructions as "Wild and Wicked Youth": "And when I am dead and taken to my grave / A decent funeral pray let me have" (Belden 1940: 284). And what I've called the Robin Hood motif—not part of the normative form but found in some version or other in ten of our sixty-four broadside-influenced texts, thus constituting a significant minority pattern—is common in several other British ballads of highwaymen: not only "Brennan on the Moor" already noted above (see Healy 1967: 1: 120–1), but also "Captain Grant" (Roud 1286 [Karpeles 1974: 2: 169]), "I Am a Wild Young Irish Boy" (Laws L19; Roud 1907 [see Doerflinger 1951: 270–1]), "Johnny Troy" (Laws L21; Roud 3703 [see Gardner and Chickering 1939: 329–31]), and "My Bonny Black Bess II" (Laws L9; Roud 620 [see Belden and Hudson 1952a: 356–7]). In short, "Wild and Wicked Youth" tends to share its imagery and language (whether lending or borrowing) with songs that not only typically treat subcultural, marginalized, even deviant personnel, but that also tend to glamorize, at times glorify, them.

The blues ballad "Rambling Boy," in contrast, tends to share verbal commonplaces not with ballads about criminals but with ballads about lovers. So for instance some versions of a Family Opposition to Lovers ballad (Laws 1957: 179–200), "Oh, Willie" (the subject of chapter 4 below), begins with a variant of the "when I was a rake and rambling boy" line which opens many renditions of Laws L12/Roud 490 (Belden and Hudson 1952a: 278). Even greater sharing is evinced with love songs of the lyric rather than ballad genre. For example, the stanza contained in John Lomax's Kentucky text given earlier ("The roses are red and the stems are green") is entirely congruent with Anglo/American lyric song conventions, as in "A Week Before Easter" (Roud 154 [see Copper 1971: 237]) and "A-Growing" (Laws O35; Roud 31). Here's another example of the same stanza, given to Josiah Combs by Tom Kelley of Berea, Kentucky:

> The rose is red, the stem is green
> The time is past that I have seen
> It may be more, it may be few
> But I hope to spend them all with you.
>> (Combs 1969: 184–5)

Traditional singer Justus Begley devoted an extra lyric stanza to describing the wife, one that's also a typical lover's panegyric (compare Sharp 1932: 2: 31):

> Oh my pretty little miss sixteen years old
> Her hair just as yeller as the shining gold
> The prettiest face and the sweetest hands
> Bless the ground on where she stands.
>> (Lomax 1960: 192)

Fellow Kentuckian Jean Ritchie learned "Rambling Boy" from Begley but varied it considerably by adding several stanzas borrowed from lyric songs like "Slighted Sweetheart" (Roud 11422; see Belden and Hudson 1952b: 307) and "My Little Dear, So Fear You Well" (Roud 464; see Schinan 1957: 429–31). Perhaps the most lyrical association of all is found in a version from Mr. C. L. Pruitt of Roanoke County, Virginia, in which the robber voices a commonplace usually reserved for betrayed maids who desperately wish the impossible—to turn back time and undo events that are past and gone:

> I've wished and I've wished.
> But it was in vain,
> I've wished and I've wished
> But it never will be
> Till oranges grow on an apple tree.
>> (University of Virginia Special Collections, box 12, accession no. 9936)

Variations such as these are usually made by particularly gifted traditional singers, like Jean Ritchie, who often possess an attitude toward their songs typical of what Eleanor Long (1973) has called a "rationalizer" and may be very revealing because they make explicit certain significations that less reflective singers in the same tradition (or singers who have little occasion to perform for outsiders) take for granted, regarding them as "obvious." These variations function as a sort of exegesis, analogous to grammatical appositions or scholarly footnotes: they duplicate, reinforce, expand on, even explain that to which they're attached (compare Renwick 1980: 43–7; Foley 1991 on "immanent meaning" and "synecdoche"). Clearly, these examples of where in folksong's generic network bearers of tradition, by association, position "The Wild and Wicked Youth" on one hand and "The Rambling Boy" on the other reinforce what we have said about the ballads' respective value systems.

Yet another kind of context is a behavioral rather than textual one, a song's *performative* setting, and on the very rare occasions collectors of "Wild and Wicked Youth/Rambling Boy" oral versions addressed the subjects of singer or of song occasion rather than just of song text, their comments seem to match what I've said of the two traditions. The Reverend Sabine Baring-Gould asserted of "Wild and Wicked Youth" that "It is a fine thing to hear the song of the highwayman sung by the sons of smugglers over a great fire in a kitchen in Cornwall. Their eyes flash, their colour mounts, and they roar out the chorus with immense excitement and enthusiasm" (Baring-Gould and Sheppard 1895: 39). These sons of former lawbreakers, although now themselves probably domesticated, evidently reveled in the fictional robber's distressing of the aristocrats by stealing their wealth and in the funeral ritual's empowering of an underclass. The singers thought in terms of group identity, not only in collaborating on the refrain but also in enthusiastically empathizing with the class of marginals and outsiders, evincing that empathy with what in today's vernacular we'd call an "in-your-face" performance "with attitude," perhaps even identify as an early prototype of "gangster rap."[20]

A southern U.S. counterpart of this southern English sensibility was provided by a song collector, Maude Minish Sutton, and occasioned by a rendition of "The Rambling Boy" from Mrs. Ann Coffey of Caldwell County, North Carolina: "It is very likely," wrote the folklorist, "that [Mrs. Coffey] felt some of the significance of the story; one of her two sons was condemned to death for murder and the other was a deserter from the army when I heard her sing it" (Belden and Hudson 1952a: 355).

Maude Minish Sutton suspected that the singer made the song meaning-ful relative to her own singular experience: it dealt with the emotional rupture incumbent upon a particular mother's losing of a particular son, not with matters of class, kind, or type and certainly not with a social theory or a social agenda.

Less speculatively, we might see represented in this contrast between the Cornish smugglers' sons and the North Carolina mother a larger "gendered" pattern: the outer-directed ethos of the Old World form of the song seems attractive mostly to men singers, while the inner-directed blues ballad is apparently just as attractive to women as to men. Of the twenty-eight oral versions of "Wild and Wicked Youth" whose singers are identified, only four were collected from women: one from Mrs. Webb in February 1906 (*Journal of the Folk-Song Society* 1930: 8: 190–1; Purslow 1972: 107–8, 143), one from Bell Robertson of Aberdeenshire in March 1908 (who'd learned it from her mother [Shuldham-Shaw et al. 1981-97: 2: 264, 554]), one from Mrs. George A. Barnett of Columbia, Missouri ("as learned and sung by her mother, Mrs. J. T. Cooper of Johnson County, Missouri, before the Civil War" [Belden 1940: 136]), and one from Mrs. Goldie Hamilton of Wise County, Virginia (University of Virginia Special Collections, box 29, folder 1192, accession no. 1547). The remaining twenty-four attributed oral texts were all gathered from men. In England, even though Cecil Sharp collected extensively from women informants, the three versions of "Wild and Wicked Youth" he recorded all came from males.

In contrast, eight of the nineteen "Rambling Boy" versions with iden-tified informants were gathered from women (one of these versions came from two women, Mrs. Lee Stephens and Mrs. Ethel Rodney of White Rock, Missouri [Randolph 1946-50: 2: 84]), while a ninth is from the singing of the three-member Carter Family, two of whom were women. In sum, across the Anglo/American spectrum, women domestic and community singers don't seem to have felt much aesthetic interest in the bravado of "Wild and Wicked Youth," while they do seem to have been attracted to the more affecting "Rambling Boy" (though see the headnote in Ritchie 1997: 91).

Yet another kind of context in which folksongs exist is, of course, soci-ety at large. Up to very recent times, a pervasive class system was an accepted fact of life for the British, including those who sang and listened to "The Wild and Wicked Youth." To working-class singers of rural Britain during the heyday of the ballad's popularity, the story must have reflected social conditions by no means unfamiliar to them. Apprenticed to a trade, the protagonist of that British ballad would have been implicitly located by a British singer and his or her audience in the lower tiers of the social hierarchy, well below the professional class of administrators like the magistrate whose "gang" or "crew" eventually captures him and of course far, far below the members of the nobility whose wealth he appropriates, Lord Golden and Lady Mansfield. Such a highly stratified—and highly marked—class system which stamps members of a community as "inferior" or "superior," which usually bears a direct correlation with birth, wealth, and power, and which is not readily conducive to personal mobility between classes is clearly a more fertile ground for the sort of biography dramatized in "Wild and Wicked Youth" and the sort of values the song's voice seems to support. In that kind of world, wide disparities in social and material standing consistently motivate actors. Thus the British robber may have turned criminal to preserve his wife's upper-class status and way of life (her class is never mentioned, but it is strongly implied: evidently, she's already accustomed to a lavish lifestyle when she marries the youth). The causal power of class divisions are more explicit in the robber's choice of victims, the aristocracy: in the great majority of texts, the wild and wicked youth robs "lords and ladies bright" in general in addition to Lord Golden and Lady Mansfield in particular (though one must not ignore the obvious fact that aristocrats owned property most worth stealing).[21] And note that the quasi-revolutionary cry toward the ballad's end is for the highwaymen's *liberty*, which seems to imply not just release from physical incarceration but the more far-reaching, more ideologically resonant release from the structural constraints that, in a hierarchical society, are imposed a priori on people by the circumstances of their birth: the wild and wicked youth yearned for the opportunity to "be somebody," yearned for "respect"—or rather, he wished it for (or projected his own desire for it onto) his fellow outcasts.

But to have any real chance of achieving all that, he had not only to emigrate but indeed to change his citizenship to "The Rambling Boy," whose song obviously reflects America's more democratic social context. For example, the robber is never identified by such externally imposed

attributes as his trade but by personal character traits, behaviors, or possessions intimate to his identity (dry goods, sword and pistol, someone
to "go his bail"). Since his victims' personas have no social or political
ramifications, those victims are virtually never identified. And despite
the precedent of Patrick Henry's memorable plea, the American robber
never uses the term "liberty," probably because unlike his British cousin
he is not constrained by the rigidities of a class system and has no need
of that word's political and philosophical resonances: "free" is the word
he uses, denoting straightforward physical freedom (from a prison cell, of
spatial movement so that he can return home) but even sometimes a
more spiritually suggestive freedom from earthly life's inevitable tra-
vails. Such freedoms have little to do with culturally constructed markers of status and class, and once again seem appropriate to an American
context. While there were certainly differences in wealth within the resi-
dent population of the southern uplands, especially after the Civil War
with the coming of industrialism—textiles, mining, lumbering—the
older agrarian pattern of small-holding land ownership and egalitarian
social organization continued to dominate the region up to World War II
(Hall et al. 1987: 114–80). Thus the American robber appropriately acts
within an American environment that lacks the sort of social and economic conditions which support deep class divisions between the Lord
Goldens and Lady Mansfields on the one hand and youths who turn thief
on the other.

Finally, the distinction between an outer-directed ethos and an inner-
directed one seems perfectly compatible with the conventional wisdom
that typifies the British cultural norm as set toward a greater awareness
of and sensitivity to the social whole as opposed to the American cultural
norm of "individualism." One of the very earliest analysts of U.S. culture,
Alexis de Tocqueville, noted that Americans in the 1830s had much less
interest in objective contemplation of the social body and for theorizing
about it than did Europeans, being much more attuned to practicality and
to individual experience and needs (1969: 2: 429). The coming of postbellum industrialism, of urbanization, and of increasing gaps between rich
and poor didn't seem to have changed this ethos much—and certainly not
in the southern uplands, where any "social philosophy" or ideological
"system" was automatically subject to suspicion and rejection, especially
when imposed from *outside.* In the first decades of the twentieth century,

southerners tended to distrust and even hate capitalists and communists with equal intensity (Fischer 1989: 650), and despite the hardships caused by the Great Depression, while organized protests certainly occurred, America did not experience anything like widespread social rebellion, for "most Americans felt the Depression as an individual, not a class experience, and, since they considered unemployment a sign of personal failure, the idle hands blamed not society but themselves" (Diggins [1973] 1992: 108). Of course, "The Rambling Boy" cast his net a bit further: for his hardship, he blamed his woman!

In sum, the textual properties of each song strain exhibit a logical match with the general properties of its several intersecting contexts. Thus may the more striking differences in the two traditions be understood. At the same time, however, we must not forget the obvious: that "The Rambling Boy" is a *variant* of "Wild and Wicked Youth" that does not really subvert its progenitor to produce a rupture in the song's Anglo/American tradition but "adapts" it. Consequently, while this investigation has highlighted the differences between the two song strains as the more interesting aspect of "The Wild and Wicked Rambling Boy's" history, we must not neglect to acknowledge there is also significant continuity, not just of narrative facts but also of feeling and idea. For instance, both strains of our ballad seem to depend on a view that urban life (London, Dublin, Columbus City) corrupts innocents of tender age and/or of rural origins.[22] This rural/urban theme—and its associated agrarian economy/industrial capitalist economy corollary—seems to transcend other contextual differences in unifying the two strains.

More interesting, however, may be a continuity of *feeling*. In 1928, the proto-Skillet Lickers from Georgia (the "McMichen-Layne String Orchestra") recorded "The Rambling Boy," ending it with a variant of the burial-instructions narrative theme that's perfectly consistent with the blues ballad sensibility:

Now when I'm dead go bury me deep
Place a marble stone at my head and feet
And on my grave place the wings of a dove
To prove to the world that I died for love.
   (Darling 1983: 109–10)

This marble-stone stanza, which originated in Britain, plays a common-place or "floating" role in anglophone lyric song tradition, though it is most often linked with the "Died for Love" (Roud 60)/"In Sheffield Park" (Roud 860)/"Butcher Boy" (Laws P24; Roud 409)/"Sailor Boy" (Laws K12; Roud 273) complex. Wherever it appears, however, its relevance is always to love's dominance over all other human emotions and experiences, and to love's power—against all reason, against all natural laws—over life itself. While the stanza and the feeling it evokes seem compatible with the blues ballad ethos, they don't seem compatible with the more ideo-logically inclined ethos of "The Wild and Wicked Youth," whose burial instructions overwhelmingly project an oppositional, countercultural posture.

In 1906, however, Charles Woodhouse of Hampshire sang for George B. Gardiner a version of "Wild and Wicked Youth" that, even though it included the most socially-conscious of all the motifs found in "Wild and Wicked Youth's" anglophone tradition, the one embodied in the "Robin Hood" stanza, lacked narrative theme (I) *burial-instructions-for-male-participants*, substituting for it a more familiar and widespread funeral request:

> So it's dig me a grave, both large, wide, and deep
> And a marble stone at my head and feet
> And in the center a turtle dove
> To show mankind I died for love.
>
> (Reeves 1960: 153)

Evidently, Mr. Woodhouse felt more than just passingly the same emo-tional pulse in the British highwayman that his distant kin in faraway Appalachia would refashion into the rambling boy's very essence.

3

The Anglo/American Catalogue Song

A survey of the more significant studies of Anglo/American folksong published over the last decade or so would reveal the ballad to be still by far the genre of scholarly choice (see, for example, Cheesman and Rieuwerts 1997; McCarthy 1990; Toelken 1995), even in the present postformalist age when text-determined topics usually take a backseat in folklorists' worldview to ethnographically determined ones; when the current taste of cultural theorists for instability, indeterminacy, relativism, anti-essentialism, and so forth regards the concept of a bounded "type" as far too rigid and reifying, a distortion of the real world; and when categories derived by library scholars smack of the dreaded canonizing.

Many reasons lie behind this continued privileging of ballads over other kinds of folksong, but surely one of the foremost is that over the last hundred-odd years such a strong foundation has been laid for ballad study that it's become a self-perpetuating activity. This foundation includes a vast store of raw materials, both published and archived; well codified, organized, and accessible databases, thanks to the efforts of such forebears as Francis James Child ([1882–98] 1963) and G. Malcolm Laws Jr. (1957, [1964] 1975) and to contemporaries like Steve Roud (1994a–present; 1994b–present); and a sense that we really understand ballad poetics, especially as laid out by such outstanding works as David Buchan's *Ballad and the Folk* (1972) and Flemming G. Andersen's *Commonplace and Creativity* (1985). These same generalizations hold for ballad study in many Continental European countries and their diasporic kin. In short, it is our mastery of the genre's textuality that has fed the strong, ongoing analytical work.

Such success usually entails a downside, however: because the ballad was made so attractive an object of ongoing study, other traditional song types were neglected, with the result that we have nothing else approaching a seminal work on any other genre. In fact, as the widely employed phrase "ballads and songs" (along with its slight permutations, such as "ballads and folksongs") attests, we often lump all other traditional songs into a catchall category after we've extracted the "ballads." True, were we pressed to identify any other genre in the Anglo/American traditional song repertoire, many folksong scholars might name the "lyric song," and indeed two recent folklore encyclopedias, Jan Harold Brunvand's *American Folklore: An Encyclopedia* (1996) and Thomas A. Green's *Folklore* (1997), have entries for lyric song as well as for ballad. But that's it! No other Anglo/American song type gains encyclopedia recognition on formal grounds, only on functional ones (for example, lullaby, chantey, hymn, worksong). And in fact, actual attempts to lay bare the poetics of the lyric song are exceedingly few (Coffin 1985; Renwick 1997).

To repeat, however, the ballad's success in engaging the scholarly imagination has been predicated on our thorough knowledge of its textual conventions and manifestations; functional characterizations have not gained folksongs sustained and widespread analytical attention. So in hope of changing this state of affairs, I make here a stab at identifying the textual conventions of a third Anglo/American traditional song genre that, even though examples exist in profusion in our many, many collections of folksongs from both the British Isles and Anglo-North America, we've virtually ignored analytically, since we've thought about them only as functional or regional types rather than as formal ones. I am even going to propose a name for this third type of traditional Anglo/American folksong—catalogue.

The textual sensibility that has so successfully established the medieval or Child ballad in ongoing scholarly consciousness conceives of genre as a way of articulating images in sung verse (Renwick 1996). The ballad articulates its images in a narrative way: the relationship between images is linear, one-dimensional, sequential, and causal. The lyric song, in contrast, articulates images in an expressive way, interrelating them associatively: for instance, a burning sun and a pair of sparkling eyes are unified at a higher level of abstraction by some shared quality, such as "intensity." In our shorthand characterizations, we say that a ballad "tells a story," while a lyric "expresses emotion." A catalogue song, in contrast, articulates its images additively: it inventories or lists them so that they constitute an assemblage of parts that, while unified by a common empirical quality such as contiguity, comprise a whole that's not much more than the sum of those parts. I hope that this characterizing of texts as generated by compositional techniques or strategies ("ways of articulating images") rather than as adhering to a fixed template ("a ballad is a song that tells a story") allows for a more fluid perception of song, one at least partially consonant with the notions of permeable boundaries and mutable form that anti-Platonists prefer. If we depict the three dominant traditional Anglo/American song "ways" as a Venn diagram, we can better visualize this somewhat more sensitive conception:

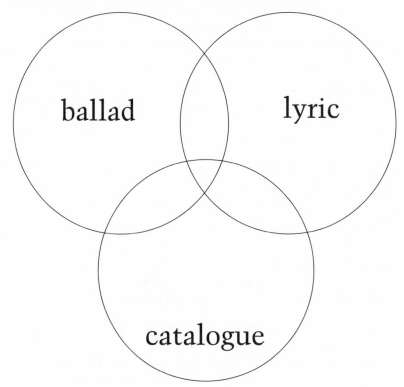

Most traditional Anglo/American song texts as actually sung can be characterized by the intersections in the diagram above: some lines, couplets, stanzas, or groups of stanzas may evince a highly lyrical idea, others a strong ballad idea. Some songs may even be informed equally by all three ideas. But the Anglo/American corpus suggests that, far more often than not, in any single song one way will dominate, and for simple categorization purposes we may surely give that song a generic designation of ballad, or lyric, or—I hope—catalogue.

To ease our transition into a closer look at the catalogue way of articulating images, let's first examine two songs on a topic that, although far more popular in francophone tradition, is also found in anglophone folksong: marriage between a young girl and an old man. The first is probably of Irish origin (from Morton 1970: 17–8):

ROLL ME FROM THE WALL (ROUD 8302)

[1] When I was young some years ago from trouble I was free
The boys they used to court me and how dearly they liked me,
They often said how happy I'd be when the winter storms would fall,
If I had for mine a youth so fine to roll me from the wall.

[2] Now an ould man came to court me and he was four score and more.
He had long grey hair and a curly beard, but he had gold in store.
There wasn't a trace in his face of a youthful sign at all,
And I was told he was too old to roll me from the wall.

[3] Ah! But when my parents heard the news sure they got very bold,
They said I'd have to marry him if he was twice as old.
Just to satisfy my parents I went without a brawl,
But sorely he rejected to lie beside the wall.

[4] This ould man was feeble and his bones were cold as clay,
And like a frozen ice-berg he there beside me lay.
I often laid in bed and prayed that the Lord would on him call,
And I'd have for mine, a youth so fine, to roll me from the wall.

[5] After six long months of married life, this ould man took sick and died,
His money and land he left me, as I stood by his side,
With money and land at my command that I might enjoy them all,
I would have for mine, a youth so fine, to roll me from the wall.

[6] When the funeral was over and all things said and done,
I got wed to a nice young man I thought the sun shone on,
But very soon sure he'd gone through my money, land, and all,
And now I suffer dearly for my rolling from the wall.

We see in this song a way of articulating images that folksong scholars know intimately, a narrative way: over time, events lead into, emerge out of, and mingle with each other to build up an evolving set of interrelated experiences that creates drama, tension, and change in the lives of the dramatis personae. The first stanza introduces the protagonist, the second a suitor whom she is reluctant to accept, the third the parents whose approval of the old man helps make up her mind. Stanza three moves forward to describe her married life, which by stanza five is over after only six months when her husband dies. As a widow she finds her circumstances significantly transformed by the money she's inherited; she marries again, this time a young man of her choice. But he turns out to be a wastrel, perhaps even a step down from husband number one! The narrator eventually ends up worse off than she'd begun, now no longer protected by parental support and saddled with the liability of a useless husband who'll impoverish her. And of course the song has a point to make, a general precept about prudence or morality or character, which the events narrated dramatize and exemplify. In short, students of folksong would have little hesitation calling "Roll Me from the Wall" a ballad.

Contrast the following song on the same topic (from Belden 1940: 264):

THE OLD MAN'S COURTSHIP (ROUD 362)

[1] There was an old man came over the lea,
Ha ha ha but I won't have him
Came over the lea a-courting me
With his old gray beard newly shaven

(REPEAT REFRAIN)

[2] My mother she told me to open the door
I opened the door and he bowed to the floor

[3] My mother she told me to give him a stool,
I gave him a stool and he sat like a fool

[4] My mother she told me to give him some pie.
I gave him some pie and he made the crust fly.

[5] My mother she told me to light him to bed.
I lit him to bed and he asked me to wed.

[6] My mother she told me to lead him to church.
I led him to church and I left him in the lurch.

Many of the images we saw in "Roll Me From the Wall" we also see in "The Old Man," but the song presents those images in a significantly different way. Certainly, there is a sequence of chronologically related happenings, but that sequencing contains no surprises, no tension, no plot. The main character, the maiden, ends up exactly where and how she began. The events are far more predictable than they were in "Roll Me from the Wall," thanks not only to the set-piece nature of the action (the old man journeys to the girl's house, enters the door, sits down at table, eats, goes to bed, goes to church, is left) but also to the formulaic language that reinforces the set piece's internal redundancy to produce a text of highly repetitive syntax and lexicon. Indeed, this is a common kind of textual architecture, often found in folklore, that we call "incremental repetition," and it puts the song's images, or component parts, together in a way that is less linear than it is vertical: the images are "stacked" one on top of the other, as it were, since any one is really a slightly different version of any other. ("Stepwise" rather than "linear" narrative progression is an epithet often used to characterize incremental repetition's structure when the technique appears in ballads.) The point, however, is that, while the ballad idea is primary in "Roll Me from the Wall," it is distinctly secondary in the "The Old Man's Courtship." What is primary in "The Old Man's Courtship" is what I wish to call the catalogue way of articulating images in sung verse. I hope to demonstrate that this model is so pervasive in Anglo/American traditional song and so rule-bound that we should call it a genre.

Of course, neither the concept nor the term "catalogue" is new: it's most commonly employed in epic studies, especially in Homeric scholarship (as in "catalogue of ships" or "catalogue of heroes") and is considered a trope in formal rhetoric. Hence you'll find the word in dictionaries of literary terms, which usually illustrate the construct with examples from Milton and Walt Whitman but which may also note that the convention's most common home is traditional oral poetry, as in—yes—Homer. Had the interests of literary critics extended further into traditional oral poetry than the epic, however, they might have added to their examples the songs of Scottish agricultural workers barracked for the season in farm bothies, of New England lumbermen in their similarly seasonal shanties, and of West Texas cowboys in their bunkhouses, not to mention such types as lullabies, worksongs, play-party and frolic songs, and the verses of children's singing games.

That's quite a diverse bunch of functional and culture-specific song-types, and I may seem to be severely stretching a point to claim that items that we feel fit under so many headings are related in more than just a trivial way. But that, to my mind, is a virtue of the construct catalogue: it brings to our awareness a distinctive set of traditional poetic competencies that are widespread and of long usage, and that cut across both empirical boundaries, such as date and place of origin or extent of diffusion, and cultural boundaries, such as age, occupation, and gender. And until we formalize these tacit compositional skills, techniques, devices, and strategies, we're not going to achieve—as we have for ballads—sustained, full-blown, nonparochial scholarly attention to what is a very substantial portion of the Anglo/American traditional song corpus.

Anyone with a more-than-passing knowledge of traditional British and anglophone North American song will recognize the distinct formal patterns that are grounded in the catalogue idea of additiveness and listing, though he or she may not have thought they constituted a set. I'll identify five such cataloguing patterns, or what by analogy we may call syntactic structures, since they're specific ways of linking the component parts of a song's topic together. The simplest one—in the sense that it manifests the least poetic shapeliness—gives a sort of roster or menu of images, the individual parts coming in no particular order and without any special verbal repetition to reinforce their obvious similarity. This is the most common technique in Anglo/American folksongs influenced by the catalogue idea. It's dominant, for example, in the geographically rooted type we call the "local song" and its many subtypes, such as the "moniker song" that identifies and characterizes each member of a team of, say, lumbermen (or cowboys, or sailors, or farmworkers, or fishermen), the collective community depicted piece by piece in phrase, line, or stanza as individuals who not only are in physical proximity with each other but also share other empirical traits, such as typical behaviors, or the same employer. Those commonalities are both a function of and a cause for membership in the same phenomenal class, category, or set. Other ubiquitous local-song subtypes, like spree songs, place-songs, and occupational songs that depict a work experience in a series of vignettes, all invariably reveal this syntactic pattern as well. For example:

OLDEN DAYS (ROUD 9951)

[1] When Kate she joined in wedlock 'twas sixteen hundred and two
They had no stoves nor funnels then, but the smoke went up the flue,
The bride-boys dressed in corduroy, the bride-girls dungaree,
Old Bob cleared out the kitchen and they started off a spree.

[2] Uncle Reuben held the fiddle, it was up and down the floor,
Swing around Jemima, but don't knock down my door!
Swing to your partner, Nell Bell Flemont, dance to your partner now John
    Twine
Right and left, me darlin' creature, now fair lady toe the line!

[3] Saul took down the flint and steel, we all shook hands with the bride,
Aunt Viner went to get some cake and her costume came untied,
We seated round the open fire when Jezz began to spin,
He took a chew of "T and B" when the juice ran down his chin.

[4] When the dance was finished it was fill your old T.D.'s
Billy crawled under the table and tickled Bessie's knees,
Saul brought in a stock of rum from a Frenchman in the bay,
He placed the jar on the table—come on, boys, drink away!

[5] Jim Hickman made some baskets, all of us bought one,
We tied them to the bride's frock tail, now didn't we have fun,
Nick had killed a great big owl and Lude had a job,
She dished the soup on table, they called it northern slob.

[6] Uncle Joshua raised an argument, he called young Clem a liar,
He made a crack at Nattie's back, then his whisker caught on fire,
Sal she rushed for water and nearly drowned us all,
We all ran home and jumped in bunk and this cleared up the ball.

"Olden Days" (from Peacock 1965: 1: 79–80) is characteristic of local song compositions. It treats, if not a real occasion, certainly one whose occurrence was entirely possible. It is peopled with what were undoubtedly very real men and women, all of whom lived within the sight, reach, and knowledge of the songmaker, the song singer (often the same person as the maker), and the song audience, despite its obvious exaggeration

and parody (like the wedding's 1602 date). The catalogue song's percep-
tual and compositional building block is usually the common Anglo/
American four-line stanza (but may be the line or the couplet), which
treats a single separable—but not isolated—component part of the event
constituting the topic as-a-whole, which in "Olden Days" is Kate's post-
wedding party. Any one component part may, within the confines of its
stanza, be itself constructed by a ballad's narrative technique, as in the
Saul/Aunt Viner/Jezz episode of stanza 3 and the Jim/Nick/Lude episode
of stanza 5, but those single lines of action are not the units of thought of
the song "Olden Days" because they cannot stand alone: the unit is the
entire vignette.

The song as a whole is constructed by the juxtaposing of such
vignettes, and for the most part that juxtaposing follows no necessary
order. That is to say, the most important relationships among the images
are the very simple ones of contiguity (the parts were physically close,
even adjacent to each other), complementarity (they were all parts of the
same whole, Kate's wedding), and/or similarity (all participants shared a
certain quality: for example, a common place of residence, a common
definition of the situation, a common mood/attitude/spirit of celebratory
participation in the ritual occasion). The best word I can think of for this
catalogue "way of articulating images" is *enumeration*: portrayal by
means of a simple inventory or list of items that are the song topic's component parts—to repeat, the least shapely of the cataloguing patterns
common in Anglo/American song tradition, one which requires the least
poetic construction (though of course not necessarily skill) and is closest
to compositional patterns of ordinary speech.

A bit more shapely than enumeration is a second, less ubiquitous pattern we can call *iteration*. In the iterative pattern, one of the catalogue's
fundamental relationship-among-parts—similarity—is built into the
actual poetry so that verbal repetition in depicting parts matches those
parts' semantic similarity, as in the shared exaggeration of items in "lying
songs" or in the common exuberance of behaviors in "spree songs." Of
course, repetition comes in degrees, and the point where simple enumeration ends and the more crafted iteration begins is open to debate, but so
many British traditional songs display substantial, structural iteration in
their stanzas that there can be little doubt they constitute a distinct sub-

genre of catalogue. The technique is very common, for instance, in meta-phorical songs of sexual liaisons (Renwick 1980: 85–96):

THE FURZE FIELD (ROUD 1037)

[1] I have got a furze field, my own dearest jewel,
Where all my fine pheasants do fly,
And if you comes a-shooting when shooting's in season
I'll tell you, love, how to proceed.
You bring your dog with you, your gun in your hand,
All loaded and primed all at your command.
When the pheasants take fright, you must take sight,
You shoot the next moment, you're sure to be right.

[2] I have got a fishpond, my own dearest jewel,
Where all my fine fishes do play,
And if you comes a-fishing when fishing's in season
I'll tell you, love, how to proceed.
You bring your rod with you, your nets in your hand,
Your hooks and your angles all at your command.
When you throws in, all the fishes will play,
It's down to the bottom, and that's the right way.

[3] I have got a warren, my own dearest jewel,
Where all my fine rabbits do play,
And if you comes a-ferreting when ferreting's in season
I'll tell you, love, how to proceed.
You bring your dog with you, your ferret in your hand,
Your hooks and your angles all at your command,
And the ferret will bolt and the rabbits will play,
For it's down to the bottom, and that's the right way.

"The Furze Field" (from Reeves 1960: 117) represents the most formal-ized use of iteration: the whole stanza is patterned, and the entire song holds rigidly to that pattern. More usual would be repetition of line or even half-line that's stuck to for only part of the song, as found for exam-ple in the ubiquitous catalogue-of-trades. Here's the relevant portion of such a song, its iteration marked by the "and there is" phrase opening each stanza (from Lomax 1910: 103–5; Roud 876):

And there is the merchant, as honest, we're told.
Whatever he sells you, my friend, you are sold;
Believe what I tell you, and don't be surprised
To find yourself cheated half out of your eyes,—
And it's hard, hard times.

And there is the lawyer you plainly will see,
He will plead your case for a very large fee,
He'll law you and tell you the wrong side is right,
And make you believe that a black horse is white,—
And it's hard, hard times.

And there is the doctor, I like to forgot,
I believe to my soul he's the worst of the lot;
He'll tell you he'll cure you for half you possess,
And when you're buried he'll take all the rest,—
And it's hard, hard times.

The repetition that constitutes the primary marker of the iterative sub-type is not the recurring end-of-stanza refrain, "And it's hard, hard times": burdens, refrains, and choruses are features of performance (encouraging audience participation, for instance) rather than of poetics. Poetic iteration is manifested most commonly in a repeated formula of stanza beginnings, representing a paradigm or template for several stanzas. This sort of repetition is cognitive and artistic, not behavioral.

The next pattern is grounded in a poetic technique we customarily consider a narrative one that's especially characteristic of the medieval or Child ballad genre that, according to the historical records, first appears in thirteenth-century Europe (we can't pinpoint just where), though in Britain it doesn't seem to have become a widely used compositional model until the fifteenth century (Child [1882–98] 1963). This technique is what, in Child ballad critical terminology, is called "incremental repetition" (Gummere [1909] 1959: 117–34). Let us call it for our purposes *incrementation*. The incremental pattern exhibits both verbal and formal repetition, as did iteration, but a repetition that brings some kind of progression, however minimal, into the catalogue's static world. (It's for this reason, of course, that the technique is congruent with the ballad's storytelling quality.) Each repetition produces a slight change in the topic's condition or state, though the change is painfully slow, redundantly predictable, and step-wise rather than horizontally linear. "The Old Man's Courtship" given earlier exemplifies a song built solely on incrementation, as does "The Foolish Boy" (Reeves 1960: 112):

THE FOOLISH BOY (ROUD 469)

[1] My father died, I can't tell 'ee how
And left me six horses to follow the plough.
CHORUS: Wim-mee—wim-mee—wobble O!
        Jiggee, jiggee, stobble O!
        Little boys a wobble lived under the gloam.

[2] I sold my six horses and bought me a cow.
I'm a going to get money but I can't tell how.
(CHORUS)

[3] I sold my cow and I bought me a calf.
By that my bargain I lost just half.
(CHORUS)

[4] I sold my calf and bought me a cat
And in the chimney corner the pretty creature sat.
(CHORUS)

[5] I sold my cat and I bought me a mouse
Set fire to her tail and her burnt down the house.
(CHORUS)

[6] I sold my mouse and I bought me a wife.
Her cut my throat with an old rusty knife.
(CHORUS)

The similarity of incrementation to iteration is patent, but the difference is just as critical, as we can see by comparing "The Foolish Boy" with the "The Furze Field" given earlier. As with incrementation's simpler relative, enumeration, the images or component parts, each embedded in a stanza that is its vehicle, can be rearranged with no loss of sense: that is to say, the air-creature, water-creature, land-creature order of this particular version of "Furze Field" could be shuffled around with no loss to the song's poetic, aesthetic, or semantic values. Such is not the case, however, with "The Foolish Boy": one arrangement makes far more sense than any others. Thus incrementation is even more complex, more "shapely" or "formalized" than the three patterns we've seen so far.

Incrementation is also more closely aligned than those other catalogue patterns with the plotted "way of articulating images in sung verse" that characterizes the ballad. For example, "Dives and Lazarus" (Child 56; Roud 477) tells a story of a poor man's begging at a rich man's house while the owner gives a feast for friends. The host, Dives, refuses Lazarus's request for food and drink, eventually in exasperation sending servants and dogs to punish the beggar, which they're unable to do, as they're mysteriously made immobile. Eventually, Lazarus dies, goes to Heaven, and is granted a permanent seat on an angel's knee. Dives too dies but goes to Hell, from where he can see Lazarus; he is forced to importune the former beggar for water to slake his "flaming thirst." The ballad ends with Dives repenting his former actions. Here is a typical threefold incremental repetition describing Lazarus's initial begging:

Then Lazarus laid him down and down,
And down at Dives' door;
"Some meat, some drink, brother Dives,
Bestow upon the poor."

Then Lazarus laid him down and down,
And down at Dives' wall:
"Some meat, some drink, brother Dives,
Or with hunger starve I shall."

Then Lazarus laid him down and down,
And down at Dives' gate:
"Some meat, some drink, brother Dives,
For Jesus Christ his sake."
    (Child 56A)

But a nonincremental, chronologically unfolding storytelling technique dominates the song of "Dives and Lazarus" as a whole, and we feel perfectly comfortable calling it a ballad, while recognizing that, for the purpose of comparative poetics, we would plot it in a different section of the Venn diagram given earlier than we would, say, another religious ballad, "The Carnal and the Crane" (Child 55; Roud 306), which is informed almost solely by a linearly narrative "way of articulating images." Indeed, when we consider the poetics of whole songs, the function of incremental repetition differs between ballads and catalogues: in ballads, the device slows the action down ("lingering," in the terminology of Gummere [1909] 1959: 91), whereas in catalogues, incremental repetition speeds things up—at least, relative to other catalogue techniques like enumeration and iteration. While I do not agree with him, Child thought the incremental syntactic pattern told enough of a story on its own to be considered a primarily narrative "way of articulating images," since some of his canonized songs—for example, the A versions of "The Bonny Earl of Murray" (Child 181; Roud 334) and "Bonnie James Campbell" (Child 210; Roud 338)—are cast solely in incrementation.

The fourth and perhaps most distinctive syntactical pattern in Anglo/American catalogue songs that I've been able to identify is a cumulative one, which I suppose we could call *cumulation*. This is the catalogue pattern exhibiting the greatest structural integrity: that is to say, if used at all, it's used for the whole song, not just for a few stanzas, which is often the case with the other techniques. Moreover, the cumulative pattern never to my knowledge combines in the same song with noncatalogue ways of articulating images in sung verse (that is, ballad and lyric), though, like incremental repetition, it can be used to bring about a change in the state of affairs depicted, however minimal and predictable that change might be. In the cumulative pattern, each stanza after the first is composed of a fresh image as well as of all the images that preceded it embedded in *their* own stanzas, so that each stanza is one stanza-unit longer than its immediate predecessor:

THE EVERLASTING CIRCLE (ROUD 129)

[1] All in the greenwood there growed a tree,
So fine a tree as you ever did see
And the green leaves flourished around around around,
And the green trees flourished around,

[2] And all on this tree there growed a branch,
So fine a branch as you ever did see
And the branch was on the tree
And the tree was in the wood
And the green leaves flourished . . .

[3] And all on this branch there growed a spray,
So fine a spray as you ever did see
And the spray was on the branch,
And the branch . . .

[4] And on this spray there was a fine nest,
So fine a nest as you ever did see
And the nest was on the spray . . .

[5] And all in this nest there was laid an egg . . .

[6] And all in this egg there was a golden yolk . . .

[7] And all in this yolk there was a gay bird . . .

[8] And all on this bird there was a fine feather . . .

[9] And out of this feather was made a fine bed . . .

[10] And all on this bed a lad did lie . . .

[11] And all with this lad a maiden she did sleep . . .

[12] And all in this maiden a baby was made . . .

[13] And out of this baby a boy did grow . . .

[14] And the boy he did lay in the ground an acorn . . .

[15] And out of this acorn did grow a great tree . . .

Like "The Everlasting Circle" (from Reeves 1960: 101–2), some of the
most widely known traditional anglophone songs are cumulative catalogues: for example, "Twelve Days of Christmas" (Roud 68), "One Man
Shall Mow My Meadow" (Roud 143), and "Green Grow the Rushes-O"
(Roud 133). It is the most complex of the four catalogue forms I've so far
discussed, always including within its pattern enumeration, iteration,
and incrementation.

Child not only thought incrementation told enough of a story that traditional songs structured entirely on its principles could be considered
ballads; he also thought the same of the fifth and final pattern I propose
here to be more consonant with the catalogue's listing, redundant style
than with a plotted, linear style: the dialogical technique—or, simply,
dialogue. In this usage, "dialogue" denotes more that just dramatic
speech; a folksong dialogue is analogous to a literary flyting (poetic turn-

taking between two "contestants," often adversaries who are abusive of each other) or *débat* (more rational disputation or argumentation, also conducted in turn and also in poetry). Folksong dialogues are invariably two-person, each discussant taking up one compositional unit-of-thought (once again, invariably a stanza) at a time, and are also more often of the alternating or turn-taking, rather than of the divided kind (but see "The Elfin Knight" [Child 2; Roud 12], for instance).

Many Child ballads exhibit throughout their texts this dialogical technique, and in fact some scholars consider extended use of dialogue, especially unascribed dialogue—that is, dialogue for which no speaker is named in the text itself—to be virtually an identifying feature of the genre (Bronson 1975). But we find the very same extended use of dialogue, both ascribed and unascribed, in many songs that we'd never think of calling ballads, even though they have just as much (or in my opinion just as little [compare McCarthy 1990: 98]) narrative implication, like the British "Keys of Canterbury" (Roud 573) and "Cutty Wren Song" (Roud 236), or the North American "Farmer and the Shantyboy" (Roud 670) and "Buffalo Boy" (Roud 313). For example, here's a Missouri version of a widely collected British song (Belden 1940: 265):

HARD OF HEARING (ROUD 467)

[1] "Old woman, old woman, won't you do my washing?"
"Speak a little louder, sir; I'm very hard of hearing."

[2] "Old woman, old woman, won't you do my ironing?"
"Speak a little louder, sir; I'm very hard of hearing."

[3] "Old woman, old woman, won't you do my darning?"
"Speak a little louder, sir; I'm very hard of hearing."

[4] "Old woman, old woman, may I come a-courting?"
"Speak a little louder, sir; I almost heard you."

[5] "Old woman, old woman, will you marry me?"
"O God bless you! O God bless you! That's the time I heard you!"

I have put dialogue last on the list because it is—or at least has the potential to be—the most complex of the five catalogue types considered, always containing within its structure enumeration (as do, of course, all five types) and quite often iteration. Even incrementation is common in dialogue songs (as in "Hard of Hearing"), though the pattern may be employed for just a portion of the song—for example, in the penultimate and ultimate stanzas only, while the rest of the text is simple iteration of parts that can be reordered without affecting sense, as in another dialogue song about marriage collected in the northeast of Scotland by Gavin Greig (Greig 1963: 98: 1):

OH, BUT I'M WEARY (ROUD 5555)

CHORUS: Oh, but I'm weary, weary, waitin;
        Oh, but I'm weary nicht and day;
        Oh, mither, gie me the man
        Will tak' this weariness away.

[1] O daughter dear, wad ye marry the man
That mak's his livin' by the ploo?
Oh, na, mither, she says,
The smell o' muck would gar me spue.
(CHORUS)

[2] O daughter dear, wad ye marry the man
That maks his livin' buildin' stones?
Oh, na, mither, she says,
He may fall to the earth and break his bones.
(CHORUS)

[3] O daughter dear, wad ye marry the man
That mak's his livin' by the gun?
Oh, na, mither, she says
He mith gang oot and never come in.
(CHORUS)

[4] O daughter dear, wad ye marry the man
That mak's his livin' by the sea?
Oh, na, mither, she says,
The ship mith sink and ruin me.
(CHORUS)

[5] O daughter dear, wad ye marry the man
That mak's his livin' by the pen?
Oh, ay, mither, she says,
My hearts delights in gentlemen.
(CHORUS)

*   *   *

I've characterized genre in general as a "way of articulating images" in sung verse. "Articulate" implies not only the sort of syntactic patterns treated so far in this essay but also semantic ones. The question we may now ask, then, is whether the catalogue exhibits regularities not just in organizing the component parts of its topic but also in representing that topic? To answer that question we need to look at catalogue as a trope and identify how it imagines the world. Five characteristics of catalogue signification strike me as most noteworthy: *boundedness, stasis, redundancy, atomism,* and *determinacy*.

The first, boundedness, denotes well-defined spatial and temporal containment. Ballad personnel have great potential freedom of movement both in space and time: "Young Beichan" (Child 53; Roud 40), for instance, sails from England to Turkey and back again, while "Lord Lovel" (Child 75; Roud 48) leaves home for a year of wandering (during which absence his true love dies). In lyric songs, not only do images move back and forth between human actors, the landscape, and even at times the cosmos, but one of the most notable thematic features of lyric song semantic is the mobility of its personnel, especially the (usually false) male (Renwick 1980: 56–69). Catalogue personnel, in contrast, are invariably confined to the same location and to the same point in time, as in courtship dialogue songs, so often of Irish provenience: such songs are "in real time"—that is to say, the actual debate that is the topic would take about as long to transpire as the song depicting it takes to sing (for example, "The True Lovers' Discussion" [Roud 2948; see Huntington 1990: 362–4])! Other common examples are catalogue songs that inventory animals or animal parts, like the cumulative "The Mallard" (Roud 1517; see Peacock 1965: 1: 16–7), which lists the parts of the bird the narrator has eaten, starting with head and ending with toe (thus the extent of the song's world is the space the animal as a physical entity occupies), and spree songs that list the various participants and goings-on at some celebratory occasion, as in "Olden Days" given earlier (its temporal boundaries are the beginning and ending of the party). Even when a song topic's geographical range may be empirically extensive it is semiotically constrained by being kept to a set route, for example to the points the good ship Dreadnought passes on the Transatlantic sea lane when journeying iteratively and incrementally from Liverpool to New York (Doerflinger 1951: 127–8):

THE DREADNOUGHT (LAWS D13; ROUD 924)

[1] She's a saucy fast packet and a packet of fame,
She hails from New York and the Dreadnought's her name,
She's bound to the westward, where strong winds do blow;
She's a Liverpool liner, bully boys, let her go!
CHORUS: Bound away, bound away, where strong winds do blow,
     Bound away in the Dreadnought to the westward we'll go.

[2] Now the Dreadnought is leaving the Waterloo Dock,
And the boys and the girls on the pierhead do flock.
They give her three cheers, while their tears freely flow.
Bound away in the Dreadnought to the westward we'll go.

[3] Now the Dreadnought is anchored in the Mersey so free,
Waiting for the Independence to tow her to sea,
Down past those black rocks where the Mersey does flow,
Bound away in the Dreadnought to the westward we'll go.

[4] Now the Dreadnought is sailing down the wild Irish Sea,
Her passengers on deck, all their hearts light and free;
And the seamen on watch pace the decks to and fro,
Bound away in the Dreadnought to the westward we'll go.

[5] Now the Dreadnought is plowing the Atlantic so wide,
Where the heavy green seas rush along her black sides,
With her sails trimmed so neatly, her Red Cross to show,
Bound away in the Dreadnought to the westward we'll go.

[6] Now the Dreadnought is crossing the Georges so grand,
Where the sea it is green and the bottom is sand;
Where the big fish swim around her and sporting whales blow;
Bound away in the Dreadnought to the westward we'll go.

[7] Now the Dreadnought is lying in New York once more.
Let's go ashore, shipmates, to the land we adore,
See our wives and our sweethearts, be jolly and free,
And we'll drink to the Dreadnought wherever she be.

[8] Here's health to the Dreadnought and to her bold crew;
Here's health to our captain and officers true.
Talk about your fast packets, Swallowtail and Black Ball,
But the Dreadnought's the clipper to outsail them all.

We can be sure that, had something unexpected happened to the Dreadnought on her voyage west—had she run into a life-threatening storm, say, or had smallpox broken out among the crew, or had she even encountered a pirate (however unlikely that would have been in real nineteenth-century Atlantic waters)—the songmaker would almost certainly have chosen a different "way of articulating images"; indeed, almost just as certainly, would have chosen the ballad method's nonrepetitive, linearly plotted way of sequencing events. And just as mathematically lengthy distances can be "bound" by fixing them within a predetermined and finite spatial grid, so too may empirically lengthy time periods be bound within the framework of a calendrical formula, such as the twelve months of the year, or the seasonal rhythm of spring/summer/fall/winter. Thus in "The Holly Twig" (Laws Q6; Roud 433) and "Dashing Away at the Smoothing Iron" (Roud 869) the preformulated sequence of days-of-the-week provide the restrictive template: on Monday such-and-such, on Tuesday this-and-that, on Wednesday so-and-so, ending with Saturday or Sunday (see Karpeles 1974: 2: 31–2, 421–4). Such temporally formulaic catalogue songs are more often than not dominated by incrementation.

Related to boundedness is a second quality of catalogue song representation, stasis. Not only is a catalogue topic restricted in time and space, but (perhaps as a consequence) it doesn't evolve, grow, or exhibit any significant transformation. At song's end, the state of affairs is much what it was at song's beginning. Narrative songs specialize, of course, in depicting change in the states or fortunes of its characters, as conflicts emerge, build up to climaxes, and are resolved, for good or ill. By definition, change always takes place in the ballad world. As for lyric songs, while in their worlds recreating the details of a memorable experience is of far less concern than recreating one's emotional reactions to the experience, the dramatis personae do move in the course of their inevitable suffering from, say, live to dead, or from a state of ecstasy to one of despair, or from being the subject of a courtship to being the victim of a desertion (though the song's presentation of these movements is seldom linear). Catalogue songs are different: even after a whole season of employment, the farmworkers in Scottish bothy catalogues are pretty much what they were at season's start—still disgruntled, still poor, and once more unemployed:

NEWMILL (ROUD 5588)

[1] It was to Newmill, ayont the hills,
Last term I did fee,
To Mr. B., a farmer there,
His servant for to be.

[2] I hadna been a week come [from?] hame
When I could plainly see,
The tables they were rather bare,
They were none suit for me.

[3] The breid was thick, the brose was thin,
And the broth they were like bree;
I chased the barley roon the plate,
And a' I got was three.

[4] So unsuccessful was my search,
My spoon I then threw doon;
The knife and fork were seldom seen
But in the carpet room.

[5] Our humble cot, as you may see,
And it stands bleak and bare;
And the chuckie-hoose stands west a wee
For to complete the square.

[6] And Mr. Langnecks is a man
Who can both cheat and lee,
And tries to put his servants off
Without their penny fee.

[7] And he wad sell his chaff and strae
The black silk goons to buy;
He wad sell the water in his dam,
If anyone wad buy.

[8] Three hundred stones of hay we cut
And drank three quarts of beer;
Two and sixpence was the cost,
Oor medicine wasna dear.

[9] Oor mistress she the silk goons wore,
As true as I do say,

And orders to the master gave
To give us every day.

[10] When we were to the barn sent
To raip and draw the strae,
She at the keyhole o' the door
To hear what we might say.

[11] And when her daughters were with us,
She did regard them right,
And always kept her eye on them
Till twelve o'clock at night.

[12] Ae day my horse did lose a shoe,
While grazing on the ley
And I was put to seek the same
The feck o' one whole day.

[13] Wi' blessed hand and happy fit
The shoe I then did find,
And safely to my master brought,
To ease his troubled mind.

[14] Now farewell, Mr Langnecks,
And to your daughters three;
But the turkey-hen that lives her lane,
I think I'll lat her be.

[15] So farewell, Mr. Langnecks,
Nae langer will I bide;
And I will steer my course again
Back to bonnie Deeside.

    (Greig 1963: 92: 2)

Even in the catalogue pattern possessing significant narrative potential, incrementation, change is minimal. For example, in "A Week's
Work" (Roud 1692), which employs the template of a week to catalogue
a man's set of daily experiences during his brief marriage, stasis is emphasized by the circularity of his history: he courts and marries Mary Anne
on Monday, arouses her ire on Tuesday, is cuckolded on Wednesday,
engages in fisticuffs with his wife of four days on Thursday, separates
from her on Friday, and buries her on Saturday, she having hanged herself

because "without me she could not live." But the protagonist has evidently learned nothing from his experience and shows no signs of changing his behavior in the weeks to come: the song's closing couplet is "I saw her into the ground all right / Latched onto another on Saturday night" (Peacock 1965: 1: 322–3).

A third notable feature of catalogue representation might be called by several names, but the one I'll use is redundancy: each component is depicted as very similar to each other, in purpose, attitude, style, form, or nature. Thus in the usually iterative catalogue type that we sometimes call "lying songs," each image is an exaggeration:

WHEN I WAS A LITTLE BOY (ROUD 1706)

[1] When I was a little boy to London I did go,
But now I've turned a roguish blade, my courage it will show.
My feet was on the table, sir, my head was hanging down,
And I jumped over Kingston's Hill and never touched the ground.
REFRAIN: With my tooral laddy, whack fol laddy, tooral looral ling.

[2] I bought myself a little bull about three inches high;
The people all admired me; it's for me to hear him cry.
The people all admired me for he made such an awful sound,
He made the steeple of St. Paul's Church come tumbling to the ground.
(REFRAIN)

[3] I bought myself a flock of sheep and most of them were wethers;
Sometimes they brought me fine wool, sometimes they brought me feathers.
They were as fine a flock, sir, as anyone could possess
Every month or six weeks' time they brought me six lambs apiece.
(REFRAIN)

[4] I bought myself a little hen, and of her I took great care;
I set her on a mussel shell and she hatched me out a hare.
The hare grew up a milk-white steed about eighteen yards high,
And if anyone tell you a bigger story, I'll tell you it's a bloody lie.
(REFRAIN)

[5] I bought myself a little box about three acres square;
I stowed it into my breeches pocket, the guineas they were there.
Now the people all admired me, thanked me for what I'd done,
And they gave me a portion of silver and gold about ten thousand ton.
(REFRAIN)

   (Vaughan Williams and Lloyd 1959: 101)

Each component part (here, as in most catalogue songs, coexistent with the stanza) is redundant with each other, sharing the common features of, for instance, being possessions, or being fantastical, whether as exaggerations (sheep that give birth once a month, a horse eighteen yards high, a box three acres square) or as topsy-turvy impossibilities (feathered sheep). Since each part is so redundant with any other, the whole which they comprise—that is, the song's topic—is itself strongly unified and internally homogeneous.

As with "When I Was a Little Boy," this semiotic feature of redundancy is often matched by one of the most characteristic textual features of catalogue: repetition in the very language of the song—not in choruses or refrains (which as I've said I regard as having a performative function, not an articulating one), but in the stanzas themselves. Such textual repetition is of course the main marker of the iterative pattern, as well as a critical one in the more complex, more shapely cumulative and incremental patterns. Verbal repetition is also often found in dialogue, though it is not a necessary aspect of that particular "syntactic structure." But whether repetition is present or not, redundancy is a pervasive feature of catalogue representation, as evidenced by its presence even in enumeration, which is the one pattern of the five that doesn't exhibit significant repetition of phrase or line (since that would, by definition, be iteration). Here's a Canadian example (from Peacock 1965: 3: 769):

THE BONAVIST LINE (ROUD 5206)

[1] As I roved out one morning in May
To view those who labour down on the railway
I saw the tear drops that fell from their eyes,
Those red roaring devils on the Bonavist Line.

[2] To sew in a button they'll charge you five cents,
Fifty to stick up their shack by the fence,
To boil your kettle they'll charge you a dime,
And these is the rules on the Bonavist Line.

[3] Down to the store your milk for to buy,
They will tell you it's the best ever come from a cow;
It's only flour water, they mix it so fine,
They sell it for milk on the Bonavist Line.

[4] It's for the pork it is so bad,
And for the molasses it would set you mad,
And for the flour it's just like slake lime,
Twould give you consumption on the Bonavist Line.

[5] Down to the store your groceries to buy,
The old woman she'll nod and wink her eye,
She will tell you about it and isn't it fine,
And she'll give you a tip on the Bonavist Line.

[6] On a fine Sunday morning turn out, turn out,
Those poor labourers will turn out their snout,
And it's all for Bertha she dresses so fine,
She's the devil for men on the Bonavist Line.

A typical example both of a local song and of a satirical song, "The Bona-vist Line" depicts an internally consistent set of experiences that the temporary residents of the locale, who are there to build a railway line, encounter: scarcity or lack of ordinary subsistence goods, inflated prices, and opportunistic natives.

A fourth defining feature of catalogue semiotic is atomism: the part is a sharply focused object of attention. This trait's prominence may stem from the very homogeneous, internally redundant, unified nature of each song's topic as a whole and, hence, of that topic's vehicle, the song as a whole. Since, unlike ballads and lyric songs, the whole of any individual catalogue song is not greater than its parts but only constitutes their aggregate, for artistic effectiveness each part has to carry significant semantic weight. Hence it has to be clearly, concretely, and finely drawn. For example (from Peacock 1965: 1: 55–6):

GRANDFATHER BRYAN (ROUD 8248)

[1] My grandfather Bryan he died,
It was on St. Patrick's Day,
He started out for the next world
Without ever asking the way.

[2] Leaving me all of his riches,
And a good deal of wealth do you see,
And a pair of his cloth-leather britches,
That buttoned up down to the knee.

[3] He left me the whole two sides of a bacon,
Only one half was just cut away,
A broomstick with the head of a rake on,
And a field full of straw to make hay.

[4] A blanket made out of cloth patches,
A breadbasket made out of tin ware,
A window without any sashes,
And a horse-collar made for a mare.

[5] He left me a mighty great clock too,
With brass wheels that were made out of wood,
A key without ever a lock to,
And a stool to set down where I stood.

[6] His beaver to sport all the summer,
His whiskers to wear in the fall,
A bagful of guinea-pig's eyebrows,
And a boxful of nothing at all.

[7] He left me some whisky for drinking
And a beautiful stick, look at that!
And a fat Jersey heifer for milking,
With a tail of B. John Thomas' cat.

[8] A pair of bone studs made of leather,
A satchel of old wedding rings;
Two earings to wear in wet weather,
With a bucket of horse-stinger's wings.

[9] He left me, poor man, a great fortune,
And a puncheon of juniper tay.
Two shares in the Rock of Gibraltar,
And a mortgage on Robin Hood's Bay.

[10] He left his trousers and waistcoat,
The tails of two shabby old coats;
A fortune to do me forever,
With a boxful of Union banknotes.

[11] He left me some pastry for eating,
Oh the creature before he did die,
Two bluchers to put me poor feet in,
And a slice of bumble-bee pie.

[12] A pair of wet cuffs for the winter,
A red nose to hang out for a sign,
So I'm fixed in grand style for the winter,
God bless you, old grandfather Bryan!

[13] Then hurrah for old grandfather Bryan,
I wish he were living I'm sure;
And every day he'd be dying,
He'd leave me ten times as much more.

We see in this enumerative catalogue the same sort of topsy-turvy humor of "When I Was a Little Boy," but as in that other "lying song" each component part—each item left in the will—is sharply focused, able to hold the listener's attention as virtually a self-contained object. Although all parts share the same redundant quality of unusability, whether because of their impossible or irrelevant or archaic nature, each is ontologically unique. This characteristic of atomism may very well be the reason for the lack in catalogue songs of what are variously called "floating stanzas," "commonplaces," "clichés," or "formulas": such ready-made epithets are common in Child ballads and lyric songs, where wholes are generated by the interaction of parts rather than equal to their aggregation.

The fifth prominent property of the catalogue idea is determinacy: since each successive image carries little additional information, a competent listener probably knows not only where the song is going after hearing two or three stanzas but, even if he or she comes in at the middle or end of the song's performance, where it's come from. Put another way, the whole (a "macrocosm") can be induced from knowledge of a part (a "microcosm"), a part deduced from knowledge of the whole. So for example, the many distinctive manifestations of the "Alphabet Song" (Roud 159; see Peacock 1965: 1: 4–5; Fowke 1970: 25–6) can be predicted both forward and backward from any letter, as can the sequence of relatives in nuncupative-will catalogue songs that we usually call ballads, like "The Miller's Three Sons" (Laws Q21; Roud 138), "The Cruel Brother" (Child 11; Roud 26), "Edward" (Child 13; Roud 200), and "The Twa Brothers" (Child 49; Roud 38). Each member of a logging crew can stand for the whole team, each image in catalogue songs of metaphorical sex (like "The Furze Field," given earlier) for the act of intercourse. Each trade in a catalogue-of-trades (physician, lawyer, merchant) stands for a social whole that is the unproductive, even exploitative, often bourgeois class. Even the successive bits of information in an incremental pattern, each of which is technically "new," can be predicted by a competent hearer once the larger paradigm that provides the song's template or framework is decoded, as in "The Old Man's Courtship" given earlier as well as in the following:

HONEST GIRL (ROUD 8156)

[1] I went to church
Like a honest girl should.
And the boys come too
Like other boys would.
CHORUS: Boys are boys
       Wherever they may be
       I will tell you by and by
       How the boys treated me.

[2] I come home
Like a honest girl should
And the boys come too
Just like boys would.
(CHORUS)

[3] I made a light
Like a honest girl should
And the boys put it out
Just like boys would.
(CHORUS)

[4] I went to bed
Like a honest girl should
And the boys come too
Just like boys would.
(CHORUS)

[5] I bare my baby
Like a honest girl should
And the boys denied it
Just like boys would
(CHORUS)
    (Henry 1934: 28–9)

                      *   *   *

As I said at the beginning of this essay, while mastery of catalogue songs' textual poetics is essential if the genre is to be imprinted in the folksong scholar's worldview, there are some extratextual or behavioral regularities that provide additional evidence that catalogue is not just a theoretical construct but in fact has some status as a "native" type. For example, while all folksongs have both an aesthetic and a cognitive function, only certain ones have a significant motor function, and whenever traditional song is, in its natural contexts of performance, intimately linked with physical activity, catalogue will be the song's most likely form. This correlation holds true not only for highly labor-intensive tasks like short-hauling on pre-twentieth-century sailing ships but also for less strenuous but still highly energetic performances, such as those required in children's singing games and adult play parties. Since for sea shanties a consistent rhythm and a participatory refrain were the most critical features, shantymen could—and did—use ballads as work songs (as witness one of the most popular of shanties in the Western ocean repertoire, "Blow the Man Down" [Roud 2624; see Doerflinger 1951: 18–9]), but any representative collection of oceangoing shanties will reveal the overwhelming popularity of catalogues, as in the following, which like so many worksongs self-referentially enumerates—with a fair bit of iteration—diverse experiences of the deep water sailor in a series of vignettes (from Doerflinger 1951: 5):

HAUL, AWAY, JOE (ROUD 809)

[1] Oh, haul away the bowline, the packet ship's a-rollin'!
REFRAIN: Away, haul away, haul away, Joe!

[2] Oh, haul away the bowline, don't you hear the cap'n growlin'?
(REFRAIN)

[3] Oh, haul away together, we'll surely make her render!
(REFRAIN)

[4] Oh, the cook is in the galley, a-makin' duff so handy,
(REFRAIN)

[5] An' the cap'n's in the cabin a-drinkin' wine and' brandy!
(REFRAIN)

[6] Oh, once I had an Irish girl and she was fat and lazy,
(REFRAIN)

[7] An' now I got a Yankee girl she nearly drives me crazy!
(REFRAIN)

[8] Oh, haul away the bowline, me hearty lads, be handy,
(REFRAIN)

[9] Haul away the bowline, Yankee Doodle dandy!
(REFRAIN)

Even the children's lullaby, though it consumes far fewer calories than do worksongs or dance songs, performs an important physical function and as a consequence is invariably a catalogue.

A related but distinct indication that catalogue may not be just a construct of the library scholar's imagination but an emic genre is that whenever a traditional song is customarily performed by a group, in consort—even when no significant motor function may be involved—catalogue is the preferred form. Sacred songs, for example, frequently draw upon catalogue technique, perhaps because repetition—the principal characteristic of catalogue—is particularly compatible with such concepts as litany and incantation that commonly suffuse worship. Also drawing habitually upon catalogue technique are songs associated with activities which, while not sacred, might be called ritualistic: I have in mind songs accompanying British calendrical customs like caroling, pace egging, hunting the wren, wassailing, and so on. Enumerative ("The Wassail Song" [Roud 209], "The Souling Song" [Roud 302]) and iterative ("The Derby Ram" [Roud 126], "The Sword Dance Song" [Roud 610]) syntactical patterns are the ones most frequently found in songs accompanying such customs of perambulation, house visit, treating, and occasionally dramatic performance (see Helm 1980; Lloyd 1967: 91–134]. "Poor Old Horse," for instance, was sung at a traditional Christmas custom in which a small group of men in homemade costume, one of which was a horse-disguise, visited local houses to sing and cavort in return for food, drink, and/or money. The song articulates its topic through iteration, incrementation, and enumeration:

POOR OLD HORSE (ROUD 513)

[1] I mind when I was a hobby colt, a hobby colt so gay,
And when my mother weaned me I thought that I should die.
REFRAIN: Poor old horse, poor old horse.

[2] I mind when I was a brewer's horse, a brewer's horse so gay.
I jumped right in the mashing-tub and drank up all the beer.
(REFRAIN)

[3] I mind when I was a gentleman's horse, a gentleman's horse so gay.
I had the best of all the corn and the primest of all hay.
(REFRAIN)

[4] But now I'm old and getting grey and fit for nothing at all.
I have to eat the sour grass that grows upon the wall.
(REFRAIN)

[5] My master rode me out one day and tied me to a stile.
While he ran away with the miller's maid when he could have rode five mile.
(REFRAIN)

[6] My flesh shall be the doggies' food, my bones they'll throw away.
My skin shall be my master's pride and so I shall decay.
(REFRAIN)

(Reeves 1960: 211)

Cumulative songs were probably most suitable as "songs of good company," in Peter Kennedy's phrase—that is, songs appropriately sung in less ritualistic contexts than calendrical customs but in the still somewhat formalized milieu of recreation-time revelry, usually featuring drinking and feasting (Kennedy 1975: 593–633). In Flora Thompson's account of an evening's socializing at a rural English pub around 1880, the various ballad, lyric, and parlor songs rendered by the farm-laborer patrons were invariably solo pieces; but then " 'Now . . . all together, boys,' some one would shout, and the company would revert to old favourites. Of these, one was 'The Barleymow' . . . [t]rolled out in chorus" (Thompson, 1954: 70). "The Barleymow's" (Roud 944) superstructure is entirely cumulative, as each stanza, incrementally increasing the size of the container from which the song's narrators will toast the harvest, projects not only a fresh image but also all images that have already preceded it in the song. And children's ensemble songs, whether or not associated with games, are also frequently built on the cumulative pattern, as witness "Old McDonald Had a Farm" (Roud 745).

In fact, even dialogical catalogue was appropriate for choral singing, despite its more natural two-person performance format. For example, the debate between "The Husband Man and the Serving Man" (Roud 873) was bawled out by the whole company at the end of a Dorset mummers' play, the servingman's part being sung by the whole troop, the husbandman's by whomever played Father Christmas (*Journal of the English Folk Dance & Song Society* 1952: 7: 11–2). And even the more sedate, more balladlike flyting kind of folk catalogue, which in most oral versions from the last hundred years and more has been sung solo, was once compatible with group rendition. Sabine Baring-Gould sent Child a version of "The Elfin Knight" he'd collected in Cornwall, noting that "This used to be sung as a sort of game in farm-houses, between a young man who went outside the room and a girl who sat on a settle or a chair, and a sort of chorus of farm lads and lasses. Now quite discontinued" (Child [1882–98] 1963: 4: 439).

Support for the generic status of catalogue can also be deduced from certain textual evidence. For example, traditional singers do seem to associate the patterns with each other—hence, evidently thinking of them as intimately related. For instance, traditional versions of "Our Goodman" (Child 274; Roud 114) are overwhelmingly in catalogue song form evincing iteration, dialogue, and more often than not incrementation: the husband comes home on a number of consecutive nights to find each time a new, unrecognized object lying around that suggests his wife's been entertaining a lover. Each time he asks his wife, "what's that x doing here where my x ought to be?" and each time the wife accuses him of being blind, stupid, and/or drunk, asserting that the object is not an x at all but a perfectly innocent y her mother gave her. Very often the song builds up incrementally to the climax that his wife does indeed have a lover: the final unrecognized object is usually a man himself in the bed where the husband ought to be but whom the wife explains away as being a milkmaid or something of the sort. Joseph C. Hickerson has drawn to my attention two versions that add cumulation to all those iterative, dialogical, and incremental patterns, the husband summarizing the entire list of fanciful answers the wife has so far deceptively proffered (Cray 1959: 25–6; Warde 1852: 118–9). Evidently the singers of this distinctive form of "Our Goodman" considered the added cumulative pattern perfectly compatible with the other already present catalogue patterns. Another example can be found in British Isles tradition, from which an animal-parts catalogue, "The Herring" (Roud 128), has been collected many times. Most versions are simple iteration (Karpeles 1974: 2: 436–9), perhaps ordered incrementally. But there is also a cumulative version sung by Bill Hingston of Devon (*An English Folk Music Anthology* 1981), as well as a dialogical one a Mr. Trump of Somerset sang for Cecil Sharp in 1906 (Vaughan Williams and Lloyd 1959: 86–7; see also Hamer 1967: 16–7). All of these versions come from English tradition and are all apparently compatible with each other. Finally, I might also suggest that while some scholars, like Child, feel that songs entirely in incremental and dialogue form can be considered ballads, singers apparently often seem to feel that they're not balladlike enough but instead need more exposition, more "plot." That would explain the traditional prose additions we often find attached to such wholly catalogue "ballads" like "Maid Freed from the Gallows" (Child 95; Roud 144 [see Coffin 1977: 91–4, 243–4]) and "Captain Wedderburn's Courtship" (Child 46; Roud 36 [see Moore and Moore 1964: 36]).

While these five catalogue patterns of enumeration, iteration, incrementation, cumulation, and dialogue are well recognized in folksong study (indeed, in folklore study, since none is exclusive to song but is found in other traditional oral forms like tale, game, and recitation), we've never acknowledged as far as I know that they might constitute a set, not only in the sense that they often interact with each other—as, for instance, in iteration's inclusion within cumulation, or incrementation's within dialogue (and of course all patterns include the least complex one, enumeration)—but also in that they are all subtypes of the same more inclusive category, whether we call that superset "catalogue" or something else.

In sum, the catalogue "way of articulating images in sung verse" encompasses a distinctive way of constructing the world, a distinctive way of representing it, and even a distinctive kind of social performance. And I don't think these features are necessarily the natural results of orality, or of limited memory capacity, or of need for group coordination, hence determined primarily by physiological demands and constraints: after all, fully oral texts exhibit noncatalogue ballad and lyric traits, and catalogue traits are common in written texts. It seems more likely that these features are motivated, that they result from choice, and that they constitute a poetics, perhaps even a genre, one that is widespread in the traditional Anglo/American folksong repertoire and that cries out for more scholarly attention.

4

"Oh, Willie"

An Unrecognized Anglo/American Ballad

The most important step in the establishment and legitimation of folk-song as a scholarly field was to amass a substantial body of data. In Britain, proponents of the emerging discipline "did fieldwork" as early as the mid-1700s, meeting with and listening to men and women who sang songs organically related to ongoing social life, both in when they were sung and in what they were about, their topics ranging from ordinary, quotidian experiences (songs of work or conviviality, for example) to rarer, life-critical ones (ballads of love relations telling ordeal-filled tales of courtship and perhaps marriage). The visitors recorded these folksongs, building up "collections" that would outlive both themselves and their singers and eventually constitute a large enough body of data to allow serious and sustained study. Of course, not all folksong investigators did fieldwork: some ferreted out such songs as preserved in other contexts and for other reasons—in handwritten diaries and personal song copy-books (often called "ballet" books), for instance, or in self-published auto-biographies and local histories, and especially in ephemeral commercial publications like broadsides and chapbooks that interacted so intimately with oral tradition. All these sources and more provided material for the growing folksong data bank. By the early twentieth century, we began to follow suit in North America, contributing our share to the ever-increasing storehouse of Anglo/American folksongs.

When eventually a large enough body of raw material had accumulated, the need for overviews arose. Overviews may take several forms, but a critical one is the organizing and codifying of a data mass, not only to bring order to the materials but also to encourage some consensus in scholarly approach toward them, some sense of engaging in a shared, productive, evolving enterprise. For Anglo/American folksong, the most successful example of such an overview was obviously Francis James Child's work on a particular subset of anglophone folksong data: narrative songs employed in everyday, face-to-face domestic performances and based on a common set of compositional principles that coalesced somewhere in late medieval Europe. Child accomplished his task so skillfully that his *English and Scottish Popular Ballads* was responsible for professionalizing the study of the folksong genre we now call, in his honor, the "Child ballad" (Child [1882–98] 1963).

When G. Malcolm Laws Jr. took his overview and published *American Balladry from British Broadsides* in the early 1950s, his motive was essentially the same as Child's. Although by the time he did his work, Laws—unlike Child—didn't have to legitimate his data as fit for serious study, like Child he sought to identify and organize a distinct corpus: all British Isles-born songs of a certain type that had been collected from American domestic singing tradition and published by trustworthy investigators, mostly under the aegis of university presses. Laws too chose narrative songs as his subject matter, but narrative songs rooted not in the compositional conventions informing the Child ballad (a genre of trans-European diffusion that became firmly entrenched in British Isles folk tradition some time in the fifteenth century) but in those of the broadside ballad, a later compositional model that didn't really jell in the oral tradition of Anglo/American quotidian performances until the eighteenth century (Laws 1957).

While his work does not have the epic quality of Child's, Laws did a very thorough job within the confines of the task he set himself. Consequently, it's hard to find a song in reputable collections available to him that he did not include in his syllabus, as long as it clearly fit his criteria for inclusion (that it exhibit a strong narrative quality and "exist in folk tradition" [Laws 1957: 1–2]). In other words, Laws seldom left out a song in error, or misidentified a ballad with its own traditional history as a *version* of some *other* item. These qualities of thoroughness and accuracy, while not manifested to the magisterial degree attained by Child, are still strong enough in Laws's work to have made his system for codifying the Anglo/American folksong repertoire of broadside ballads a standard of reference that later scholars automatically employ.[1] Laws systematized both the typical topics anglophone North American folksingers have preferred in songs they accepted into their performance repertoires (songs of Sailors and the Sea, for instance, or of Lovers' Disguises and Tricks) and the identity of individual songs that kept their integrity throughout oral tradition, assigning each song both a letter designating topic category and its own number within that category: thus "The Loss of the *Ramillies*," which tells of that vessel's sinking off the coast of Southwest England in 1760, is a ballad of Sailors and the Sea bearing the unique identifying code, Laws K1.

Since *American Balladry from British Broadsides* (along with its companion *Native American Balladry* [Laws (1964) 1975]) has come to represent such an important and authoritative overview systematizing a large part of our Anglo/American folksong repertoire, however, it is essential that any serious inaccuracies it exhibits be made known, especially since such errors continue to pass into other important overviews, such as Steve Roud's electronic database, *Folksong Index* (in which system "The Loss of the *Ramillies*" mentioned above is Roud 523 [see Roud 1994b–present]). This essay, therefore, proposes that we recognize one such inaccuracy in *American Balladry from British Broadsides*: a failure to identify, and consequently to codify, a British ballad in American tradition that had been first published, interestingly enough, in one of the earliest anthologies of American folksong to contain a significant number of field-collected items, John A. Lomax's *Cowboy Songs and Other Frontier Ballads* (1910). Strictly speaking, Laws inherited the error, for it had already been made by several of the scholars whose raw data he drew upon in composing his overview, but the privileged position of overviewer should have enabled Laws to see and correct it.

Here's a text of the ballad as it appeared in the pioneering *Cowboy Songs* (Lomax 1910: 397–8):

RAMBLING BOY

[1] I am a wild and a roving lad,
A wild and rambling lad I'll be;
For I do love a little girl
And she does love me.

[2] "O Willie, O Willie, I love you so.
I love you more than I do know;

And if my tongue could tell you so
I'd give the world to let you know."

[3] When Julia's old father came this to know,—
That Julie and Willie were loving so,—
He ripped and swore among them all,
And swore he'd use a cannon ball.

[4] She wrote Willie a letter with her right hand
And sent it to him in the Western land.
"Oh, read these lines, sweet William dear.
For this is the last of me you will hear."

[5] He read those lines while he wept and cried,
"Ten thousand times I wish I had died"
He read those lines while he wept and said,
"Ten thousand times I wish I were dead."

[6] When her old father came home that night
He called for Julia, his heart's delight,
He ran upstairs and her door he broke
And found her hanging by her own bed rope.

[7] And with his knife he cut her down,
And in her bosom this note he found
Saying, "Dig my grave both deep and wide
And bury sweet Willie by my side."

[8] They dug her grave both deep and wide
And buried sweet Willie by her side;
And on her grave set a turtle dove
To show the world they died for love.

In addition to this *Cowboy Songs* version, Laws would have encountered the ballad in a journal article by Arthur Palmer Hudson, "Ballads and Songs from Mississippi" (1926: 124–5); in Mellinger Edward Henry's *Songs Sung in the Southern Appalachians* (1934: 173–4); and twice in volume 2 of the *Frank C. Brown Collection of North Carolina Folklore* (Belden and Hudson 1952a: 278–9). Since Laws completed *American Balladry from British Broadsides*, at least three more texts have been published, by Thomas G. Burton and Ambrose N. Manning (1969: 2: 59), Anne Warner (1984: 219), and Texas folklorist William Owens (1976: 61–

2). Since the first two of those are from the same informant, we should treat them as a single version, so all told we now have access to at least seven distinct published versions of the song I propose we call "Oh, Willie."

Judging by the substantial number of times it has been published, the ballad must have been quite popular in oral tradition, though that popularity was limited in a geographic sense, since "Oh, Willie" has been found only in the southern United States. The version in Hudson's essay was gathered by a University of Mississippi student, T. A. Bickerstaff, from his sister, Audrey Hellums, of Tishomingo, Mississippi, while William A. Owens was given his version from Rod Drake of Silsbee in East Texas. Four versions come from North Carolina: one is from Buna Hicks, whose singing of "Oh, Willie" was recorded first by Anne and Frank Warner in 1941 (Warner 1984: 218) then again twenty-five years later for the East Tennessee State University folklore archives (Burton and Manning 1969: 2: 59).[2] A second North Carolina version can be considered a close genetic relative of the Buna Hicks one, both on textual and ethnographic grounds: it was recorded in December 1933 by Mellinger Edward Henry and his wife from another member of the extended Hicks family, Mrs. Nathan Hicks of Rominger, North Carolina (Henry 1934: 173), whom I take to be Buna's niece, Rena.[3]

The remaining two North Carolina versions are found in the extensive *Frank C. Brown Collection of North Carolina Folklore*: one, "Black Birds," came from the manuscript collection of a Miss Wagoner, while the other, "Sweet William," was "written down about July 1, 1915, by Miss Mae Smith of Sugar Grove, Watauga County, from the singing of her stepmother, Mrs. Mary Smith, who learned it over forty years ago" (Belden and Hudson 1952a: 278). The seventh and final published text is in Lomax's *Cowboy Songs*, as reproduced above, for which no source information is given but which we know from Lomax's papers at the University of Texas at Austin's Center for American History was contributed by C. C. Straley of Commanche, West Texas (slightly collated with a version collected from Clarence C. Carpenter of nearby Erath County; see Lomax [John Avery] Family Papers, box 3D177, folder 9).

If Laws did not recognize "Oh, Willie" as a song in its own right, what *did* he recognize it as? Strangely, it's difficult to say. I'll explain that opaque statement shortly, but first let's ask what folksong scholars in general, including Laws's predecessors, the earlier collectors and editors of the raw data he organized and codified in taking his overview, considered it to be. We don't know what predecessors John Lomax and Mellinger Edward Henry thought, since their books have no comparative notes, but Arthur Palmer Hudson in his 1926 *Journal of American Folklore* essay identified it as a version of "The Butcher Boy" (Laws P24; Roud 409), as he and his fellow editor Henry M. Belden did again later on in 1952 in *The Frank C. Brown Collection of North Carolina Folklore*, where "Black Birds" is given as the L text of "Butcher Boy," "Sweet William" as the M text.

Laws's successors have continued the pattern: Burton and Manning unequivocally label their Buna Hicks version Laws P24, while Anne Warner calls hers a "truncated" P24. Only William A. Owens seems to have considered "Oh, Willie" to be distinct from Laws P24/Roud 409, since he gives a text of "Butcher Boy" just seven pages later (1976: 68–9) and does not cross-reference the two songs. Unfortunately he makes no comments on the textual similarities between them, and in fact his Source Notes appendix (183–6) provides at least one comparative reference for most of his texts but gives none for "Oh, Willie." As for editors who do not have their own versions of "Oh, Willie" but who refer to it only in headnotes, they too seem to consider the song a version of "Butcher Boy": for example, John Harrington Cox in *Folk-Songs of the South* (1925: 430) includes the Lomax text in his comparative references to that ballad.

Which brings us to Laws. We know, of course, that he didn't codify "Oh, Willie" as a distinct piece in his syllabus, but did he agree with earlier folksong scholars that it was a version of "Butcher Boy"? It's difficult to say because, for whatever reason, Laws did not include in his references to P24 three of the five "Oh, Willie" texts he knew about: those from Lomax, Henry, and Hudson. He *did* include the other two from *The Frank C. Brown Collection of North Carolina Folklore*, but since that volume gives several versions of "Butcher Boy," one gets the impression that Laws was treating them as a more or less undifferentiated set, citing them in *American Balladry from British Broadsides* as "Brown, 272, 9; 9; add. sts.; 7; add. sts.; 13; 6; 5 (N.C.)," the 6 and 5 referring to the two versions of "Oh, Willie" that are texts L ("Black Birds") and M ("Sweet William") in the collection (Laws 1957: 260). In fact, not only did Laws fail to reference the more individuated texts of Henry, Hudson, and Lomax, but Hudson's version of "Oh, Willie" is one of *three* texts given together as versions of "Butcher Boy," and Laws cited *none* under P24, even the two unambiguous "Butcher Boy" ones.

Is this *pattern* of gaps happenstance? I'm willing to speculate that Laws, recognizing at least a degree of uniqueness to "Oh, Willie," may have set aside these texts for further study as to whether they constituted a distinct ballad or whether earlier editors were right in deeming them "Butcher Boy" variants. For some reason or other, he may have never decided on the matter—or perhaps, determining that they were indeed versions of P24, he made the simple clerical error of neglecting to add them to the relevant list of references.

If we cast our gaze at the whole Anglo/American oral song tradition, we see that "Oh, Willie" and "Butcher Boy" do not constitute a more or less independent duo but are part of a more inclusive network, or "song complex," of several interrelated—but distinguishable—songs that include, in addition to those two, a pair of lyric pieces (quite unstable in tradition and given a variety of titles by folklorists) that I'll call "Deep in Love" [Roud 87] and "Died for Love" [Roud 60], and three ballads, "Love Has Brought Me to Despair" (Laws P25; Roud 60 [same as "Died for Love," indicating the difficulty analysts have distinguishing the two]), "In Sheffield Park" (Roud 860; not found in North America), and "Sailor Boy" (Laws K12; Roud 273).[4] But while "Oh, Willie" clearly shares episodes and textual formulas with others in the complex, there's no doubt that it is most closely related to "Butcher Boy," as a representative text of that ballad will show (from Brewster 1940: 198–9):

THE BUTCHER BOY

[1] In Jersey City where I did dwell
A butcher boy I loved so well;
He courted me my life away;
In Jersey City I cannot stay.

[2] There is an inn in yonder town;
There my love goes and sits him down.
He takes a strange girl on his knee,
And tells to her what he won't tell me.

[3] 'Tis grief for me, I'll tell you why;
Because she has more gold than I.
But her gold will melt and silver will fly,
And such true love will always die.

[4] She went upstairs to make her bed,
And nothing to her mother said;
"O Mother, O Mother, you do not know
What pain and grief and sorrow and woe!"

[5] And when her father he came home,
He said, "Where has my daughter gone?"
He went upstairs; the door he broke,
And found her hanging upon a rope.

[6] He took his knife and cut her down,
And on her breast these lines he found:
"O what a silly girl am I,
To hang myself for a butcher boy!"

[7] "Go dig my grave both wide and deep;
Place a marble stone at my head and feet,
And on my breast a turtle dove
To show this world I died for love."

Putting aside the obvious fact that both songs treat unhappy love affairs
(as do the majority of Anglo/American folksongs treating love relations),
the most noticeable narrative similarities between this ballad and "Oh,
Willie" lie in the father's returning home to discover that his daughter
has hanged herself for a reason that is love-related; his taking down her
body, to find a suicide note in her bosom; and the note's instructions for
her burial. Verbal similarities reside principally in the same stanzas that
contain the above shared episodes: in both ballads the father "runs
upstairs," "breaks the door," "finds her hanging by a rope," "draws his
knife and cuts her down," and "in her bosom finds these words," the
words themselves invariably asking that the grave be dug "wide" as well
as "deep." These verbal similarities seldom occupy more than two stanzas, however (stanzas 6 and 7 of the Lomax cowboy text above).

   "Butcher Boy" and "Oh, Willie" also exhibit consistent differences,
and it is this consistency that leads me to argue for distinctive pieces.

One of the more obvious differences lies in point of view: whenever "Butcher Boy" is introduced by a first-person narrator, that narrator is always the girl, whereas in five of the six published "Oh, Willie" versions with a first-person narrator (Rod Drake's East Texas version is narrated entirely in third person), that narrator is the boy. The first-person narrative voice is embedded in a recurring verbal difference between the two songs: "Oh, Willie" never opens with some rendition or other of "Butcher Boy's" characteristic scene-setting line, "In Jersey City where I did dwell" (or, when narrated in third-person, "In Jersey City there did dwell"); in the five first-person versions mentioned above, the opening line is Willie's character-defining assertion, "I am a rude and rambling [rake and rambling, rowdy rambling, wrecked and rambling, wild and roving] boy."[5]

Another recurring difference is that "Butcher Boy" invariably *ends* with the suicide note's burial instructions, whereas "Oh, Willie" usually continues on to a final stanza treating the burial's aftermath—another commonplace, of course, but once again manifesting clear patterns of absence and presence, as in the "Black Birds" version from North Carolina:

> He drew his knife and he cut her down
> And in her bosom these lines he found:
> "Go, dig my grave both deep and wide
> And bury sweet Willie so near my side."
>
> Well, now she's dead and under ground
> While all her friends go mourning around.
> And o'er her grave flew a little white dove
> To show to the world that she died for love.
>   (Belden and Hudson 1952a: 278)

Also quite distinctive to "Oh, Willie" is the father's reaction when he hears of the love affair: he swears he will "use a cannon [pistol] ball"—one assumes on the young man. This threat of direct interference with the love affair is quite different from what happens in "Butcher Boy," where the parents are figures of support for their daughter in her distress and not obstacles to her happiness. In fact, in "Butcher Boy" the mother's presence is critical to the supportive-parents idea, as she tries to comfort her disturbed daughter (but encounters only filial rejection). The mother appears in none of "Oh, Willie's" seven published versions.

Also characteristic of "Oh, Willie" is the girl's declaration of love in direct speech, usually going something like "Oh Willie, Oh Willie, I love you well," as in stanza 2 of the Lomax text above. Like many stanzas in the whole song complex in which "Oh, Willie" and "Butcher Boy" participate, this "I love you well" stanza is a lyric commonplace, found in both Old and New World tradition (Randolph 1946–50: 4: 262–3; Shuldham-Shaw et al. 1995: 6: 254). It even turns up once attached to a four-stanza "Butcher Boy" collected from Mrs. Charity Lovingood of North Carolina (Scarborough 1937: 288). But it is far more strongly associated with "Oh, Willie" than with any other song, especially any other ballad. Indeed, it's logically out of place in the story "Butcher Boy" tells, since its lovers virtually never meet face to face: by the time the ballad takes up their story, the boy has long since left for what he considers greener pastures, such as a "tavern in yonder town."

Even "Oh, Willie's" rendition of the girl's commonplace burial instructions tends to be individualistic: in "Butcher Boy," she invariably makes the familiar request to "Dig my grave both wide and deep / Put a marble stone at my head and feet," while in "Oh, Willie" she makes an equally formulaic but typically distinct plea: "Dig my grave deep and wide / And bury sweet Willie by my side" (stanza 7 of the Lomax text). The "Butcher Boy" suicide note also includes a piece of information entirely absent from the note in "Oh, Willie": the girl's anguished realization that she was a fool to hang herself for such a man.

What we might call the most important summative quality of "Oh, Willie's" individuality, especially within Laws's standardized frame of reference, is that it is a ballad of Family Opposition to Lovers rather than of Unfaithful Lovers, the category of American ballads from British broadsides to which Laws quite rightly assigned "Butcher Boy." The Family Opposition theme is vividly expressed in what may be "Oh, Willie's" most (perhaps *only*) unique textual attribute, exemplified in the third stanza in the Lomax version above, where the father threatens to employ "cannon ball" violence. This image appears in six of our seven published versions and is the least formulaic feature of what is from beginning to end a very formulaic ballad of the broadside type. I can think of no other instance of this image in the Anglo-American traditional song inventory.

The motif's importance to "Oh, Willie's" identity is evidently so strong that Rena Hicks was willing to sing for Mellinger Edward Henry what she must have known he would have difficulty understanding: "She swore among them all / That she would join his cannon ball" (Henry 1934: 173).

Other evidence, in addition to the textual kind, reinforces "Oh, Willie's" status as an independent ballad. The musical record certainly does, though it is fairly negligible, since only three of the published versions we have identified so far offer tunes with their texts, and two of those three are from Buna Hicks. As was the case with her words, Buna Hicks's two tunes, even though given twenty-five years apart, are virtually identical: the only significant difference is that, in the 1941 version, the midpoint of the tune—the end of the second line—falls on the second of the scale, while in the 1966 version it falls on the third. The other version with tune was sung by Rod Drake of Silsbee, Texas, in 1952. Its tune has the same shape as Buna Hicks's 1966 one, the main difference being at the end of each verse, where the final note is the tonic rather than, as in Buna Hicks's two versions, the fourth below the tonic. Both tunes exhibit "gapped" or pentatonic scales, with no half-tone intervals. Despite the paucity of the musical record, these tunes suggest that "Oh, Willie" is independent of "Butcher Boy," the dominant tune for which is of quite a different character: the scale is diatonic; the first three lines end, respectively, on the tonic, the fifth, and the second; and the tune both begins and ends on the tonic note.

Yet further evidence of "Oh, Willie's" identity as a song can be adduced from singers' repertoires: the bearers of tradition whose songs we study do not seem to make the connection so many folklorists have that "Butcher Boy" and "Oh, Willie" are *versions* of each other. If they did, then we should expect to find texts of "Butcher Boy" that have incorporated lines that are specific to "Oh, Willie" or vice versa—not just the sharing of the pervasive and overt commonplaces like the suicide stanzas, but what more resembles a purposeful borrowing of reasonably unique, noncommonplace lines. After all, this sort of convergence has occurred between other items forming part of the larger Anglo/American network of commonplace-sharing unhappy love songs to which both "Butcher Boy" and "Oh, Willie" belong. For example, sometime around the turn of the twentieth century a Mrs. Hollings of Lincolnshire sang for

English folksong collector Frank Kidson a version of "The Sailor Boy" fus-
ing that song's customary form (in which a girl goes to sea in search of
her sailor-lover, finds out from a passing vessel that he's drowned, dies
by sailing her boat onto rocks, and gives the formulaic "turtle dove"
instructions for her burial) with "Butcher Boy" to the extent that the seafaring girl, rather than dashing her boat against the rocks, comes ashore
to commit suicide in the "Butcher Boy" manner: she hangs herself and is
discovered by her father, who cuts her down and finds the suicide note in
her bosom (*Journal of the Folk-Song Society* 1906: 2: 293–4). Or to take
another example, on September 15, 1908, Charles Ash of Crowcombe,
Somerset, sang for Cecil Sharp an unusual amalgam of the lyric "Died
for Love" and the more narrative "In Sheffield Park" (like "Butcher Boy"
without parents: the girl's mistress acts as support figure, actually inter-
ceding with the cruel lover on her behalf; he scornfully rebuffs her over-
tures, and she returns home to find the girl hanged) that could fairly be
called a version of either song (Karpeles 1974: 1: 604–5).

Syntheses such as these two unusual renditions of traditional songs
constitute a sort of folk exegesis: traditional singers have gone out of
their way to render implicit semantic associations explicit. But apart
from Mrs. Charity Lovingood's highly compressed, ambiguous version of
"Butcher Boy" mentioned above, no traditional text I know of synthesizes "Oh, Willie" and "Butcher Boy," certainly not in any way significant
enough to support the folklorist's propensity to treat them as one song.[6]

One final bit of evidence for our ballad's independent status can be
called meta-analytical: a folklorist can recognize "Oh, Willie" on the
basis of a very partial text. For example, in *English Folk Songs from the
Southern Appalachians*, Sharp prints only one stanza of a song given to
him by Mrs. Fanny Coffey of White Rock, Virginia, on May 8, 1918. Sharp
considered Mrs. Coffey's offering to be a version of "Died for Love," publishing it as the C text under that rubric (Sharp 1932: 2: 77). But the one
stanza printed manifests the highly suggestive "I love you well" set of
lines (here, from the male's point-of-view: "Oh Saro, Saro, I love you
well") that we've come to see is a common "Oh, Willie" marker. And
sure enough, Sharp's field notebook contains all six stanzas Mrs. Coffey
actually sang for him: they constitute yet another version of our "unrecognized"—even by Sharp—ballad (Cecil Sharp Collection: Folk Words,

no. 3048). Its tune is also more closely related to the two other "Oh, Willie" tunes we have than to either "Butcher Boy" or "Died for Love."

In fact, even excerpts much shorter than a stanza can be accurate markers of "Oh, Willie," as my experience with two folksong indexes indicate: Arthur Kyle Davis's *Folk-Songs of Virginia* (1949), which lists titles and collecting information of songs gathered under the auspices of the Virginia Folklore Society between 1914 and 1936, and Bruce Rosenberg's *Folksongs of Virginia*, a checklist of songs collected under Work Projects Administration auspices during the Roosevelt administration. Rosenberg's checklist has nine items under "Butcher Boy" (1969: 13–14); none is given a local title, but first lines are provided for three, one of which is "When our old parents become to know," a line immediately recognizable as integral to "Oh, Willie" (see stanza 3 of the Lomax text above: "When Julia's old father came this to know"). And, once again, when the full text is examined, it proves to be a very compressed "Oh, Willie," containing both the "Oh, Willie, oh Willie, I love you well" narrative idea as well as a reference to the critical opposition-to-lovers one ("When our old parents came to know"; University of Virginia Special Collections, accession no. 1547, box no. 18).

Davis's Virginia Folklore Society collection checklist has twenty-six entries for "Butcher Boy," most of which give local titles and/or first lines. The majority are typical "Butcher Boys," sporting that title and possessing the well-known first line that proclaims where one of the lovers lived: "In London City [Boston City, Jersey City, Johnson City, New York City, yonder city, Richmond Town] where I did [there did] dwell" (Davis 1949: 72–5). Four, however, have local titles and first lines that by now we recognize as indicators of the distinct "Oh, Willie": item #7, "Sweet Mollie," begins "Good-bye, good-bye, my old sweetheart" (compare stanza 4 of the Lomax text); item #23 has no title but begins with the familiar "William, William, I love you well" (as in Lomax's stanza 2); item #22, "Sweet William," begins "When I was a rake and rowdy boy" (Lomax stanza 1). When the full texts of these three items are examined, they all turn out to have one or more markers distinctive to "Oh, Willie," though of course all also possess one or more of the features that link members of the whole song complex we've discussed—the father's discovering his dead daughter, the cutting down of her body, the stating of burial instructions.[7] As for the fourth promising-sounding item in Davis's checklist, this was called by the informant "Willie Dear" and began "Oh, Willie dear, I love you well" (Davis 1949: 74, item #12). The staff of the University of Virginia Special Collections (which contains both the Virginia Folklore Society and the WPA material) were unable to find this item, but there is little doubt in my mind that, when found, despite the commonplace potential of its opening line, this text too will turn out to be not a version of "Butcher Boy" but of what several kinds of evidence have shown is a song with its own identifiable characteristics of plot and wording, "Oh, Willie."

The three new texts from the University of Virginia Special Collections and the one from Sharp's unpublished Appalachian notebooks now give us eleven reasonably separate versions (as with Buna Hicks's two renditions, I will treat the Smith brothers' two contributions as a single version; see note 7. I'm also treating the two Lomax manuscript texts as a single version, as Lomax himself did). So far I have talked about them as if they constituted one consistent text; but while they do evince a common identity, as folklore they obviously also exhibit variation, so it is appropriate to look at the larger tradition composed of the interrelationships among all ten—which is to say, look at them as a *network* of similarities and differences.

Only two narrative elements, each one usually embedded in a stanza, appear in all eleven versions: the father comes home to find his daughter has hanged herself, cuts the body down, and reads her suicide note's burial instructions (stanza 6 and 7 of the Lomax version). For the singers and their communities of song, "Oh, Willie's" emotional core is clearly embedded in these events, as is undoubtedly true for some of the other ballads of the Anglo/American song-complex in which "Oh, Willie" is most at home—"Butcher Boy," for example, or "In Sheffield Park," or "Love Has Brought Me to Despair." The next two most popular narrative elements are represented in Lomax's stanzas 8 and 3: stanza 8 describes the actual burial and is an integral extension of stanza 7's suicide note, while stanza 3 contains the father's discovery of the liaison and his threat to end it (usually with the unique "cannon ball" oath). The Oh-Willie-I-love-you-well declaration appears seven times (in four of those it opens the song), while some version or other of the I-am-a-rude-and-rambling-boy assertion appears in five texts, always—as in the Lomax text—as the opening stanza. Appearing only three times is the girl's letter to Willie telling of her father's opposition and making her farewells (Lomax's stanza 4), while Willie's reading of the letter and wishing he were dead appears only once—in the Lomax text, in fact, where it's the fifth stanza.[8] Also appearing only once is a stanza depicting the girl's actual suicide, once she has discovered her parents' opposition to the affair. This onstage depiction of the suicide is unique, though the phraseology is not (compare stanzas 3 and 6 of the Lomax "Oh, Willie" and "Died for Love"):

> When this young lady came this to hear,
> She wrung her hands, tore down her hair,
> She ran upstairs, no more she spoke
> And hung herself on her own bed-rope
> (Cecil Sharp Collection: Folk Words, no. 3048)

In sum, the moments in "Oh, Willie's" story that bearers of tradition have found most compelling are the girl's declaration of love; the father's discovery of the affair and threat of violence; his coming home at night to find that his daughter has hanged herself; the cutting down of the girl's body and reading of her suicide note's burial instructions; the girl's actual burial.

For this essay, I've used the Lomax cowboy version as a model text because it contains just about all the stanzas and associated episodes that make up "Oh, Willie's" entire tradition, hence has been useful for exemplification. In addition to lacking the suicide stanza, however, the cowboy text also lacks an image found in three versions, an image that, when it does appear, tends to produce the closest thing to a *significant* change in the normative story. Most often, its textual vehicle is a somewhat formulaic lyric stanza:

> I wish I was a blackbird among the rush;
> I'd change my note from bush to bush
> That the world might see
> That I love sweet Willie, but he don't love me.
> (Belden and Hudson 1952a: 278)

This stanza is significant because it brings into our ballad of Family Opposition to Lovers a note of Unfaithful Lovers. While in the above version *he* is unfaithful, in the other two containing the stanza *she* is.[9] In fact, in one of those latter two, a minimal textual variation has produced a maximal narrative change, resulting in the most unusual of the ten "Oh, Willie" versions we have: *she* "courts him" in stanza 1 but then in stanza 2 (the "I wish I was a blackbird" stanza) apparently does not love him anymore. *Willie*—not the father—comes home to find that she's hanged herself. This version comes closest of all to diverging from a Family Opposition to Lovers theme and toward an Unfaithful Lovers one, since no parents appear, or for that matter, are even mentioned.

Still, "Oh, Willie's" move away from the Family Opposition theme brings it no closer to "Butcher Boy" than it ever was, since (1) *she* is more often the unfaithful one than is he; (2) a more accurate description of the love relations in "Oh, Willie" would be *unrequited* rather than *unfaithful*, which is not the case with "The Butcher Boy," whose male lover is indisputably a cad; and (3) her burial instructions usually call for Willie to be buried by her side, whereas in "Butcher Boy" she invariably wants to be buried alone. In short, even the most variant of "Oh, Willie" texts still maintain a strong connection with what's normative to its tradition as a whole, further indicating that what we have here is a distinct and vibrant ballad deserving of its own place in our canon of American balladry from British broadsides.

The phrase "American balladry from British broadsides" is, of course, the title of Laws's justly famous book containing the invaluable overview of one hugely important segment of the traditional Anglo-North American folksong repertoire, mostly post-1700 ballads that originated in the British Isles and diffused to the United States and Canada, among other English-speaking countries. Most of the time, Laws had clear evidence of that British origin, such as the song's existence on a pre-twentieth-century English broadside, or its appearance in repertoires of late-nineteenth- and/or early-twentieth-century British traditional singers. The question now before us is this: even though its content and style is entirely "British," did "Oh, Willie" actually take shape as a distinct song in the New World?[10]

Once again, in order to track down an Old World ancestor, we are forced to navigate the scholarship on the ballad with which "Oh, Willie" has been consistently confused, "Butcher Boy." That journey produces two very promising leads: in his very thorough headnote to Laws P24/ Roud 409 in *Ballads and Songs Collected by the Missouri Folklore Society,* Belden mentions a broadside from London printer John Pitts (1765– 1844) called "The Rambling Boy" that is an "analog" of "Butcher Boy" (1940: 202). That broadside's title is, of course, familiar to us: it is the title of Lomax's "Oh, Willie" text. The second lead comes from George Lyman Kittredge, who—once again, in reference to "Butcher Boy"—cites what is almost certainly the same Pitts broadside, calling it an "absurdly confused (but quite singable) piece" (see Tolman 1916: 170).

Thanks to Steve Roud and the Vaughan Williams Memorial Library, here is a reproduction of that broadside:

THE RAMBLING BOY

J. Pitts, Printer, and Wholesale Toy Warehouse

Great st. Andrew Street 7 Dials

[1] I am a wild and a rambling boy,
My lodging's are in the Isle of Cloy,
A wild and a rambling boy I be,
I'll forsake them all and follow thee.

[2] O Billy! Billy! I love you well,
I love you better than tongue can tell
I love you well but dare not shew,
To you my dear let no one know,

[3] I wish I was a blackbird or thrush,
Changing my notes from bush to bush,
That all the world might plainly see,
I lov'd a man that lov'd not me,

[4] I wish I was a little fly.
That on his bosom I might lie.
And all the people fast asleep,
Into my love's arms I'd softly creep,

[5] I love my father I love my mother,
I love my sisters and my brothers,
I love my friends and relations too,
I would forsake them all to go with you

[6] My father left me house and land,
Bid me use it at my command,
But at my command they shall not be,
I'll forsake them all and follow thee,

[7] My father coming home at night,
And asked for his heart's delight,
He ran up stairs the door he broke
And found her hanging in a rope.

[8] He took a knife and cut her down,
And in her bosom a note was found,
Dig me a grave both wide and deep,
And a marble stone to cover it.[11]

While none of our eleven U.S. traditional renditions of "Oh, Willie" faithfully mimics this British broadside (Roud 60; see Roud 1994a–present), they're all obviously close genetic relatives. As we've seen, the broadside's first stanza appears in half of our U.S. versions; the Lomax *Cowboy Songs* text has the same adjectives, "wild and rambling," but the Mississippi text better matches the stanza as a whole, at least in the first three lines:

I am a wrecked and rambling boy,
My dwellings are both near and far;
A wrecked and rambling boy I'll be,
To love a girl that don't love me.
(Hudson 1926: 124)

The Mississippi text again presents the closest match to the broadside's second stanza, but only to the first two lines, which are also, as we have said, possible generic commonplaces (see Randolph 1946–50: 4: 263–4):

"I love thee, Willie, I love thee well,
I love thee better than tongue can tell. . . ."
(Hudson 1926: 124; compare Owens 1976: 62)

No U.S. text matches the second couplet's idea that the love must be kept secret, though that is implied in the parental disapproval common in U.S. versions.

The broadside's third stanza is recognizable as the stanza found in three U.S. versions and discussed above as a marker of what is the greatest divergence from "Oh, Willie's" normative American form. The best match is with the North Carolina "Black Birds" version, which like the English broadside takes the girl's point of view:

> I wish I was a blackbird among the rush;
> I'd change my home from bush to bush
> That the world might see
> That I love sweet Willie, but he don't love me.
>
> (Belden and Hudson 1952a: 278)

Only a portion of the next three stanzas in the British broadside, 4, 5, and 6, has what could be called a direct counterpart in the American versions: in a Virginia text of "Oh, Willie" we find in the Oh-Willie-I-love-you-well stanza, the closing lines "I love my father and my mother, too, / But I'll leave them both to go with you" (University of Virginia Special Collections, accession no. 9936), which of course match parts of stanza 5, even 6, of the Pitts "Rambling Boy." Once again, these three stanzas all are, in varying degrees, commonplaces found in other songs (for example, Browne 1979: 69; Lloyd 1967: 214–5; Shuldham-Shaw et al. 1981–97: 5: 267; Woods 1983: 111, 139), but their presence here is strongly suggestive of a direct line rather than of independent borrowing from another source. The remaining broadside stanzas, 7 and 8, which consist of the father's finding his daughter's body, cutting it down, and reading the suicide note's burial instructions—and which we infer contain the emotional core of "Oh, Willie" (as well as of other ballads in the complex like "Butcher Boy," "In Sheffield Park," and "Love Has Brought Me to Despair")—are found in all eleven American versions of our ballad.

The American preference for a (usually closing) stanza that, somewhat redundantly with the suicide note, describes the actual burial (found in seven of the eleven "Oh, Willie" versions) is absent from the British broadside. But the most significant difference between the British broadside and the American oral versions is that U.S. singers make the parental disapproval explicit, whereas it is more nuanced in the British broadside, only suggested in the girl's assertions that she must keep her love secret, that to be with her sweetheart she must forsake family and friends, and that to take possession of her patrimony—house and land—she will have to disavow her lover. American singers evidently felt a greater need to emphasize family opposition to the match, and they did so most explicitly by adding an image that is particularly American: the father's cannon ball threat, as in stanza 3 of the Lomax text above.[11]

In general, we might say that the U.S. domestic singers strove to disambiguate the song by clarifying its story as one of Family Opposition to Lovers. The British broadside ancestor seems ambiguous: are the lovers separated by family disapproval or by unrequited love? If the former, why doesn't the girl forsake her family and go with her love, as she claims she is willing to do? If the latter, which lover is the unfaithful one?[12] That in its ambiguity the British broadside is probably representing love quite realistically appears to have held no appeal for American singers. They liked the song, but only after adapting it to suit their tastes.

How did the Pitts broadside fare with British traditional singers? It doesn't seem to have appealed to them at all! One will scan Anglo/American folksong databases for a field-collected British version without much success, even though songs of love affairs with clearly delineated tragic roots—a male's inherent falseness, the refusal of family members to sanction the match, a crisis of either human (war) or natural (shipwreck) design—abound, as do other members of the song-complex like "Died for Love," "Sailor Boy," and "In Sheffield Park." There just may be one exception, though; in 1932 the English collector E. J. Moeran published *Six Suffolk Folk-Songs*, which contained the following text:

THE ISLE OF CLOY

[1] It's of a lady in the Isle of Cloy,
She fell in love with her serving boy.
Soon as her parents came to hear,
They separated her from her dear.

[2] So to disgrace her whole family,
They sent this young man across the sea,
On board "The Tiger," a man o' war,
To act his part like some gallant tar.

[3] This young man hadn't been long upon the main,
Before a cruel fight began,

It was his sad luck for to fall,
He got struck dead by a cannon ball.

[4] This very same night this young man was slain,
Close to her father's bedside she came.
With heavy sighs and bitter groans
Close to her father's bedside she stole.

[5] As she stood weeping, scarce could refrain,
The tears roll'd down from her eyes like rain.
All weeping sore for her own true love,
She hang'd herself from the beam above.

[6] The squire's servants they stood around:
They viewed this lady and cut her down,
And in her bosom a note unsealed:
A girl of sorrow it revealed.

[7] "My father is one of the best of men,
But he's drove me to this disgraceful end.
And of this vain world pray a warning take:
I died a maid for my true love's sake."

   (Moeran 1932: 22–5)

Collected from oral tradition (the book's six songs were "taken down from the singing of Mr. George Hill of Earl Stonham and Mr. Oliver Waspe of Coddenham" [Moeran 1932: 1]), "The Isle of Cloy" shares with the Pitts broadside not just the usual elements shared by several ballads in the song-complex—a girl's killing herself because of disappointment in love, the cutting down of her body, and the discovery of a death note, the contents of which are given—but also the parents' opposition to the match. These are all, of course, the same narrative elements the Pitts broadside shares with the American "Oh, Willie." Narrative differences, however, are just as if not more pronounced: the parents have the boy pressed into the navy; he dies in battle; her body is found by servants rather than by the father; and her death note contains no burial instructions. More critically, unlike the case with "Oh, Willie's" relationship with its obvious genetic relative, the Pitts "Rambling Boy," this "Isle of Cloy" from oral tradition shares virtually no phraseology with the London broadside, though the fact that the two protagonists share a dwelling place, the Isle of Cloy, that is not found in any dictionary of official British place names (and hence may be a "folk" name) is certainly suggestive.

Nor at first glance does "Isle of Cloy" share any significant wording with "Oh, Willie," other that what is suggested by the faint resonance between the Cloy lover's death in battle from a "cannon ball" and the father's threat in "Oh, Willie" to "use a cannon ball" on his daughter's lover. I say "at first glance" because it is indeed true that the English song has little in common with the phraseology of stanzas that have proved most popular with American bearers of tradition, as indicated by the earlier discussion of internal relationships among the ten known versions. As often happens in folklore, however, one will find evidence of genetic connections in a non-normative text. Such is the case here: on March 18, 1932, Mary Lou Bell of Staunton, Virginia, sent to the Virginia Folklore Society's collection a four-stanza version of "Oh, Willie" contributed by Staunton's Thursday Morning Music Club:

(NO LOCAL TITLE)

[1] William, William, I love you well.
I love you more than tongue can tell.
I love you so, I dare not show,
If you do so, let no one know.

[2] But when the parents came to hear.
They parted William and his dear.
And sent him on board of the "Ship of War,"
To act his part as a gallant tar.

[3] When her father came home 'twas late at night.
He called for Sarah, his heart still light.
Up stairs he ran, and the door he broke,
And found her hanging by her own bed rope.

[4] Go dig my grave both wide and deep.
Put a marble stone at my head and feet,
And on my heart put a turtle dove.
Let the wide world see I died for love.

(University of Virginia Special Collections, accession no. 9936)

In stanza 2 of this Virginia version we have clear evidence of a familial relationship between the "Isle of Cloy" from British oral tradition and

"Oh, Willie" from American oral tradition: that second stanza is almost certainly a variant of the second halves of stanza 1 ("Soon as her parents came to hear, / They separated her from her dear") and stanza 2 ("On board 'The Tiger,' a man o' war, / To act his part like some gallant tar") of the Suffolk oral version. Moreover, although the wordings differ, we see narrative similarities with Sharp's unpublished Virginia version of "Oh, Willie," which shares with "The Isle of Cloy" not only the parents' pressing of the lover but also the so-far unique image of the girl's hanging herself onstage. And since "Oh, Willie" is obviously a genetic relative of the broadside "The Rambling Boy," we must conclude that so too is "The Isle of Cloy."

If, however, "The Isle of Cloy"—which as far as I know has been collected from no other traditional singer, British or North American—is, like "Oh, Willie," a reworking of the broadside ballad, it is obviously a much more radical one. In Eleanor Long's terms, the American bearer of tradition who reinvented the British broadside (or, more likely, reinvented an oral manifestation of it that bore a closer resemblance to "Isle of Cloy" than the record shows) was a "rationalizer": he or she respected the received text's identity but adapted it to prevailing cultural norms, with the result that it appealed to other singers, who in turn learned it, sang it, and passed it on. In contrast, the British bearer of tradition who reworked the broadside (or an oral rendition of it) into "The Isle of Cloy" was an "integrator," one who stayed within the norms of traditional ballad poetics—story types, motifs, prosody, meter—but who fashioned a *new* song. Why, unlike its American cousin, it apparently never passed into the repertoires of other domestic singers can only be guessed. I would suggest that, like the Pitts broadside of "The Rambling Boy," it is too ambiguous, but in a quite different way: it depicts the father as causing the tragedy by actively opposing the love match but at the same time as a figure of respect ("my father is one of the best of men"). The traditional song aesthetic doesn't usually like things both ways. Perhaps if the British "integrator" had respected traditional aesthetic norms a bit more, "The Isle of Cloy" would have enjoyed, like its American relation "Oh, Willie," a measure of at least regional popularity.[13]

While we can't do much more than speculate on such matters, I certainly think we can now assert confidently that "Oh, Willie" is its own ballad: even though—as folklore will do—it dialogues with other songs in the Anglo/American traditional repertoire, most notably "Butcher Boy," it enjoys its own life in oral tradition. More than that, it also has its own ancestry, inheriting its dominant genes from a song surviving in at least one form, John Pitts's early-nineteenth-century London broadside. At some point in its history, it also interfaced directly with a British song of oral circulation, the only known example of which was collected seventy-odd years ago as "The Isle of Cloy." In short, "Oh, Willie" has the right we have failed to recognize and grant: separate membership in our database of American balladry from British broadsides.

5

"The Crabfish"

A Traditional Story's Remarkable Grip on the Popular Imagination

At the address http://www.harrier.net/hashes/, an internet surfer will find the website of the Pike's Peak, Colorado, chapter of the Hash House Harriers, an organization with branches all over the world whose core membership has historically been composed of British expatriate and British Commonwealth citizens. Even in the present day's more globally interconnected world, that membership still generally shares an orientation that could be described as Anglophile, even when a chapter is as far away from Britain as Colorado Springs, where the Pike's Peak group makes its home. A social club, the Hash House Harriers emphasize outdoor activities, especially long-distance communal runs, but they are also known for their parties, at which much beer is drunk and bawdy songs are sung, a custom common among other traditionally male-centered organizations with British ancestry, like rugby football clubs and college societies. Not untypically, the Harriers have even put out their own anthology of such bawdy songs, accessible at a link to the address above.

This essay is about a risqué story, a version of which appears in the Hash House Harriers' collection versified as "Lobster Song." What folklorists call a ballad, the "Lobster Song" (Roud 149) has a tale to tell: a man buys a lobster for the family dinner, brings the creature home, and stores it temporarily in the toilet bowl—but without telling his wife. When she unknowingly uses the commode, the lobster attaches itself to her pudendum. She calls to her husband for help, and together they loosen the crustacean's grip by attacking it with a broom, eventually killing it (Roud

1994b–present). I first heard this song as an undergraduate almost forty years ago at my McGill University fraternity house, where one of the members—an Englishman—occasionally broke into a "Lobster Song" refrain ("Roll tiddley oh / Shit or bust / Never let your bollocks / Dangle in the dust"). But he sang it only in the confines of our fraternity house and only on all-male occasions, since we dubbed it "obscene" in its employment of language and topics considered inappropriate in "mixed company." Of course, that was in 1960. Today, that "fraternity" has both men and women members, as does the once all-male Hash House Harriers, a modernization reflected in the Pike's Peak chapter's full name, Hash House Harriers and Harriettes. Has the latter's presence altered the bawdy quality of the group's social song repertoire? Evidently not; as we shall soon see, however, the "Lobster Song's" ability to cross the barrier dividing different gender tastes is not really surprising, since throughout its lengthy life it has crossed all kinds of other boundaries.[1]

Additional MS 27879 ca. 1650 is another "address," though of a handwritten manuscript occupying physical shelf space in the British Museum rather than of a digitally encoded assemblage of information in cyberspace. Also known to bibliophiles as "Bishop Percy's Folio Manuscript," the literary artifact, probably compiled between 1620 and 1650, contains what David Fowler (1968: 132–3) thinks were typical minstrel performance pieces from an even earlier age. On its four hundred and sixty-second page is the following song:

THE SEA CRABB

[1] ITT: was a man of Affrica had a ffaire wiffe,
ffairest *tha*t euer I saw the dayes of my liffe:
    with a ging, boyes, ginge! Ginge, boyes, ginge!
    Tarra didle, ffarradidle, ging, boyes, ging!

[2] This goodwiffe was bigbellyed, & with a lad,
& euer shee longed ffor a sea crabbe.
    ginge &c.

[3] The goodman rise in the morning, & put on his hose,
He went to the sea syde, & ffollowed his nose.
    ginge &c.

[4] Sais, "god speed, ffisherman, sayling on the sea,
Hast thou any crabbs in thy bote for to sell mee"?
    Ging &c.

[5] "I haue Crabbs in my bote, one, tow, or three;
I haue Crabbs in my bote for to sell thee."
    Ginge &c.

[6] The good man went home, & ere he wist,
& put the Crabb in the Chamber pot where his wiffe pist.
    Ging &c.

[7] The good wiffe, she went to doe as shee was wont;
vp start the Crabfish, & catcht her by the Cunt.
    Ging &c.

[8] "Alas!" quoth the goodwiffe, "that euer I was borne,
the devill is in the pispott, & has me on his horne."
    Ging &c.

[9] "If thou be a crabb or crabfish by kind,
thoule let thy hold goe with a blast of cold wind."
    ging &c.

[10] The good man laid to his mouth, & began to blowe,
thinkeing thereby that they Crab wold lett goe.
    Ging &c.

[11] "Alas!" quoth the good man, "that euer I came hither,
he has ioyned my wiffes tayle & my nose together!"
    ging &c.

[12] They good man called his neigbors in with great wonder,
to part his wiues tayle & his nose assunder.
    Ging &c.
    (Furnivall 1868: 99–100)

Despite some obvious differences in wording and narrative detail, this seventeenth-century "Sea Crabb" is indisputably the "same" song as the twentieth-century "Lobster Song" sung by the modern-day joggers and partygoers in Colorado.

The two texts represent but two points in the very substantial life of the story they both tell, which I shall call "the Crabfish story." The range of its appeal is astonishing: after all, in Anglo/American culture alone, very few popular songs have remained vital, meaningful, functional, still-evolving performance items over an almost four-hundred-year span, able to serve such widely separated interests as those of a Stuart minstrel in his tavern repertoire as well as those of 1990s middle-class Coloradans in a convivial Saturday-night singsong. But "The Sea Crabb/Lobster Song" has. And in fact the historical span of its underlying *story's* popularity includes more than just these two eras, for if we expand our purview to Continental Europe and its diasporic traditions, we find in addition a fourteenth-century prose version, as well as eighteenth- and nineteenth-century ones. In other words, the Crabfish story can cross not only boundaries between gender tastes but also those between distinct histori-cal periods.

The first documented versions of the story told in our English-lan-guage ballad come in prose form from Europe, the earliest being an Italian literary retelling by Franco Sacchetti, ca. 1330–1400 (Poggiali 1815: 243–8). A later version, more or less contemporaneous with the English min-strel's "Sea Crabb" song, is found in a Late Renaissance/Early Modern French jest book (ca. 1620), where the story is set in an actual tale-telling session, a convention often found in print technology's early years of reproducing visually the medieval norm of face-to-face oral storytelling (Beroalde de Verville n.d.: 89–90).

The boundary between the pre-1650 Late Renaissance period and the eighteenth-century Enlightenment presented no challenge to our story either—at least not in England, and the same is doubtless true elsewhere in Europe: what seems on the surface to be a coarse jest, an old-fashioned fabliau, appealed enough to Charles Churchill, a highly educated, cosmo-politan London man-of-letters, that sometime in the early 1760s he was moved to re-create the story in a lengthy narrative poem, "The Crab" (Bertelsen 1986: 269–74). The story's popularity in anglophone cultures also survived the Industrial Revolution and Victorian prudery, existing in nineteenth-century singing tradition both in a somewhat bowdlerized form (with such lines, for example, as "Middle of the night / Missus gave a grunt / There was the lobster / Hanging on her foot" [Lamb 1958]) as well as in its longtime idiomatic, nonbowdlerized one ("The old woman got up the piss-pot to hunt . . . / The sea crab jumped an' caught her by the cunt" [Randolph 1992: 68]). The Crabfish song has also turned up many times in post–World War II repertoires in English-speaking countries.[2] And as the Pike's Peak Hash House Harriers and Harriettes' songbook shows, it is still popular at the turn of the millennium. In short, the Crabfish story has enjoyed continuous appeal from at least late medieval times to postmodern ones.

Nor has the story been constrained within artistic boundaries. Most notably, it has flourished as both prose tale and song. We find the song form in English-speaking countries—Britain, Canada, Australia, and the United States—whereas in Continental Europe and eastward the story exists only in prose form. Like the song, the prose versions—especially oral ones—are short and simply structured, telling a very similar story. The Crabfish also passed into poem form with Charles Churchill's "The Crab," which versifies the story in twenty-four stanzas of six-line *rime couee*—that is, rhyming AABCCB and accented 4/4/3/4/4/3. The poet never published the piece, which has several contemporary satirical allusions and was probably meant for recitation within his circle of literary friends and colleagues:[3]

THE CRAB

[1] Whoever studies Humankind
Devoid of prejudice, will find
    Whatever Priests pretend,
That they like us are flesh and blood,
And were before and scince the flood,
    And will be to the end,

[2] This truth scince all the Learned own,
Without excepting pious Stone,
    E'en let the Bigots rail
Their rage but shows them in the wrong,
Then not to make my prelude long,
    Why here begins my Tale,

[3] A priest of more than Irish fame
Tradition says, but hides his name,
    Who in his younger days
Instead of mumbling over beads,
Had done in Love surprizing deeds,
    And cropt immortal bays,

[4] Began to find at fifty five
That though each member seem'd alive
    And each in vigour still,
Yet one would often droop its head,
And spite of what he did or said,
    Refuse to work his will,

[5] A sad discovery you'll say
For one who in the Month of May
    Had fix'd upon a night
To meet an healthy buxom bride
Whose wants an Husband ill supply'd,
    And yet who knew her right,

[6] Not go was to proclaim his case,
But then to suffer a disgrace!—
    'Ne'er fright yourself good Sir
(Said Doctor Ward) when Nature halts
Experience shews us certain Salts
    Will set her on the spur,

[7] This Doctrine Cleopatra knew,
And thence luxuriously drew
    Exstatick draughts of pleasure,
Crabs, Cockles, when the Queen was lewd
The Roman's appetite renew'd
    And Oysters were a treasure,

[8] In May th' inhabitants of Cloysters
Are too well fed to look for Oysters,
    Ay true but Crabs are plenty
So quick to Billingsgate he goes
And of the largest pick'd and chose
    And sent the Lady twenty,

[9] So many Crabs the wond'ring wife
Had never seen in all her life
    Quick to her room she fled,
And not to leave them in the way
For fear of what the world might say,
    Hid them beneath the bed,

[10] There long they lay in Silent state
'Till one impatient of his fate,
    Or urg'd by Lord knows what,
Crawl'd out with many an awkward stride,
And waiting the return of tide
    Stole in a neighbouring pot

[11] The rest they stew'd with spice and wine
In proper time, and broil'd the chine,
    I'd swear no grace was said
He gave no respite to his jaws
By his advice she suck'd the claws,
    Then hurried up to bed

[12] While he was fumbling at his hose,
Madam was whip'd between the cloaths
    And squat on that machine
(In vain we talk of style or mode)
From whence the royal favours flow'd
    Of great Pomonqué Queen,

[13] And where the Crab lay snug and still
Who having quickly drank his fill
    Would eat as well as drink,
And fearless of the rattling shower
Stretch'd forth a claw with all his power
    And seiz'd the mossy brink

[14] What stubborn Amazonian heart
But must have fail'd at such a smart,
    In such a tender spot,
Mercy! she shrieking cry'd dismay'd
O Man of God! quick lend me your aid,
    There's death within the pot,

[15] The Priest to her assistance flew,
Pull'd up her shift in haste to view
    From whence those cries arose,
And whilst he mus'd on what he saw
The pendant Crab stretch'd th' other claw
    And caught him by the nose,

[16] God's wounds he cry'd (for priests will swear)
Then groan'd as if his end was near
   Like Florimel in labour,
The Dame too now with fresh surprize
Redoubled quick her treble cries
   And fright'ned ev'ry Neighbour,

[17] Both pull'd and tugg'd with might and main,
Us'd ev'ry art, but all in vain,
   To heighten their disaster
The more they pull'd the more they cry'd
The wicked Crab with cruel pride
   Still grip'd and clung the faster,

[18] Now all the Street was in a clatter,
All wond'ring what could be the matter,
   Half drest ran Aunts and Cousins,
Some one thing some another swore
Howe'er at length they burst the door
   And tumbled in by dozens,

[19] And now while all suppos'd a rape,
Or Murder in some dreadfull shape
   And ev'ry cheek grew pale
Imagine how air once they grinn'd
To see the Prelate's nostrils pinn'd
   So close to Madam's tail,

[20] Imagine their surprize to hear
Such oaths which not a Turk would swear
   With now and then an Ave
While Madam wriggling to and fro
Now labour'd to dislodge the foe
   Now tired cry'd peccavi

[21] Consider too the Husband's face
To find a Crab in such a place
   So curiously suspended
And then conceive—but what a jest
Without my aid you'll guess the rest
   And so my Story's ended.

[22] Your Story ended! prithee friend
This never sure can be the end
    In spite of what you say
You stop because your spirits fail
Now Durfey would have told this tale
    In quite a diff'rent way,

[23] We want to know the Prelate's shame
And of the Crab too what became
    And can't compound for less,
But you in strange pretended haste
For want of wit bid Men of Taste
    Conceive imagine guess

[24] What Moral then would you infer?
A Tale Should have a moral Sir,
    A Moral! thus it flows,
On him misfortunes still attend
Who in the secrets of a friend
    Imprudent thrusts his nose.
    (Bertelsen 1986: 269–74)

Despite its richer rhetorical texture, its more extensive exposition, and the many intrusions of its narrator (not unexpected in written texts informed by a strong literary sensibility), Churchill's "Crab" tells a story that's remarkably like the one told in the many oral, amateur versions of everyday enactment, whether they're in song or prose.

Geocultural boundaries have also presented no challenge to the story's dissemination: as a tale, the crabfish narrative has been noted in the Far East (Korea, Indonesia, India), in the Near East (Turkey, Bosnia), and in both southern (Italy, France) and northern (Finland, Norway, Germany) Continental Europe, while the song has been documented with even greater frequency throughout much of the anglophone world: England, Scotland, Canada, the United States, and Australia.[4] Clearly, the range of languages, habits, and beliefs prevalent in the cultures whose members accepted the Crabfish story into their active repertoires is impressive. Here is a nineteenth-century prose version from Turkey that, except for a probable bowdlerizing (foot for vagina; such a substitution could have been made either by the informant or by the folklorist/editor), contains very typical motifs. The events are attached to Hodja Nasreddin, a cleric and trickster figure who appears in a large number of Turkish traditional tales. The text was translated for me by Jeffrey Barnouw: "One day the Hodscha and his wife went to the river to wash linens. But as the wife inadvertently put her foot in the water, a crab grabbed it. 'Help, Hodscha,' she cried, 'Help.' He said: 'Sit down, so that I can see what it is.' He bent and saw what sort of animal it was; but as he crouched lower to see better, the crab caught his nose with the other claw. In that moment the wife, whose fear was growing, released a fart; the Hodscha cried: 'You don't need to open that [bodily orifice] up, but rather [open up] the foot of this beast' " (Wesselski 1911: 178).

Yet another boundary that has in no way constrained the popularity of the picaresque crab's adventures is a socioeconomic one. Charles Churchill, the London wit who remade the story into the long poem above, moved in elite circles of mid-eighteenth-century writers, artists, and thinkers, numbering among his acquaintances people like Dr. Johnson's biographer, James Boswell, and the poet William Cowper. Similarly, in twentieth-century America many people who sang "The Crabfish" on their own diverse festive and ritual occasions moved in comparably exalted social milieux. For example, "The Crabfish" appears in a songbook put out by a University of Illinois student group, probably a male fraternity (Cray 1992: 4; Randolph 1992: 1: 70–1). A few years ago when I read a paper on the song to representatives of North America's intellectual elite, a roomful of Ph.D.s at a scholarly society's annual meeting, one of my colleagues on the panel, a professor of English at a Canadian university, asked if I would like him to sing me "his" version! And when I delivered yet another Crabfish paper at the 1998 conference celebrating the hundredth anniversary of the English Folk-Song Society's founding, another university instructor—this time at a European institution—was moved to versify the story on the spot in Chaucerian style.[5] Obviously, the Crabfish story holds appeal for the most highly educated and cosmopolitan stratum of a population.

At the same time, the song's been collected from Arkansas hill farmers of little formal education and completely rural backgrounds (see Randolph 1992: 66–70), as well as from working-class residents of English country villages, like Harry Cox of Catfield, Norfolk, who sang it for Peter Kennedy in 1953 (Kennedy 1975: 452). Even subsistence-level tribal cultivators have evidently told and heard the story with satisfaction and delight (Elwin 1947: 589). Clearly, then, "The Crabfish" is also unrestrained by yet another kind of boundary, socioeconomic class, being known on the one hand to creatures of privilege like university professors, economically secure and trained to think abstractly, and on the other hand to underprivileged, economically marginal, more practical thinkers from wholly rural environments.

In sum, the Crabfish story has flourished in a number of diverse contexts, whether those be of communicative medium (from oral tradition to the internet), of historical period, of literary vehicle, of geographical location, of cultural milieu, or of social class. Yet, despite that diversity, we find a remarkable consistency in its central image of a man and a woman joined, female genitals to male face, by a crustacean. The wide-ranging popularity of the story combined with its remarkable consistency forces one to ask, what on earth is there about this humiliating, absurd incident that can so transcend cultural specificities as to appeal not only to the late medieval mentality but also to the Y2K one; not only to Muslims but also to Buddhists, Christians, and aboriginal polytheists of central India; not only to a learned, sophisticated, urban writer like Charles Churchill but also to "an old Texas trail driver named Ambrose Bull," from whom Arizona rancher Riley Neal learned the song during Theodore Roosevelt's presidency (Logsdon 1989: 245–8)? It is to that question I now turn.

One reason for our story's ubiquitous appeal may be the obvious: it's funny. This is the explanation America's now-foremost authority on obscene song, Ed Cray, offered in the first edition of his *Erotic Muse* (Cray 1969: 2). While it is true that "what's funny" is culturally relative, Cray undoubtedly realized that certain kinds of ideas seem to break the rule. One such idea is that of the gluing together of objects and/or persons who are normally, or empirically, quite separate; such a bonding manifests the general quality of incongruity that's said to elicit laughter cross-culturally (Berger 1993: 3; Gutwirth 1993: 84–99). Informally, folklorists call this image the "stick-fast" motif, and clearly our Crabfish story consistently evokes the idea by the couple's unnatural adhesion and their inability to break apart. (Verrier Elwin immediately follows his Indian Crabfish version with a stick-fast tale [1947: 589–90].)

Indeed, the idea that stick-fast's many manifestations "naturally" elicit laughter is encoded into Motif H341.1, Princess brought to laughter by people sticking together (Thompson 1966: 3: 407), as dramatized, for example, in versions of Tale Type 571, All Stick Together, in which the king's daughter, who has never laughed, is finally induced to do so by the sight of an incongruous joining. To quote the generalized summary from *Types of the Folktale*, "To the magic goose the innkeeper's daughter, who has stolen a feather at night, sticks fast, as do also the parson, the sexton, and three peasants" (Thompson 1964: 211). Like the Crabfish story, Type 571 enjoys cross-cultural popularity.

Moreover, because body parts like bottoms and genitalia are almost universally regarded as private and hence subject to social taboo, images of stick-fast that include such organs being made public would add to the incongruity, evoking a particularly intense response.[6] It is not too surprising, then, to find not only that a substantial set of stick-fast motifs are common in global tale tradition because they portray the idea of incongruity (see the various submotifs of D1413, Magic object holds person fast, and D2171, Magic adhesion), but also that several of them prominently feature human private parts (D1413.5, Bench to which one sticks; D1413.6, Chair to which one sticks; D1413.7, Basin to which one sticks; D1413.8, Chamber-pot to which one sticks [Thompson 1966: 2: 224–6, 396–7]). Indeed, this aspect may play a significant causal role in what is evidently the Crabfish story's fairly modern ability to transgress the boundary between gender tastes: by taking to what used to be called a "dirty song," the postmodern Harriettes in Pike's Peak, Colorado, are liberating themselves from older constraints against social indecorum ("fit topics for song") as much as they are from other traditionally gendered taboos, such as those against women's indulging in "too much" physical exertion (a "hash"—that is, a Saturday run—can be very physically demanding). In other words, the story's stick-fast incongruity in a sense parallels the "incongruity" of middle-class women embracing a song of traditionally masculine appeal, "unfit for ladies' ears."

The evidence is strong, indeed, that throughout most of its five-hundred-and-more-year history, the Crabfish story *has* been overwhelmingly a male performance piece. For example, virtually every time an informant is credited as the source of a Crabfish text, that informant is male, and even though a female plays *at least* as prominent a part in the narrated events, two of the three explicit morals that end Crabfish texts (the Italian one and Charles Churchill's poem) are directed to men. In fact, even as objective an observer as the most eminent of folktale scholars, Stith Thompson, seems to have assumed a male point of view to the story, for he titled its central motif, J2675, "Bungling *rescuer* caught by crab" and characterized it thus: "He tries to rescue woman caught by crab. Is caught himself and found in embarrassing position" (Thompson 1966: 4: 229; italics added).

Granting that the Crabfish story is predominantly men's folklore, is the humor of its surface motifs enough to account for its hold on males of vastly different historical eras, cultures, and social classes? I doubt it. I suspect that the story evokes in the male psyche some more deep-seated, probably subconscious semantic associations to make it so compelling. And indeed, one need not possess very great imagination to suggest that the Crabfish speaks to an intense male concern with the female genitalia that stems not so much from desire or awe or even from an innate procreation drive as from anxiety.

If so, then our corpus of Crabfish texts suggests that the anxiety takes two interrelated forms, hostility and fear. Hostility seems to dominate in a strain of the anglophone song's textual tradition that is marked by its lack of the male-capture episode: the wife is bitten, she calls her husband for help, and together they dispose of the dangerous creature. Other traits often found with this subtype—but not exclusive to it—are that (1) the creature (as in the Pike's Peak Harriers' songbook version) is a lobster; (2) the human(s) physically attack and often kill it; (3) there is a moral tag about making sure to look before urinating. More rare, is (4) the song's language tends to be euphemistic rather than idiomatic: for example, the wife may be caught by the "front" rather than the "cunt." I suspect that this subtype is relatively recent, probably linked to pre-1860 British performance of the Crabfish song before more heterogeneous audiences and in more public places, like early music halls, but whatever its provenience, by omitting the crab's biting of the husband, this "lobster" strain intensifies attention to the wife, particularly in her role as recipient of a very painful, very aggressive attack. Whether or not the man himself is responsible for her victimization is ambiguous in the Crabfish song; at the very least, one is tempted to see the overt agent, the crab, as a projection of the man, since he placed the creature in the commode. (In fact, the projection may be even more specific: the crab may represent the male phallus as the inflictor of pain, an image that's rampant in anglophone "dirty songs" in general [see Cray 1992].)

Here's a typical version of this more modern Anglo/American "lobster" song-strain:

THE LOBSTER

[1] "Good morning, mister fisherman." "Good morning," said he.
"Have you a lobster you can sell to me?"
CHORUS: Singing row diddely O, row diddely O.
        Row diddely O, riddely O, toe, toe.

[2] "Oh, yes," said the fisherman, "I've got two;
One is for you and the other is for me."

[3] I took the lobster home, I put it in the dish;
I put it in the dish where the misses used to wish.

[4] First I heard her grunt, then I heard her scream;
There was the lobster a-hanging on her front.

[5] The missus grabbed a brush and I grabbed the broom;
We chased the bloomin' lobster round and round the room.

[6] Now the moral of my story, the moral is this,
Always have a shufti before you have a wish.
        (Palmer 1981: 220)

While male hostility evidently dominates this relatively modern Anglo/American "lobster" strain, male fear seems more prominent in versions containing the globally widespread episode of the crab's subsequent attack on the husband. In this strain of the Crabfish story, the creature would be a female rather than male trope, metonymically signifying the woman's vagina. Semantically, then, this form of the Crabfish story might reflect males' fear of losing control in their relationships with women—by being "caught" in a romantic relationship, for example, even in some sort of contractual bond (vide the common notion of the male's affection being "captured," or of his being "trapped" into marriage by a partner's pregnancy). Such general fear of female sexuality may lie behind occasional Crabfish versions in which the man is caught on a body part like the lip that has no particular phallic resonance (though the also-found "beard" and "moustache" *do*). In most cases, however, the man is caught by the nose, which Gershon Legman, who possessed magisterial knowledge not only of the Crabfish tradition itself but of all folklore of tabooed subjects and was a leading proponent of the thesis that male sexual fears lie at the root of such material's popularity, insists is a "standard" metaphor for the male phallus (Legman 1975: 619; see also 568–9). Hence throughout the Crabfish story's worldwide manifestations, we have what is apparently a much more specific fear of female sexuality: the crab, which metonymically stands for the female vagina, attacks the nose, which metaphorically represents the male penis.[7]

While many ideas in Legman's two extraordinarily dense volumes on sexual folklore (1968, 1975) could be explored as bearing on our topic, I think three of his referents have the most credible link with the Crabfish story—especially its Anglo/American song form, since anglophone folklore in general provides us with some well-known parallels. The first is a male concern that's commonly projected onto folklore, according to Legman: the phenomenon of a "stuck penis" that purportedly occurs during intercourse with a woman whose tenacious vagina imprisons the male member and won't let go. In Anglo/American folklore, examples of this motif can be found in superstitions, in legends (like the one about the lovers sticking together during intercourse because the woman suffers a spasm; as in many American versions of the Crabfish song, only a physician can separate them), and even in a European tale, Type 1159, The Ogre Wants to Learn to Play. To quote Thompson's summary, "Finger caught in a cleft of a tree. Later he is terrified by the man's wife with her legs apart. He thinks he is to be caught again" (Thompson 1964: 365; these examples come from Legman 1975: 427–8). We can certainly see more than a hint of this fear in our story, as the woman's crab/vagina grips the man's nose/penis in a hold that cannot be broken by ordinary means. (This referent also links the realm of unconscious, anxiety-laden meanings to the realm of conscious, humorous ones discussed above.)

A second common male fear centered in the genitals and in heterosexual coition, according to Legman (1975: 447–9), is of venereal disease. (Our English-language song versions of the story add linguistic fuel to this interpretation by the choice of "crab" as the creature attaching itself to the woman's genitals, "the crabs" being English slang for one kind of venereal disease.) Parallel manifestations of this motif in Anglo/American folklore are well-known, particularly in the contemporary urban legend about a young man's female sexual partner who, only recently met and whose name and address he has been unable to elicit, quits his bed early one morning leaving the lipstick-scrawled greeting, "Welcome to the world of AIDS," on the bathroom mirror for the horrified victim to see when he wakes up (Fine 1987). The tale implies that she is on some sort of sociopathic crusade against men, using her sexuality as a death-dealing weapon. A similar legend about incurable strains of venereal disease with such exotic names as "The Black Rose" (which often crosses with the AIDS tale) have also been common in the last two decades or so, particularly in reference to U.S. soldiers' experiences in Southeast Asia (Gulzow and Mitchell 1980: 311-4). Once again, the Crabfish story's dramatization of the female vagina's sharply painful attack on the male phallus may very well be a projection of this general male fear of venereal disease.

A third, related male anxiety, also ubiquitous in folklore and also credibly implied in the Crabfish, is of castration. Folklorists are familiar with this concern's dramatic manifestation in the F547.1.1, *vagina dentata* motif (Thompson 1966: 3: 164), common in native North and South American Indian folklore, but also found in South Pacific and Asian Indian folklore. While the literally toothed vaginas of tribal folklore do not to my knowledge appear in Anglo/American or even European materials, what can plausibly be considered functional analogues do, as in the Crabfish story, where a clawlike extension of the woman's vagina bites the man's nose/penis. The most striking contemporary kin to the *vagina dentata* motif in our culture is found once again in Vietnam War legends, particularly in tales of Saigon prostitutes and Viet Cong sympathizers placing razor blades, broken bottle necks, and other such objects in the vaginal cavity before seeking U.S. soldiers as customers (Gulzow and Mitchell 1980: 306-11). The motif, whose popularity of course predates the war in Southeast Asia, is also common in jokes (Legman 1975: 429-34). In short, comparative evidence suggests that the Crabfish story has enough traditional analogues to indicate a widely held, deeply rooted phobia among anglophone males—and perhaps among males of many other cultures as well.

That the Crabfish story may evoke unconsciously the same referents in males all over the world is an arresting notion, but many folklorists will view it skeptically, since they don't buy into the classic Freudian model of the mind that informs such interpretations, or even believe that such topics—sexual intercourse, body parts—are traumatizing (or anxiety-causing, or socially tabooed) enough to be sublimated in members of non-European, or even nonbourgeois cultures. Moreover, in the language of some contemporary critics, such a theory constitutes a "master trope," which, by its very assumptions of universality, determinism, and stability—its extreme insensitivity to contextual differences, to human agency, and to the nature of how meaning is communicated and interpreted—is suspect. True, Charles Churchill's poem seems to validate the association by bringing sex into consciousness: the lover, now in his mid-fifties, is worried about his virility, and the well-known aphrodisiac property of shellfish leads him to plan the meal of crab, though perhaps Churchill's capacity for irony bore greater responsibility for this motif, since rather than enhancing the cleric's sexual experience the crab aborts it by incapacitating both his partner and himself.

That his poem undoubtedly had a real-world correlative may also have been a sufficient motive for Churchill's creative variation, so perhaps an indisputably folk version of the Crabfish story from the Muria, a subset of central India's aboriginal Gond peoples, may help the skeptical feel a bit more kindly toward psychologically inclined explanations. The Muria version is, I think, the most distinctive of the fifty-odd Crabfish songs, tales, and poem I've seen. The distinctiveness doesn't lie in the tale's first half, which contains nothing unusual, exhibiting plot details found in other Eastern texts: the action takes place outdoors, the woman gets bitten while washing in a stream, and a passerby tries to help by biting off the crab's claw but is instead himself caught by the nose. Another passerby, also male, responds to the couple's plight, eventually freeing them with a pair of tongs. Just before he does so, however, this Muria version begins to depart from the common Crabfish story: the stranger extracts a promise from the imprisoned woman that she will repay him with her sexual favors! The tale proceeds, in the collector's synopsis: "Some days later he comes to her house to claim his reward. She is busy cooking and asks him to lie down on a cot until she is ready. He lies on his face, but is so excited that his erect penis goes through the strings of the cot and protrudes below. A cat thinking it a bit of meat, catches it. . . . The woman comes out and refuses to release [him] unless he declares her quit of her debt" (Elwin 1947: 589).

From a psychological perspective, we can see that this second section of the tale literalizes—and hence, decodes—the figurative first section. It lays bare such "hidden" referents as (1) the woman as a sexual figure (not just an unfortunate victim of an animal attack, to be pitied and assisted); (2) the male phallus (not just its metaphorical substitute, the nose; more-over, the phallus appears in its explicitly sexual aspect, erect); (3) the woman's palpable threat to the man's sexual well-being (he is attacked by her household pet, not by some stray wild creature); even perhaps (4) the vagina-as-castrating-weapon (it's highly likely that to the Muria the cat was as much a vaginal symbol as "pussy" is in English-speaking ver-nacular).[8] In short, this ethnic Indian version gives a sort of "folk interpre-tation" of the Crabfish story that is surprisingly consistent with a classi-cally Freudian interpretation, providing support for the idea that the story's grip on the imagination of males, whatever their cultural back-ground, may be rooted in subliminal anxiety about the dangers of female sexuality.

While the female genitalia, the male face, and the crustacean that joins them in a most incongruous way are the elements of the Crabfish story virtually universal in their popularity and hence representative of what one might call a global or "transnational" culture, other narrative fea-tures that are not as primal in their resonances *are* subject to adaptations in their travel from place to place. While this aspect of our story—its nar-rative variations—is the one most often addressed in Crabfish scholar-ship (on which I've depended enormously for bibliography: see Cray 1992: 3–11; Gershon Legman's notes in Randolph 1992: 1: 70–3; Meade 1958: 91–100), I think it is worth at least touching on again, since several more texts—and some especially interesting ones—have come to light in recent years and since even the most sophisticated of existing compara-tive discussions, that of Legman, limits itself to a portion of the story told. Moreover, for our purposes, familiarity with the story's narrative range will provide a context for better appreciating the fourth section of this essay yet to come, where I will narrow my focus even more and examine in depth a single English version of the Crabfish song.

Let's look first at the diversity of the story's characters. In virtually all western European and North American examples I've seen, the relation-ship between the absurdly bonded couple is that of husband and wife. A prominent exception is Churchill's poem, in which the two are adulter-ous lovers, undoubtedly Churchill's own variation and motivated by cer-tain social and political events: the poet was targeting, in his combina-tion of satire and farce, a real clergyman and topical sex scandal. In marked contrast to western European versions, Eastern Crabfish tales prefer the joined couple to be in-laws or even strangers. In-laws are asso-ciated with Muslim countries: in one Balkan text, for example, sister-in-law is attached to brother-in-law (Krauss 1904: 152–3), in another, daugh-ter-in-law to father-in-law (151–2), while in an Indonesian version the attached couple are mother-in-law and son-in-law (Coster-Wijsman 1929: 43). In the two Southeast Asian versions, the attached couple are strang-ers: in a Korean text, a housewife carrying provisions to fieldworkers at noontime is caught and yoked to a passing Buddhist monk (Janelli 1997), while in the Muria Indian rendition the two are similarly unacquainted travelers who encounter each other by chance (Elwin 1947: 589).[9]

Many versions—especially the prose tales—have additional charac-ters, invariably minor, who witness the couple's embarrassment. In Con-tinental European tale versions (and in the older, pre-Victorian British texts), their exposure to others who must help them in their plight or simply laugh at it (strangers, neighbors, servants) is a prominent motif. In America, the role of helper is assigned to a doctor, though that charac-ter never actually appears: the story ends with his summoning. In our one Indonesian version, the Muslim in-law emphasis is extended: the helper is father-in-law, who frees his wife from the couple's son-in-law. Very common in the American tradition of the Crabfish song is a peculiarly New World variety of this involvement-of-another-family-member motif: the stuck parents are exposed to their children, who find the sight of their "dad's nose in ma's a——— hole [sic]" hilarious.[10]

The animal itself is overwhelmingly a crab. (In British and British diasporic song tradition it is often a crabfish, which I take to be the same thing.) As mentioned above, the lobster is, I think, a relatively modern variant of the crab and indicative of a subtype (though indistinct and unstable); except for a single Norwegian tale version, this creature is found only in anglophone song tradition, but found quite often, so often that I suspect it to be a nineteenth-century substitution for the earlier crab. Two versions (between which textual evidence suggests, though weakly, a genetic relationship) are unique in making the creature a codfish: one is from American college student singing tradition (Cray 1992: 5), while the other, a typical example of a bowdlerized version, is from British army tradition;[11] the bowdlerization in this case is probably the editor's, but there are examples of very similar folk bowdlerization as well.

While the creature itself varies little, the reason for its presence in the same place as its victims differs a fair bit. In the oral tale versions from precapitalist agrarian economies, mostly in the East, the action takes place outdoors, often at a river where the couple may be engaged in what is apparently a subsistence activity, crab hunting. Since this is the crab's natural environment, the reason for the creature's presence is purely empirical. Only slightly less empirical is what is found in more technologically advanced, more urbanized Western versions, an indoor setting. Usually, the crab is at hand simply because, having been purchased or caught outdoors by the husband, it is to be served for dinner as a more or less everyday meal, but we find in anglophone versions (one Scottish and several English) a slightly more complex motif: the wife is pregnant and craves a meal of crab, which sends the accommodating husband out to fetch some. This motif, understandably, appears only in conjunction with a man/wife relationship.[12] The most elaborate reasons for the crab's presence appear, as might be expected, in two literary versions: in the early-seventeenth-century French tale, the husband is a provincial governor, and the crabs come from local fisherman as a sort of typical bribe of public-sector civic authority by private-sector self-employed people (Beroalde de Verville n.d.: 89), while in Charles Churchill's more topically resonant eighteenth-century poem, where the couple consists of a well-known cleric and his married mistress, the lover has purchased the crabs for their aphrodisiac property and brought them to the rendezvous, as his sexual powers are on the wane.

The methods employed to loosen the beast's grip are somewhat diverse as well. In general, the nontechnological methods do not work, the "some-tech" ones do. In the three Far Eastern versions, for example—Korean, Indian, Indonesian—pulling or biting off the crab's claw is the favored method of release, though in two of the three cases it does not work but in fact makes matters worse by bringing the puller/biter within striking distance of the crab, thus facilitating the male-female joining. The same thing usually happens with the similarly "nontech" method of blowing air on the crab, which reputedly causes it to loosen its hold (evidently, a "folk belief"): when the blowing is from the mouth, the attempt in all but one version also results (like pulling and biting) in the blower's capture by the crab's free claw. When a cognate blowing technique, farting, is employed, the results are more complicated, though the primary purpose, release from the crab, is just as seldom achieved as by huffing and puffing. Technology, however simple, is more successful: a pair of tongs or pliers is used in three versions (Indian, Early Renaissance Italian, and Late Renaissance/Early Modern French) and is successful in every case. In America, the more hyperbolically burlesque motif of separating the joined couple by pulling them free with horse-and-cart is quite common.

Related to the method of release is the crab's eventual fate. An apparently modern motif, found to my knowledge only in song texts collected after World War I but probably dating back to nineteenth-century pub, perhaps even music hall, versions, seems to elevate the creature from deus ex machina status to that of dramatis persona: in a scene that would distress our modern-day enlightened urban sensibility, the creature is punished with a severe beating after its hold has been broken. Evidently originating in England and diffusing from there to Australia and to the United States, where it is very common, this motif has the husband and wife pursuing the beast around the room while beating it with some household implement or the other (most often a broom, but also a poker, a shovel, a scrubbing brush, a fork, a spoon, or a ladle) as if to punish its hubris. This animal-abuse motif is very strongly associated with what I have called the "lobster strain" of the Anglo/American Crabfish song. In America, the couple's children join in or even take charge of the punishing. In several texts, mostly British, the crab/lobster's death from the punishment is specified (for example, "They kicked him on the head, they kicked him on the side / They jumped upon his back, boys, until the poor crab died" [Kennedy 1975: 452]), though just as often that death seems to be implied.[13] In contrast, pre-twentieth-century song versions, Churchill's poem, and almost all prose tale versions usually portray the crab as less anthropomorphically pathetic or demonic: the death is simply assumed to be integral to the joined couple's release and is of no dramatic or moral moment per se.

While I suspect that any traditional story, whether told in prose tale, poem, or song form, contains *some* instructional point, however covert it may be, only a few of our Crabfish texts have explicit moral or practical tags. Songs that contain this feature all have the same moral, aimed presumably at females: inspect a commode's insides carefully before urinating, the Kentucky "codfish" text adding the explanatory caveat that "none of us has an eye on our behind" (Cray 1992: 5). Just as tongue-in-cheek but a trifle more clever perhaps is Charles Churchill's male-directed moral that misfortune will attend anyone who thrusts his nose in a friend's business (in his version, remember, the couple are a pair of adulterous lovers, not man and wife; by versifying a topical scandal, Churchill was himself thrusting his nose into others' business, and this irony no doubt added to the poem's effect). Even more ironically tongue-in-cheek, and once again predictably more complex, is the earliest surviving version we possess, the late-fourteenth-century Italian literary retelling of the traditional tale. Its moral, also directed to males, seems to satirize the very notion that a story should make a point (a "meta-moral"?): it's an intentionally verbose mishmash of the vacuous, the pseudoprofound, and the tautological (the translation is by Moyra Byrne): "And thus it often befalls careless people, or rather, one should say, forgetful people, because this man, having returned from the sea with the crabs, laid them on the bed, and then got what he well deserved. . . . And thus in this life are men often overtaken by a variety of events, and such events are so numerous that it would be impossible to imagine them all. However, one should never trust in one's luck, as many times a small spider's bite has felled a mighty man" (Poggiali 1815: 247–8). A few American texts contain a tag that's a dirty-song formulaic closure rather than a moral: "That's the end of my story, there isn't any more, / There's an apple up me arse, boys, an' ye can have the core."[14] This type of rhetorical figure is widespread in folklore, whether as a performer "signature" or simply as a generic "framing" device.

Yet another narrative feature subject to interesting culturally relative manipulation falls into the category of what we might call "bodylore," which in America at any rate has become almost a genre of its own in a burst of recent folklore scholarship (see Young and Babcock 1994). Many

Crabfish texts have a scatological motif depicting the woman's inability to control her own bowel functions: she farts from surprise or fear on being first seized by the crab's claw. In the three Near Eastern versions, the man is critical of the woman's farting—even though it is caused by her distress—either because it is of no help to the problem at hand (Turkish: don't open "that" up [presumably her anus], he says peevishly, but open the crab's claw instead [Wesselski 1911: 178]) or because it will anger the crab and worsen their plight (the two Balkan versions). In America, as mentioned above, the flatulence may be represented as a method of blowing wind on the crab, which purportedly causes the creature to let go. But in all instances, Eastern or Western, tale or song, the attempt fails: in fact, in several American song versions, in trying to fart she unintentionally defecates instead, right into her husband's face. Only in one of the three French versions is the result favorable: her fart unexpectedly blows the crab to pieces and gains the couple their release (Bouchet [1873] 1969: 36–7).

As for the bodylore of genitalia, the early-seventeenth-century French version makes much of the sexual nature of the female anatomy: her urine's warmth and freshness arouses *le paillard cancre* (the licentious crab) hunkered down in the chamber pot, so that it stretches forth its pincers in what may be mimicry of male sexual stimulation. While one shouldn't make too much of a single motif within a fairly complex story—and an ambiguous one at that—this image is unusual in that it links the crab semantically to *male* sexuality in a way that makes the female organ an object of male desire and attraction, whereas—as we've suggested—the crabfish is more commonly linked semantically with *female* sexuality in a way that makes the female organ an object of male fear and avoidance.[15] Also somewhat prurient are song versions with the codfish rather than crab/lobster, found in a British army rendition and a Kentucky college fraternity one. Unlike crabs and lobsters, the cod has no claws and in the U.S. college student version does its mischief by slipping inside the woman's vagina. Since the husband is safe from a codfish's attack, his role is confined to helping his wife in her plight (though the husband is unbitten in a large number of crab/lobster versions as well). Emphasized here is the penetration of the woman by a phallic object, which seems particularly apposite in the late adolescent social context of a small, pre-sexual-revolution-era U.S. southern college.[16]

In contrast to Western versions, Eastern versions of the Crabfish story take a more *explicitly* pejorative view of the female sex organ: the Indonesian son-in-law complains of having to smell his mother-in-law's vagina all the way from the river, where they'd been bitten, to home, where father-in-law frees them with a pair of pliers, while the Korean monk remarks disparagingly on the strong taste of the woman's vaginal secretions. In a Bosnian version, father-in-law (like the Turkish Hodja Nasreddin) enjoins daughter-in-law not to fart, which will inflame the beast, but instead (unlike the Turk) to emit "sexual odor," which will calm it down, a strange inversion of the French crab/man analogy that may, I suppose, tell us something of the two cultures' respective attitudes toward women and toward sex (Krauss 1904: 152).

As for the male body, whenever the husband/in-law is caught by the crab—thus joining the two humans—it is almost always by the nose in the anglophone song tradition, though we do also find "toes, "balls," and "lip." In the tale traditions of Europe and Asia nose dominates slightly, but lip is common, while beard and moustache each appear once. The lip is a key image in a topsy-turvy motif found in two versions, the Korean and the Norwegian: when the couple are eventually freed, somehow or other she ends up with his lip, he with her labia major. The Norwegian synopsis suggests that their anatomical parts were removed in the couple's freeing and sewed back on in error (Hodne 1984: 348), but the informant who provided the Korean version, when asked about this feature, would only say "That's the way the story goes" (Janelli 1997).

These are the more substantive kinds of variations in the Crabfish story one finds throughout its appearance in folklore and in popular literature. While the story's consistency cross-culturally is astounding, one assumes that the variations discussed correlate functionally with the contexts of their popularity. For example, the American image of the whole family, possibly representing "civilization," battling as a corporate unit the animal that represents "wilderness," could arguably evince a "frontier" pioneer-settlement mentality; the Muslim predilection for making the joined couple in-laws may possibly reflect Islamic beliefs in the sanctity of marriage and resulting taboos against vulgar secular jokes that defile it; the Kentucky college student "Codfish" version may indicate the late-adolescent fixation on heterosexual fornication as a topic of huge interest in and of itself, as reflected in the codfish's actual penetration of the female vagina.

From such a culturally relative point of view—which of course contrasts with the universal perspective adopted in the last section—one of the more interesting texts is, once again, the Muria version, especially in the way it empowers the woman. Elsewhere in Crabfish narrative tradition the woman is invariably a subordinate figure, victim of the crab's attack and dependent on others for her release. The Muria version's first half, which matches the full story told in most Crabfish versions, is perfectly consistent with that pattern; in fact, it seems to overdetermine the woman's usual powerlessness with an up-to-that-point unique motif: she has to prostitute herself to compensate her rescuer. Having set her up for complete debasement, however, the tale in its second half introduces the tables-turned device that empowers the woman and subordinates the man in at least three ways: first, his male anatomy puts him at risk, just as her female anatomy put her at risk when she crossed the river; second, attacked by the cat's claws, he now feels the same sort of pain in his private parts she felt when attacked by the crab's claws; and third, rendered helpless, he must agree to her terms if he wants to be freed, just as she, helpless in the crab's grip, had to agree to his demands for sexual favors. The biter is indeed bit, and while narrative symmetry as a compositional trait is of course quite common in folklore in general, we must surely conclude that this particular example is the result not simply of widely found oral stylistics but of intentional, motivated, axiological variation that is functionally related to the cultural context of its popularity. (Note that even the collector's summary of the tale as quoted earlier takes the man's point of view, matching the bias suggested in Stith Thompson's title and description of the story's central motif J2675 given earlier.)

What is there about Muria culture that could logically fit this version's far more egalitarian portrayal of relationships between the sexes than that evinced in other Crabfish texts, which are consistently male-centered? The answer apparently lies in a remarkable custom of the Muria that frees young people from at least certain aspects of gender bias found in other societies, Eastern as well as Western: the custom is to bring young people of both sexes together for most of their nonworking hours in communal dormitories called *ghotuls*. Theoretically comparable, I suppose, to post-World War II Israeli *kibbutzim* or to post-sixties U.S. college coed dorms, the *ghotul* living contributes to an unusual sense of egalitarianism within the social order, including relationships between sexes (for example, Elwin 1947: 57–8, 325, 365, 431).

The Muria text does more than *Muria* cultural work, however; it also does some analytical work for *us*, by revealing continuity between, on the one hand, the more or less universal and unconscious meaning psychological interpretation brings to light, and on the other hand, the more culture-specific and tacit meaning suggested by a more ethnographic sensitivity. These two kinds of analysis, psychological and ethnographic, are often treated as warring paradigms, often as mutually exclusive, but the Muria Crabfish tale integrates them logically, by making the covert male fear of dangerous female genitals overt, deconstructing the model of gender relations built on such a fear, and offering a new model of what might be called balance of gender power.

So far, we have looked at the relationship between the Crabfish story and the people who learn it, tell or sing it, and listen to it on two levels, the globally shared and the culturally distinctive. Let us now look at a third level, that of a specific occasion on which the Crabfish story was enacted by an actual (rather than typical) performer to an actual audience. Present-day folkloristics favors such microstudies of particular performances over macrostudies of texts as quasi-independent artifacts divorced from situations of use for several reasons, but one of the more important is the belief that an item is seldom simply reproduced each time it is enacted. Instead, it is in a sense "reinvented": the performer manipulates its content and/or its intent to fit his or her perceptions of what we might call "journalistic" variables—the who, the where, the when, the why, and so forth of the circumstances at hand. Meaning, in short, is not so much *transmitted*, ready-made and predetermined, from a "sender" to a "receiver," as it is *negotiated* among participants, thus "emerging" in the very act of performance. Hence microfolkloristics avoids talking about "the" meaning of a story like "The Crabfish," for that would presume an entity that is stable, consistent, and universal; to do so would be falsely to "essentialize" the Crabfish story by focusing only on some part of it and treating that part as somehow standing for the diverse complexities of its multiple uses and reuses. More interesting, in contemporary thinking, is what is unstable and unique, perhaps even "reflexive" in that the text turns back upon itself and "interrogates," possibly subverts, "previous" meanings. In this section, I will try to employ this more performative, situation-sensitive, microfolkloristic perspective toward a Crabfish datum.

In the summer of 1904, Mrs. Emma Overd of Langport, a village in the west of England county of Somerset, sang "The Crabfish" for Cecil J. Sharp, a visiting folksong collector from London. A traditionally macrofolkloristic understanding of the event would be that she was for the most part transmitting information to Sharp: that is to say, he (a folksong collector) had asked her to sing him an old song, and she (an informant and member of a category of English society—rural and working-class—that could be called "the folk") was obligingly retrieving one from her memory and reproducing it as an artifact that he could record in his notebook. A more progressively minded "performance-oriented" folklorist would, however, see this transaction as more personally motivated, more unique, more communicative, and certainly more expressive than that characterization suggests.

Here is the text Sharp recorded in his field notebook of what Mrs. Overd sang for him on August 15, 1904 (Cecil Sharp Autograph Field Notebook Collection: Folk Words; Vaughan Williams Memorial Library Microfilm Collection, reel 1):

CRABFISH

[1] There was a little man & he had a little wife
And he loved her as dear as he loved his life
  Musha row dow dow dow diddle all the day (*bis*)

[2] One hr. in the night my wife fell sick
And all that she cried for a little crab fish

[3] Then her husband arose & put on his clothes
And down to the seaside he followed his nose

[4] O fisherman O fisherman canst thou tell me
Hast thou a little crabfish thoust cd. sell me

[5] O yes O yes I've one two or three
And the best of them I will sell thee

[6] So they had no pot to boil him in
So they whipped him in the pot where his wife used to
   Row dow

[7] O husband O husband I pray thee come hither
For the devil's in the pot & he got me by the leather

[8] & the baby were born with the crabs on his belly
   Row

Even in a performance-oriented analysis, the "what" of the song—or tale, or recitation—is the most important matter, since a folklorist's task, whatever his or her theoretical stance, is to explain folklore. But just what constitutes the text—just what *is* that "what"—is by no means straightforward, for reasons that may range from simple to complex. For example, on the simple end, there is the matter of accurate recording: did Sharp's field notes' text above represent what Mrs. Overd actually sang him? It does seem truncated, incomplete, very much unlike the vast majority of Mrs. Overd's song offerings.[17] Mrs. Overd was clearly a superior tradition bearer whose repertoire was fresh in her mind, who cared about the quality of her performance, and who did not sing fragmented, irrelevant, or disjointed texts; she evinced an artistic sensibility typical of what Eleanor Long (1973) has dubbed a "rationalizer." It is possible that Sharp (this was, after all, 1904), put off by the song's vulgarity, wearied by stanza 7 of transcribing the highly indelicate stuff.

It is my opinion, however, that Sharp did indeed record accurately and thoroughly the words (and tune) Mrs. Overd sang. Remember that before the modern era of 1960s liberation—before the days of the Hash House Harriettes—"The Crabfish" was a man's song, so it is very likely that Mrs. Overd knew it only casually, probably seldom if ever singing it, privately or publicly, so that it stayed fresh in her memory. As for Sharp, his lack of prudishness is evident: he published the song not long afterward, including—with some stylistic emendations—all of Mrs. Overd's seven full stanzas. He did bowdlerize some content, but minimally: he changed the wife's "leather" to "nose" and expurgated the "baby it were born" closing line (Sharp 1904–9: 3: 12–3).

But even if Sharp did document Mrs. Overd's text accurately, the "what" that was actually communicated in the performance event of

August 15, 1904, entailed more than just the words and tune manifested in the recordable (and recorded) text. It has become a truism, for example, that all kinds of extralinguistic and paralinguistic features of performance—voice tone, for instance, or bodily gestures—signify, in addition to the linguistic text. Moreover, even unspoken but mutually known information may be tacitly invoked by the manifested text and hence also be communicated (Foley 1995: 29–59). Since even in 1904 the Crabfish song was old, widespread, and well-known in anglophone tradition, not only Mrs. Overd but Sharp himself (who had been a Cambridge undergraduate for four years) was probably familiar with the lineaments of the ballad's larger, more extensive plot; they both "knew how it went," even if neither could necessarily recall all the words. Indeed, when Sharp published the song, his one substantive addition was a stanza that Mrs. Overd *did not* sing him but that is ubiquitous in the story's tradition: a stanza depicting the husband's capture.[18] Mrs. Overd's fragmented part may have brought into both their minds, and in effect "stood for," a whole that was the fuller story.[19]

We can feel some confidence, then, that the "what" that Mrs. Overd communicated to Sharp that day was the full traditional narrative of the British Crabfish song: a husband buys a crabfish to satisfy his wife's pregnancy craving, temporarily storing the creature in the chamber pot. Upon using the pot, the wife is caught on the genitals by the crab's claw; she calls to her husband for help, and he is in turn caught on the nose by the crab's other claw. Their absurd plight is exposed to others—neighbors, servants, and/or family members. After they're freed, husband and wife may punish the creature by beating it with some household implement, like a broom. The wife eventually gives birth to a baby bearing the mark of her traumatic experience.

A glance at Sharp's entire collection of English folksongs, a collection numbering in the thousands that, we assume, accurately reflected rural amateur singers' quotidian performance repertoires, indicates that Mrs. Overd's "Crabfish" is an anomaly: treating normatively taboo material, it belongs to the same class ("obscene" songs) as other British ditties that I remember from my fraternity house days as an undergraduate in Montreal forty years ago, songs like "The North Atlantic Squadron" (Roud 5666) and "The Ball of Kerriemuir" (Roud 4828). Such stuff was undoubtedly sung by English working-class males in Cecil Sharp's day, but except for Mrs. Overd's "Crabfish," Sharp collected not a one, not even from men. One reason for this lacuna, no doubt, was rooted in the social differences between the folklorist and his informants: Sharp was a "gentleman," formally educated, whose dress, speech, and deportment all signaled upper-class status. For a working man to have sung him an obscene song would have been a severe breach of etiquette, implying a most disrespectful attitude of equality and camaraderie.[20] Consider, then, how much more pronounced the breech for Mrs. Overd to sing "The Crabfish," since she was not only working-class (she stripped willow saplings for a local chair manufacturer), but also elderly (she was born in the late 1830s and was about sixty-seven in 1904), a rural dweller (hence a "rustic" or a "yokel"), and female (thus lacking, on the basis of sex alone, many "rights," such as the vote). Sharp was of respectable and authoritative middle age (he was forty-four at the time), an urban dweller, a professional musician/teacher/author, and male; by most prevailing definitions, Sharp was what Mrs. Overd's friends—if not necessarily she herself—would have called her "better."

In sum, both the "what" and the "who" of Mrs. Overd's performance to Sharp suggest that the singer had a pretty compelling motive in singing the clearly off-color "Crabfish" that summer's day in 1904. In fact, even the "how" variable supports that assertion: while Mrs. Overd's style was often unusually animated for a traditional singer, Sharp made a special point of noting that her "Crabfish" "was sung to me very excitedly and at breakneck speed, the singer punctuating the rhythm of the refrain with blows of her fist upon the table at which she was sitting" (Sharp 1920: 2: xi). In other words, Mrs. Overd sang this particular song neither tentatively nor reticently but purposively.

Which brings us to the question of "why." What almost certainly intuitive, felt rather than clearly understood motive impelled Mrs. Overd to cut blithely through common convention with her unparalleled performance of a naughty song? I suggest that the significance of the Crabfish story to Mrs. Overd lay not in its explicit, guffaw-producing images of unrelated objects incongruously stuck-fast to each other, nor in its resonance with unconscious anxieties about female sexuality invoked primarily in the male psyche, but of certain cultural principles: in particular, of the prevailing social definition of gender identities, both male and female, and of the relationship between them.

Mrs. Overd, I submit, intuitively felt the force of unstated premises underlying her song. One such premise, for example, is that woman is defined by her physiology: in "The Crabfish," it is her condition of pregnancy and the physical craving it produces which brings the creature into her house; it is her need to urinate that moves her into striking distance of the beast; it is her most womanly anatomical feature that is the crab's target; and it is her physical helplessness that prevents her doing anything to extricate herself. In contrast, yet another "Crabfish" premise asserts, society grounds its construction of male identity in cultural properties: it is he—the husband—who acts as customer in bargaining with the fisherman to purchase his catch; as household manager in deciding how to keep the crab fresh till mealtime; as the one who, by employing thought and skill (not just instinct, which is all the woman employs by screaming her pain), attempts her release; and as the one whose dignity is subjected to public ridicule when he is viewed by outsiders with his nose attached to his wife's pudendum. In the semiotic of Mrs. Overd's song, then, the most powerful signifiers are synecdoches rather than metaphors: the vagina stands for woman's identity as a physiological entity, while the nose stands for male "face," which is to say (metonymically) his social persona, standing, and reputation. In sum, it seems that, in singing "The Crabfish" to Sharp, Mrs. Overd was appropriating a traditionally male possession—a dirty song—and revoicing it from a woman's point of view to imaginatively empower her sex: the crabfish, a surrogate for the most prominent signifier of female identity (and warrant for her low status), the pudendum, both unmasks and subverts the most prominent signifier of male identity (and warrant for his high status), the nose.

With a little imagination, we can see this apparent subtext of Mrs. Overd's "Crabfish" paralleled in the immediate context of the song's occurrence—that is, her actual singing of it to Sharp on August 15, 1904. In the context of that "performance event," the song itself was like the crabfish in the ballad narrative, and by singing it, Mrs. Overd, like the wife in the song, was the source of a hostile attack on Sharp's self-possession—indeed, on the whole male-determined, middle-class idea of good breeding, good manners, good taste, and sense of generally being in control of a situation. In fact, if certain conditions of "where" and "who" also obtained that day (we don't know because they weren't documented), the analogy may be pressed even further: if, as is distinctly possible, Sharp recorded Mrs. Overd in her own home, then we may speculate that, just like the crabfish in the song emerged from the meanest living quarters in the house (the toilet), so too did Mrs. Overd's song emerge from Langport's humblest dwellings, one in a row of four attached cottages (probably two-up and two-down) on Knapp's Lane, all sharing the same outdoor privy and communal washhouse, where Mrs. Overd lived with her husband, William, and children. It is also distinctly possible that, just as in the Crabfish story's wider tradition, there was an audience present at the singing to witness Mrs. Overd's piercing of Sharp's face: her row-house neighbors Mrs. Sarah Trott (whose family, which included eleven children, occupied two of the four cottages) and Mrs. Eliza Hutchings, from both of whom Sharp also collected songs (see Karpeles 1974).[21]

Do I have any further reason for thinking that, to Mrs. Overd, "The Crabfish" had implications of gender politics (and even associated class politics) that were ahead of their time? I do indeed, and it is this: in singing Sharp "The Sea Crab" on August 15, 1904, Mrs. Overd was actually re-enacting an event that had occurred on the couple's first meeting a fortnight before and that *also* paralleled the Crabfish narrative. In the words of Sharp's biographer, Maud Karpeles, the event concerned

> an encounter with a woman who had a great reputation as a singer. She lived in a mean street, which was inhabited—so he was told—by "bad people." She was out when he first called upon her, but was said to be at the public-house round the corner. As he approached the public-house he saw a group of women standing outside and chatting. "Is Mrs. Overd here?" he asked. "That's my name," an elderly woman replied, "and what do you want of me?" Cecil Sharp explained that he was hunting for old songs and hoped that she would sing him some; whereupon without any warning she flung her arms around his waist and danced him round and round with the utmost vigour, shouting, "Lor, girls, here's my beau come at last." (Karpeles 1967: 40)

Consider that, as a provincial, elderly, working-class woman, Mrs. Overd had almost certainly been subject to a life of hardship, poverty, and powerlessness that was common to her kind before the days of the welfare state. Suddenly there came within her reach a stranger from the big city of London, a male of superior speech and dress and with polite but undoubtedly authoritative air. Ignoring all accepted rules of deportment,

Mrs. Overd stepped out of her expected role as subordinate, deferential underling: in crabfish fashion she employed the very physicality ("the utmost vigor") that so defined and subjugated her kind to reach out, pincerlike, and imprison Sharp in her grip, dancing him around in the public street, and almost certainly puncturing his reserved, genteel, middle-class, male "face" in front of her working-class women friends. To make matters worse for Sharp but to enrich the analogy with the "Crabfish" story, who would appear at that very moment but *his* significant social Others: "In the middle of this terpsichorean display Cecil Sharp heard a shocked exclamation, 'But surely that is Mr. Sharp,' and looking around he saw the vicar, with whom he was staying, and the vicar's daughter, both gazing with horror on the scene" (Karpeles 1967: 40)—further denting, undoubtedly, Sharp's already well-pierced "face."[22]

This event must have occurred at least sixteen days before August 15, 1904, at which time Mrs. Overd again broke through barriers that convention decreed to sing a dirty song, "The Crabfish," for the song collector.[23] I don't think I am stretching credibility too far in seeing these three highly unusual phenomena as structurally and semantically isomorphic: the content of the only obscene song Sharp ever collected; Mrs. Overd's act of singing such a vulgar, tabooed, inappropriate item for the London gentleman; and her crude display of public familiarity on their very first meeting.

Moreover, we may now see Mrs. Overd's "The Crabfish" as continuous with the global tradition of the story. At the most general level, the very unusualness of her action illustrates once again the story's ability to pass easily through all sorts of boundaries, with little change in its outward form. More specifically, though, we can view Mrs. Overd, in resisting patriarchally constituted norms of propriety, as a forerunner of today's feminist-savvy Harriettes of upscale Colorado. It also bears similarity with the most unusual version of all, the Muria Crabfish tale from central India: like Mrs. Overd, the tellers of that tale have appropriated what in the larger worldwide tradition invariably takes a male point of view to deconstruct and revoice it in the service of gender equality. In fact, Mrs. Overd's performance even exhibits continuity with the Freudian explanation of the crabfish story's subliminal hold on the male psyche: that it is rooted in men's fear of what harm women may do to them.

*   *   *

The Crabfish story, even in its anglophone song form, was born hundreds of years before either Mrs. Overd or Cecil Sharp, and as the Pike's Peak Hash House songbook indicates, it remains popular as a quotidian performance item many decades after their deaths. Its ability to transcend boundaries that normally signify difference, keeping material outside the premises they demarcate, is remarkable. If our understanding of what Mrs. Overd was saying tacitly to Sharp is correct, then it seems that she was being adversarial, engaging in a battle of conflicting ideologies. I like to think, though, that at a deeper, unconscious level in *her* psyche— the level where, in males, the Crabfish's poison-female message is processed—Mrs. Overd may have been subliminally *testing* Sharp rather than battling him. When on Monday, August 15, 1904, she sang him "The Crabfish," might not Mrs. Overd have recognized that Sharp in fact had sought her out not for her physical properties (as a factory "hand," or a sexual object, or even as a social statistic—representative, say, of rural poverty) but for her *cultural* ones—that is, as someone possessing knowledge ("knew old songs") and skill ("would sing him some")? And even on their initial meeting at which she sought to embarrass him, might she not have unconsciously been in fact extending to the London gentleman the hand of true friendship, saying that, really, can't culturally constructed identities such as male/female, upper class/lower class, superior/inferior be transcended, however temporarily, by a breakthrough into more meaningful, more profound, more authentic human relations—of the sort that result, for instance, when two lovers of traditional English folksong, like we two, meet in a perfect fusion of matching sensibilities ("Lor, girls, here's my beau come at last")?[24] And could Sharp have not only earned but even understood Mrs. Overd's gesture, since his immediate response to the sudden appearance of his social peers in witness of his embarrassment was to "shout . . . to them to go away—and they went" (Karpeles 1967: 40)? And could not Mrs. Overd, two weeks later, have reinforced the idea by offering Sharp the most secret traditional song she knew, one that a folksinger would normally never give an outsider, an "obscene" one containing within its text a dramatic rendition of her "thesis"? And could not Sharp have appreciated the offering and reciprocated by in fact recording what Mrs. Overd sang in his notebook, rather than suppressing it? And could he not even, in fact, be said to have "rescued" Emma Overd from the inevitable anonymity accompanying a life of marginal subsistence by preserving her songs in his field notes, so that today she lives on in thirty-seven excellent sets of words and even more sets of airs preserved in the Vaughan Williams Memorial Library, in the performances of folksong revival singers, and in the ongoing scholarship of admiring folklorists?[25]

AFTERWORD

D. K. Wilgus was actually one of my teachers when, in 1969, I enrolled in UCLA's graduate folklore program and learned a healthy respect not only for texts but for lots of them. Eventually, I earned my M.A. and departed for the doctoral program at Penn. There I was inundated with new folklore paradigms like "ethnography of communication" and "structuralism," to which, like everyone else, I was attracted, for they helped me expand my understanding of Anglo/American folksong; but I tried to make sure that they did so *without* compromising the integrity of those songs as represented in our great collections. What *didn't* attract me was that, in the then-intellectual environment of graduate school, these "new perspectives" were too often explained and legitimized within the terms of Thomas Kuhn's *Structure of Scientific Revolutions*, which—at least, according to our understanding of them—stressed the importance of radical disjunction between paradigms: hence you could only embrace the new if you rejected the old.

Many of my fellow students and teachers bought into this notion of discontinuity and "chose sides," seeming to agree that "the gap between the present day student of popular culture and the material produced by his or her antiquarian/collector ancestor can seem so complete that meaningful dialogue about problems and theories appears almost impossible" (Merricks 1988: 178). But I found myself unable to stigmatize the supposedly discredited approaches, like comparative study or psychoanalytical readings of folklore materials, finding it difficult to believe that their capacity for illuminating folksong had all of a sudden disappeared. I simply couldn't abandon my primary loyalty to folksong—that is to say, I couldn't "decenter" the subject matter as a favored object of devotion and substitute for it loyalty to a theory (or even, for that matter, to the act of theorizing, or to the lure of novelty). For me, theoretical loyalty had to be secondary, had to emerge from subject loyalty: if a theory didn't make folksong interesting; if, however elegant and compelling, it didn't fit the obvious facts of the data; if it directed attention away from song and toward explanatory construct, then it wasn't for me. And indeed, later on, my first two major endeavors as a professional scholar were the strictly comparativist *Supplement* to *The British Traditional Ballad in North America*, which could just as comfortably have been published in 1877 as in 1977, and the ethnographically and semiotically informed *English Folk Poetry*, which was definitely a creature of newer paradigms.

Despite their differences, the two works gave me equal pleasure in researching and writing, and I'm still just as fond of one as I am of the other. The same has been and is true of this book. "We'll be finished as a discipline when we lose our sense of the continuities linking us with Sir Walter Scott . . . and instead identify and legitimate our work solely on the grounds of its opposition to 'previous' work,' " I wrote a few years ago (Renwick 1992: 81). It's not too hard to see in those words the same sensibility that guided D. K. Wilgus throughout his career: the scholarly "discourse" that he championed most strongly was one he called "rational," one that respected and tried its hardest to discover what the evidence of folksong itself had to say, not what we—however well-intentioned—devoutly wished it to say. I hope I've been true to that ideal.

NOTES

FOREWORD

1. I use "Anglo/American" throughout this volume to denote a cultural continuum or network; I reserve the more usual "Anglo-American" to denote Americans of British (anglophone English, Scots, Irish) ancestry.

CHAPTER 1

1. Actually, even within the terms of creolization theory's own linguistics-induced vocabulary, insofar as I understand it, "creole" does not seem to me the applicable concept for Nora Bristol's adaptation. "Ideolect" would seem more apposite, or perhaps even "pidgin," a pidgin being an ad hoc language with no "native speakers."

2. Also resonant is a Bahamian version in which, while each relative is appealed to only once, the lover stanza is repeated twice, since he was too far away at the first call (Bronson 1959–72: 2: 472–3). It is highly unlikely that these three versions possessed any direct historical link with each other, however.

3. One might also argue that as the ballad becomes more subject to lyric conventions it becomes correspondingly more subject to transformation from third person to first person, since first-person point of view is an integral feature of the lyric genre. Artistic unity and convention, therefore, becomes as much a determinant of textual change as more general cultural forces.

4. Two other essays on African American songs related to "Barbara Allan," both of which are influenced by "creolization" concepts, are Doyle and Kelley 1991 and Minton 1995.

5. For examples of talking birds in British West Indian cante-fables, see Jekyll [1907] 1966: nos. 3, 31; Beckwith 1924b: nos. 71, 73b; Roberts 1925: 154–5; Parsons 1918: no. 113 (Child 274; Roud 114). For talking birds in postcolonial Jamaican tales (most entirely in prose) see Dance 1985: nos. 22, 57C, 75, 111, 146, and 157.

6. Again, there is a theoretical concept in creole linguistics scholarship that

claims to explain this kind of different-contexts/similar-texts phenomenon in language. It posits polygenetic origins and physiological causation, incompatible with the premises of the "relexification" model underlying the study under discussion. See Bickerton 1984.

7. I might also add that the name Matty Groves appears only in American tradition, never in British. While American culture certainly diffused to the colonial Caribbean (especially through such channels as whaling and merchant shipping), British West Indian song traditions were more likely to have been influenced by British Isles song traditions than by American ones.

8. Yet again, if we follow Abrahams in looking to creole linguistic studies for conceptual models to apply by analogy to ballads, "decreolization" rather than creolization may be the more apposite concept here (that is, the French ballad was "creolized" in England, the English version later "decreolized" in the Caribbean). But the analogy would be very inexact. See Holm 1988: 9.

CHAPTER 2

1. I will use "broadsheet" throughout this chapter to denote the (usually) single sheet of paper on which texts of "Wild and Wicked Youth" were printed and sold in major cities of England, Scotland, and Ireland; I'll reserve the synonym "broadside" as a modifier to denote the particular subgenre of traditional poetry we call the "broadside ballad." ("Broadside" and "broadsheet" may be distinguished in more technical usage; see Shepard 1962: 23–4.)

2. On the eighteenth century as the apogee of the highwayman era, see McLynn 1989: 68, 81–2; on the explosion in housebreaking during the same period, see 87–9.

3. Madden Collection: London Printers 4, item no. 606; Vaughan Williams Memorial Library Microfilm Collection, reel no. 77.

4. It is of some interest, though, that bearers of tradition have other ways of resolving textual features they consider, for whatever reasons, unsatisfactory. For instance, two oral versions contain the two stanzas but do not have the redundant "went robbing on the highway" idea: instead, to maintain his wife "fine and gay," the narrator is "resolved that the world should pay" (Reeves 1960: 152; Baring-Gould and Sheppard 1895: 39). One broadsheet version uses "highway" in one stanza, the presumably distinct "high road" in the second.

5. An added incentive to the seeker of a historical referent comes from musical rather than textual evidence: the tune to which "Wild and Wicked Youth" is most often sung in tradition first appears as a traditional piece in Edward Bunting's collection of Irish airs (no words are given) under the title "Charley Reilly, or the Robber," which provides an even more concrete and nonformulaic detail,

an actual name for the possible protagonist! That this is by far the earliest reference to an oral (rather than broadsheet) variant of "Wild and Wicked Youth" adds to its interest: Bunting collected the tune in Drogheda in 1803 (Bunting 1840: xi, 48).

6. Moreover, since crime and criminals are ubiquitous subjects of traditional song, Bunting's robber and the wild and wicked youth need not have been the same person. As for the tune similarity, unfortunately for the tracer of direct genetic connections, the air is also common in the singing tradition of a host of other British Isles folksongs, such as "Lady Franklin's Lament" (Laws K9; Roud 487), "All on Spurn Point" (Roud 599 [see Broadwood and Maitland n.d.: 180]), "The Sailor Boy I" (Laws K12; Roud 273), "The Croppy Boy" (Laws J14; Roud 1030), and even the more modern "McKaffery" (Roud 1148 [see Seeger and Mac-Coll 1960: 73]), so its attachment to "Wild and Wicked Youth" cannot be convincingly considered an "original" or genetic one (compare *Journal of the Folk-Song Society* 1906: 2: 178: "It is a favourite air amongst country singers, and is met with in England and Scotland very often").

7. Even though the song may not have had an empirical referent, could it at least have originated in Ireland? One is tempted to make that hypothesis (and some folklorists have) on the grounds that both broadsheet and oral versions of "Wild and Wicked Youth" overwhelmingly give the robber an Irish identity by claiming that he was born in Ireland, occasionally asserting that he died there as well. A handful seem to locate his whole criminal career in Ireland, one broadsheet even affirming that his specified robbery of "lords and ladies bright" took place in "Crosshowden Square" rather than in the far more common "Grosvenor Square" (Shields 1988: 24–5). But the strongest evidence for an Irish origin seems to have been Bunting's 1803 "Charley Reilly" tune, by far the earliest report of what *may* have been our ballad in traditional usage. Yet, over and above the possibility that "Charley Reilly" was some *other* robber, the tune as we've seen is not only far more popular in England than Ireland but also acts as vehicle for texts that have overwhelmingly an English, not Irish, origin. Of the many songs this tune customarily accompanies in oral tradition, only "The Croppy Boy" can be said to have a primarily Irish association, but it too was widely sung in England. The most convincing argument against an Irish provenience, however, is based on popularity: though "Wild and Wicked Youth" appeared on Irish broadsides, it hasn't been found in Irish oral tradition, whereas it's been widely reported as traditional in England. (The words in *More Irish Street Ballads* are evidently from an English source; see O'Lochlainn 1965: 70.) In short, an English origin for "Wild and Wicked Youth" seems most likely.

8. The forty oral and twenty-four broadsheet texts of this British "Wild and

Wicked Youth" strain that I've examined cannot be convincingly divided into subtraditions. The same is true of the American "Rambling Boy" strain, of which I've examined twenty-three versions. In fact, distinctive varieties of image, line, couplet, and stanza at times seem so multi-formly distributed throughout the population of texts that one is tempted to dub the distribution "random" (though a more analytical explanation would be that any one version is an amalgam of several sources: that is to say, each singer was continually hearing or reading varying renditions of the same song as well as other songs of the crime-and-criminals type and continually borrowing a motif from here, a line or even stanza from there, adding to these his or her own innovations). What *is* a recurring and significant trend is the difference between the essentially Old World "Wild and Wicked Youth" strain and the southern U.S. "Rambling Boy" one.

However, it's worth recognizing a distinctive couplet that appears in five (all traditional) of the sixty-four "Wild and Wicked Youth" texts—"I went to London both blithe and gay, / My time I wasted in bowls and play" (Reeves 1960: 152)—since a version with these lines was clearly the immediate model for the later American "Rambling Boy" remake of "Wild and Wicked Youth." Thus Lee Monroe Presnell's North Carolina version of "Wild and Wicked Youth," one of the five oral versions with the line, may very well represent the closest ancestor of most "Rambling Boy" versions (Warner 1982: 249–50). As for which of the twenty-three "Rambling Boy" versions is closest to its broadside ancestor, my vote would go to the one sung by Emma Dusenbury of Arkansas; resemblance is most notable in the opening stanza's second couplet (Randolph 1946-50: 2: 85).

Another interesting aspect of our ballad's possible history is a hint—and that's about all the evidence amounts to—of an Irish-influenced oikotype, whose markers tend to be the following: (1) the robber's place of birth is Dublin (most commonly, it's Newry); (2) a line which says that, in order to maintain his wife in luxury, the robber "made the world pay" (in oral versions) or "made Lords, Dukes, and Earls pay" (in broadsheet versions); (3) the presence of what I shall identify shortly as a general-mourning-and-resignation-to-fate stanza; and—a weak marker—(4) the robber's apprenticeship to a baker rather than to the much more common saddler. Based on these criteria, the best examples of the (very tentatively hypothesized) Irish oikotype would be three broadsheets—"The Dublin Baker" (Shields 1988: 24–5), "The Irish Robber (UCLA Special Collections), and "The Bold and Undaunted Youth" (National Library of Ireland Broadside Collection)—and three oral versions, one from England (Reeves 1960: 152) and two from Scotland (Shuldham-Shaw et al. 1981-97: 2: 264–5 [A and B versions]). The two southern U.S. versions of the broadside strain, from Lee Monroe Presnell of North Carolina and Goldie Hamilton of Virginia, share their first stanzas (Dublin birthplace, baker's apprentice) with this oikotype (Warner 1984: 250; University of Virginia Special Collections, box 29, folder 1192, accession no. 1547).

9. For example, Josiah Combs (1967: 184–5) included "Rambling Boy" in his section on "Native American Songs" rather than in "Songs of British Origin," even though he must have been familiar with published British versions of "Wild and Wicked Youth."

10. Of course, there are several instances in oral versions of stanzas being reduced by half so that only a couplet of a usual stanza appears combined with another couplet more commonly found in a different stanza. Sometimes, only a line of the more usual stanza is present, having been combined with another narrative theme in three-line form. Such instances are not representative of the corpus as a whole, however.

11. In addition, a two-line version—"But all the tears they shed for me / Won't bring me back from the gallows tree"—is found once, attached to the stanza that depicts what I'll call family-reaction-to-robber's-fate stanza (Becket 1952).

12. For discussion purposes I use the names in Harry Cox's text above, but of course names differ from version to version: for instance, in the population of "Wild and Wicked Youth" texts, the robber burglarizes—other than Harry Cox's Lord Golden and the Catnach broadsheet's Lord Golding—Lord Goldingham, Lord Goldring, and Lord Goldwin, as well as Lord Bately, Lord Dukses, Lord Edgecumbe, Lord Leicester, Lord Mansfield, Lord Mornington, Lord Nelson, Lord Sandford, and Lord Thomas. He is captured by Fielding's gang, Lord Fielding's gang, Ned Fielding's gang, Fieldmen's gang, "old blind Ferdling," and "two bold policemen."

13. This may, of course, be rationalization: unconsciously he may be commodifying his wife as a "trophy" for his own ends, a common form of projection.

14. On railroad tropes and their relationship to heaven in wider Anglo-American popular song, see Cohen 1981: 596–644.

15. In the remaining three examples of letter writing, the robber writes to "Frankfort Town," the state capital of Kentucky and probably a metonym for the governor.

16. And even some British-born ones; see "The Irish Mail Robber" (Laws L15; Roud 1905), "Botany Bay/The Boston Burglar" (Laws L16; Roud 261), and "Van Dieman's Land" (L18; Roud 519).

17. See also Brightwell 1975; Dunstan 1933 [1974]: 24; Hall 1994; O'Lochlainn 1965: 70. More usually, as in the normative version, the wife tears her hair despairingly and asks, what shall I do?

18. Madden Collection: Country Printers, sheet no. 384; Vaughan Williams Memorial Library Microfilm Collection, reel no. 88.

19. While W. A. Barrett's English text is the most idiosyncratic in the corpus and may have been subject to a very intrusive editorial hand, at least some of its quite unusual features are matched in one broadsheet from a Birmingham printer, S. W. Russell (Madden Collection, vol. 8 [County Printers], sheet no. 384; Vaughan Williams Memorial Library Microfilm Collection, reel no. 88) and in two oral versions: in the first stanza and chorus of Mrs. Webb's text cited above, and in stanza 5 of a version sung by Charles Ash of Crowcombe, Somerset, in 1908 (Karpeles 1974: 2: 161).

20. Regarding refrains: some broadside-ballad versions repeat the first hemistich of each stanza's fourth line, some repeat the last two lines of each stanza, and some have a distinct four-line chorus after each stanza; for examples, see Gundry 1966: 30; *Journal of the Folk-Song Society* 1901: 1: 15; 1930: 8: 190; Kennedy 1975: 712; Shuldham-Shaw et al. 1981-97: 2: 264.

21. Four broadsheet texts have the more inflammatory statement that, to maintain his wife, the robber makes "Lords, Earls, and Dukes to pay," but in oral texts (three in all) this comes out as "Resolved I was that the world should pay." See note 8 above.

22. And indeed, there is a corresponding contextual link between eighteenth-century England (the most likely date of "Wild and Wicked Youth's" composition) and the postbellum U.S. South (the most likely date of the British broadside ballad's "Rambling Boy" remake): swiftly increasing urbanization and industrialization brought with them increase in a relatively modern kind of economic or property crime, like robbery (McLynn 1989: 299–319; Fischer 1989: 767–8). As a period of transition in England from early modern to modern (from a precapitalist, agrarian economy to a capitalist, manufacturing one), the eighteenth century provided a generative context for the wild and wicked youth to conceive of an alternative kind of social organization—and to conceive of one's ability to change position within its hierarchy—as not only desirable but even possible. Conservatives like Henry Fielding would have put a different spin on the same phenomenon, espousing a version of the rural/urban theme: that the new economy was corrupting the working class by creating desires for luxuries ("consumerism")—for instance, for balls, plays, gaming, fine clothes, and other self-indulgences far exceeding the meeting of basic needs—that its members couldn't afford by honest means. See Fielding [1751] 1988.

CHAPTER 4

1. Laws's system has even come to be employed as a frame of reference for British Isles versions of the relevant ballads: see, for example, Shuldham-Shaw et al. 1981–97; Huntington 1990.

2. Despite this lengthy interval, the two texts are virtually identical and may be treated for analytical purposes as a single version. Their differences are truly trivial: the 1941 version contains in its opening line two indefinite articles—"A rude and a rambling boy I am"—that the 1966 version lacks, while the 1966 rendition possesses an adverb in its second line—"A rude and rambling boy I'll still be"—not found in the 1941 text.

3. The two were related both by marriage and by blood ties: Buna's husband, Roby, was the brother of Rena's father, Andy, as well as brother of Ben, father of Rena's husband Nathan. See Burton 1978: 1–25; Warner 1984: 185–250. The two versions are similar enough to suggest a very close genetic connection, if not a direct one.

4. "Deep in Love" goes by a variety of titles, including "The Water Is Wide" and "Waly, Waly," while "Died for Love" may be "A Brisk Young Lover," "I Wish, I Wish," or "Tavern in the Town." For discussion of this song complex, see Belden 1940: 201–3; MacColl and Seeger 1977: 194–5, 237–8. Neither discussion recognizes "Oh, Willie" as a distinct member of the set.

5. These lines the ballad shares with Laws L12/Roud 490, "The Rambling Boy" (subject of this book's chapter 2), though it shares little else.

6. Ethnographic evidence supporting my argument here would be the existence of both "Oh, Willie" and "Butcher Boy" in the repertoire of the same singer, but I have not been able to find such an instance.

7. In fact, item #22, "Sweet William," turns out to be from the same source as—and hence textually almost identical with—text M in *The Frank C. Brown Collection of North Carolina Folklore.* For the North Carolina compilation, the text, contributed by Thomas Smith, "was 'written down about July 1, 1915, by Miss Mae Smith of Sugar Grove, Watauga County, from the singing of her stepmother, Mrs. Mary Smith' " (Belden and Hudson 1952a: 278–9), while for the Virginia collection it was "Contributed by R. E. Lee Smith, of Palmyra, Va. Sung by his brother, Thomas P. Smith, of Palmyra, Va., and himself. Fluvanna County. July 6, 1915. Learned from the singing of Miss May Smith" (University of Virginia Special Collections, accession no. 9936).

8. Though it is not unique to that singer, because in one other version, the stanza has been dedicated to the father and repositioned in the story: he reads his daughter's suicide note and wishes he were dead (see Owens 1976: 62), thus making explicit what in all versions is implicit—that the parents should not have separated the lovers and that they lived to regret their action. They were indeed "sorry when their daughter was dead," though by then of course "it was too late."

9. This unrequited love/unfaithful lover idea appears in two other texts, tacked on to stanzas other than "I wish I was a blackbird." In one, the boy is the

narrator and complains to Saro that she doesn't return his love (Cecil Sharp Collection: Folk Words, no. 3048). In the other,

> I am a wrecked and rambling boy,
> My dwellings are both near and far;
> A wrecked and rambling boy I'll be,
> To love a girl that don't love me.

> "I love thee, Willie, I love thee well,
> I love thee better than tongue can tell;
> But all this world can plainly see
> I love a boy that don't love me.["]
>> (Hudson 1926: 124)

10. Which seems to have been the case with its closest relative, Laws P24/ Roud 409, "Butcher Boy."

11. From a copy in Cambridge University's Madden Collection (volume 8 [London Printers no. 2], sheet no. 1194; Vaughan Williams Memorial Library Microfilm Collection, reel no. 75).

11. Stanzas 3 and 4 of the cowboy version reproduced at the beginning of this essay, in which the lovers' forced separation is communicated by letter, are also absent from the British broadside version; but those two stanzas are very close to being Anglo/American commonplaces, whereas the "cannon ball" stanza is unique.

12. The Mississippi Type A version might seem ambiguous at first glance: the boy narrates the first stanza, claiming that his love is unrequited; the girl narrates the second, asserting that she does indeed love him but that he doesn't love her. This seems to me to be lovers' verbal play of mutual testing. The father certainly recognizes it for what it is, as stanza three makes clear:

> When Julia's father came this to know,
> That Julia and Willie were loving so,
> He ripped and tore among them all
> And swore he'd use his cannon ball.
>> (Hudson 1926: 124)

13. Within Long's conceptual framework, whoever reworked "The Isle of Cloy" might be seen as a "confabulator," one who employs traditional materials but who produces idiosyncratic texts that do not have much appeal to anyone other than the confabulator himself or herself. It is also possible, of course, that Moeran exercised editorial privilege and rewrote considerably what he collected.

But neither of these explanations seems convincing enough to me, since the text in most ways typifies British folksong poetics.

CHAPTER 5

1. Grady Hillman, a former graduate student of mine who spent part of 1990 in Peru on a Fulbright Fellowship, heard the "Lobster Song" sung at a party given by the Lima chapter of the Hash House Harriers.

2. For example, in the Meade Collection: Don Laycock, "The Lobster," *The Best Bawdry* (Melbourne: Angus & Robertson, 1982), 257–8; "Jimmy Johnson," *National Folk* (1970) 40:4; Bob Pegg, "The Lobster," *Folk: A Portrait of English Traditional Music, Musicians and Customs* (London: Wildwood House, 1976), 81–2. See also Richards 1982: 39; Richards 1992: 125; Yates 1980: 15.

3. The Crabfish story may also have crossed into a fourth genre: drama. Folklorist Joseph C. Hickerson of the Library of Congress has told me of encountering a published version of the story as a children's play—highly bowdlerized, of course—but I've been unable to find this text.

4. For this study I have examined more than fifty renditions of the Crabfish story, though within that population the anglophone tradition is predominant: three-quarters of the texts are song versions from Britain and North America, several of which come from photocopies in the Guthrie T. Meade Jr. collection at the University of North Carolina. Thanks to archivist Michael Taft for his help in obtaining these.

5. The poem, by Andy Rouse, is handwritten on exercise book paper:

A crabbefishe was ther in a chambrepot
What he soghte ther I knowe not
But ther iwas, and that, with clawes twain
Yat clikket-clakket:—twice, ay twice ymain.

'O, I am caughte, methink me ende is nye'
So calld ye godwif, and, godwot, tis pleyne:
The crabbefishe mad a wondrous divers catch
With clikket, claket, snitch . . . ay forsoth snatch.

The godwyf's quim, firm, in ye crabbefishe claw
Mad her crye shrille, 'Husband! Cum der, as I calle
The divil hav me in hys lechrous grypper!'
The husband loiked. Snappe! His upper lyppe
Is coghte harde ner hys godwyfe's assehole.
Lack. Alas, May God delyvre us alle!

6. The intensity may stem from other sensibilities than a comic one—for example, from the same concern underlying the popularity of legends about alligators in sewers making their way through city conduits and into home toilet bowls. This concern does seem more prominent in the psyche of children than of adults, however, though it may underlie a Crabfish song version from Virginia in which no wife appears: man buys crab, puts it in commode, is bitten on "the nose" when he goes to urinate (Yates 1980: 15).

7. See Leach 1949–50: 2: 803; Hand, Casetta, and Thiederman 1981: 1: 177 (item no. 4313). Support for the equivalence may come from the tradition of the Crabfish song itself: in several U.S. versions, the wife replies to the husband's complaint that he is now caught with his nose close to her private parts that "You've had your nose there many a time" (Randolph 1992: 1: 66–7) or "You've been that close to it many a time" (67–8). See also Babad 1972: 101. Some British versions have a semi-nonsense refrain that includes the name "Jimmy Johnson," which is a slang term for penis.

8. According to Miss Maiden, a character in David Lodge's novel, *Small World,* and someone we would call a "literary folklorist," the association is "very ancient and widely distributed" (Lodge 1984: 36).

9. I've not seen any versions in which the joined couple are of the same sex but wouldn't be at all surprised, given the story's transgressive capacity, to find one.

10. Frank Hoffman, collector, "The Sea Crab," Pennsylvania, n.d., Meade Collection.

11. F. T. Nettelinghame, "Tee, I, Ee, I, O," *More Tommy's Tunes* (London: Erskine MacDonald, [1918]), 28, Meade Collection.

12. In a couple of English versions, the pregnancy also effects a unique conclusion: long after the wife's experience with the crab is past, she gives birth to a baby "with a crabfish on his titty" (Cox 1964). This may imply that, ever since the fateful day, she'd harbored one of the creatures in her womb; more likely, however, is that it illustrates the common folksong idea of a genetic marker, as in "Knife in the Window" (Roud 329) and "The Bold English Navvy" (Roud 516; for representative texts, see Kennedy 1975: 406, 397). These typify a more general belief concerning the effect on an unborn baby of phenomena seen or experienced by the pregnant mother. See Porter 1969: 12–3.

13. A unique stanza implying triumph-in-death appears in a 1913 manuscript version from "Ollie" in Ohio, preserved among Robert W. Gordon's papers but taken here from the Meade Collection: "But the sea crab he did laugh up his sleeve / For he knew that he had taken French leave."

14. "Whiskey Johnny" in "Sailing Ship Shanties, 1928–1956," manuscript prepared for Gershon Legman in 1956 [by Stan Hugill?], Meade Collection.

15. Of course, we should not ignore the possibility that it is the inextricable linkage of both desire and fear, attraction and repulsion, that makes the female vagina so great a focus of male concern.

16. The British army version—at least in its published form—is much less vagina-centered than the college student version because of its apparent bowdlerization: the codfish catches the wife by her knee.

17. Of the twenty-five songs from Mrs. Overd reprinted in full in Karpeles 1974, only one other, in addition to "The Crabfish," seems fragmented.

18. By the ear! Sharp (or perhaps his textual editor, Charles Marson—or more likely, both in conjunction) probably rejected the nose from sensitivity to the male nose/penis association. He had the *wife's* being caught by the nose (again, probably because the more logical mouth or lip would have suggested what he was bowdlerizing—the vagina).

19. It is unclear which of the two main strains of the Crabfish Anglo/American song tradition Mrs. Overd's version belonged to: the "lobster" strain in which the man is not caught (much more popular in modern British tradition) or the "crab" strain in which he is (the only form found in our three pre-1850 British texts). Statistically, the former is more likely, but textually the latter seems more probable, since Mrs. Overd's text contains two markers of the "crab" strain: the creature is a crab rather than a lobster, and the female pudendum is called by a vulgar name ("leather") rather than bowdlerized; moreover, the wife is pregnant, which is a motif found only in the two pre-1850 British versions of the Crabfish song we possess. The two strains do intermingle in tradition, as English singer Harry Cox's repertoire suggests: one of his renditions has the killing and the marked baby but no nose capturing (Cox 1964), while another has the killing and the nose capturing, but no marked baby (Kennedy 1975: 452). Otherwise, the two versions are very much the same. Cox's 1964 text may help us understand Mrs. Overd's because they seem quite closely related: they are the only two with the "genetic marker" motif of the baby's being born with a crab attached to its body. Cox's 1964 text may also explain an anomaly in Sharp's original transcription of Mrs. Overd's stanza 6, where the word for urination is missing. Cox's version substitutes for such end-of-line tabooed words the first word of the refrain, a rhetorical device found in other Anglo/American traditional songs (see Abrahams and Foss 1968: 76). Thus where the listener expects to hear "where his wife used to piss," she gets instead "where his wife used to row-dow-dow."

20. Perhaps the most normatively tabooed topic country singers did provide visiting collectors was that of sexual intercourse, but the language of such songs was symbolic, metaphorical, or euphemistic, never idiomatic, as is the case with "The Crabfish's" language (see Renwick 1980: 54–112). Kathleen Williams of Dry-

brook, Herefordshire, sang a three-stanza "Crabfish" for Sharp on September 9, 1921 (Karpeles 1974: 2: 359), the second stanza of which is borrowed from "The Tinker" (Roud 863), suggesting that the idiomatic "Crabfish" had been converted into a more socially acceptable song of sexual liaison in the metaphorical (perhaps euphemistic) mode.

21. In fact, Mrs. Overd sang duets with both Mrs. Hutchings and Mrs. Trott (Karpeles 1974: 2: 516; 626 [note to no. 310]). Biographical information on Mrs. Overd and her neighbors comes from the Cecil Sharp file in the Vaughan Williams Memorial Library Collection, particularly from the database on Sharp's informants. (See Cecil Sharp Collection: Folk Words, no. 3343.)

22. This story, no doubt because of its very excellence, is almost certainly embellished. Sharp evidently told it more than once, not always the same. Besides, the vicar may have been no stranger but his very good friend, Charles Marson, a companion in Australia where they had both lived for a while, "perpetual curate" (= vicar) of nearby Hambridge, the person who first introduced Sharp into the society of rural Somerset bearers of tradition, and collaborator on the first three parts of Sharp's first major folksong publication, *Folk-Songs from Somerset* (Sharp 1904-9). See Karpeles 1967: 28-30.

23. Probably on July 30, 1904, the date Sharp first collected a song from Mrs. Overd.

24. Consciously, Mrs. Overd probably meant by "come at last" that she knew the folksong collector had been working in the district and that, as a prime bearer of tradition herself, she had been expecting his visit.

25. This idea would fit another motif common in the English crabfish song's "Lobster" strain that may have been known to both Mrs. Overd and Sharp, constituting part of their shared knowledge: the motif of husband and wife engaging in a cooperative act to accomplish a mutually beneficial goal. See Karpeles 1967: 31-45 on Sharp's rapport with informants.

WORKS CITED

Abrahams, Roger D. 1968. "Charles Walters—West Indian Autolycus." *Western Folklore* 27: 77–95.

———. 1983. *The Man-of-Words in the West Indies*. Baltimore: Johns Hopkins University Press.

———. 1987. "Child Ballads in the West Indies." *Journal of Folklore Research* 24: 107–34.

Abrahams, Roger D., and George Foss. 1968. *Anglo-American Folksong Style*. Englewood Cliffs, N.J.: Prentice-Hall.

Andersen, Flemming G. 1985. *Commonplace and Creativity*. Odense: University of Odense Press.

Atkinson, David. 1995. " 'Up then spoke a bonny bird,' or Lady Isabel's Secret: Transformation in 'The Outlandish Knight.' " *Southern Folklore* 52: 231–49.

———. 1999. "Magical Corpses: Ballads, Intertextuality, and the Discovery of Murder." *Journal of Folklore Research* 36: 1–29.

Babad, Harry. 1972. *Roll Me Over*. New York: Oak Publications.

Baring-Gould, Rev. Sabine, and H. Fleetwood Sheppard. 1895. *A Garland of Country Song*. London: Methuen.

Barrett, W. A. 1891. *English Folk-Songs*. London: Novello.

Barry, Phillips. 1936. "The Psychopathology of Ballad-Singing." *Bulletin of the Folk-Song Society of the Northeast* 11: 16–8.

———. 1961. "The Part of the Folk-Singer in the Making of Folk Balladry." *The Critics and the Ballad*. Ed. MacEdward Leach and Tristram Potter Coffin. Carbondale: Southern Illinois University Press, pp. 59–76.

Barry, Phillips, Fannie Hardy Eckstorm, and Mary Winslow Smyth. 1929. *British Ballads from Maine*. New Haven: Yale University Press.

Beckett, Amos. 1952. "The Gallows Tree." Sound recording. BBC 23930; Vaughan Williams Memorial Library, London, Audio Collection, no. 3041.

Beckwith, Martha Warren. 1924a. "The English Ballad in Jamaica: A Note upon the Origin of the Ballad Form." *Publications of the Modern Language Association* 39: 455–83.

————. 1924b. *Jamaica Anansi Stories*. American Folk-Lore Society Memoirs Vol. 17. New York: American Folk-Lore Society.

Belden, Henry M. 1940. *Songs and Ballads Collected by the Missouri Folklore Society*. Columbia: University of Missouri Press.

Belden, Henry M., and Arthur Palmer Hudson. 1952a. *The Frank C. Brown Collection of North Carolina Folklore*. Vol. 2: Folk Ballads from North Carolina. Durham, N.C.: Duke University Press.

Belden, Henry Marvin, and Arthur Palmer Hudson. 1952b. *The Frank C. Brown Collection of North Carolina Folklore*. Vol. 3: Folk Songs from North Carolina. Durham, N.C.: Duke University Press.

Berger, Arthur Asa. 1993. *An Anatomy of Humor*. New Brunswick, N.J.: Transaction Publishers.

Beroalde de Verville, Francois. N.d. *Le Moyen de parvenir*. Paris: Édition de belle étoile.

Bertelsen, Lance. 1986. *The Nonsense Club: Literature and Popular Culture, 1749–1764*. London: Oxford University Press.

Bickerton, Derek. 1984. "The Language Bioprogram Hypothesis." *Behavioral and Brain Sciences* 7: 173–221.

Bouchet, Guillaume. [1873] 1969. *Les sérées*. Vol. 2. Geneva: Slatkine.

Boyes, Georgina. 1986. "New Directions—Old Destinations: A Consideration of the Role of the Tradition-Bearer in Folksong Research." In Russell 1986: 9–17.

————. 1993. *The Imagined Village*. Manchester: Manchester University Press.

Brewster, Paul G. 1940. *Ballads and Songs of Indiana*. Bloomington: Indiana University.

Brightwell, Jumbo. 1975. *Newry Town*. Phonodisc. Topic 12TS261.

Broadwood, Lucy, and J. A. Fuller Maitland. N.d. *English County Songs*. London: J. B. Cramer.

Bronson, Bertrand Harris. 1959–72. *The Traditional Tunes of the Child Ballads*. 4 vols. Princeton: Princeton University Press.

————. 1975. "The Dialogue Song; Or, Proteus Observed." *Philological Quarterly* 54: 117–36.

Browne, Ray B. 1979. *The Alabama Folk Lyric*. Bowling Green, Ohio: Bowling Green University Popular Press.

Brunvand, Jan Harold. 1981. *The Vanishing Hitchhiker: American Urban Legends and Their Meaning*. New York: W. W. Norton.

————. 1996. *American Folklore: An Encyclopedia*. New York: Garland Publishing.

Buchan, David. 1972. *The Ballad and the Folk*. London: Routledge & Kegan Paul.

Bunting, Edward. 1840. *The Ancient Music of Ireland*. Dublin: Hodges & Smith.

Burns, Tom. 1970. "A Model for Textual Variation in Folksong." *Folklore Forum* 3, 2: 49–56.

Burton, Thomas G. 1978. *Some Ballad Folks.* Johnson City, Tenn.: Center for Appalachian Studies and Services, East Tennessee State University.

Burton, Thomas G., and Ambrose N. Manning. 1969. *The East Tennessee State University Collection of Folklore: Folksongs.* Vol. 2. Johnson City, Tenn.: Research Advisory Council of East Tennessee State University.

Bush, Michael E. "Jim." N.d. *Folk Songs of Central West Virginia.* Vol. 5. Ravenswood, W.V.: Custom Printing Company.

Cambiare, Celestin. 1934. *East Tennessee and Western Virginia Mountain Ballads.* London: Mitre Press.

The Carter Family. 1941. *Rambling Boy.* Phonodisc. Bluebird 33–0512.

Cheesman, Tom, and Sigrid Rieuwerts. 1997. *Ballads into Books: The Legacies of Francis James Child.* Bern: Peter Lang.

Child, Francis James. [1882–98] 1963. *The English and Scottish Popular Ballads.* 5 vols. New York: Dover Publications.

Coffin, Tristram Potter. 1952. "A Tentative Study of a Typical Folk Lyric: 'Green Grows the Laurel.' " *Journal of American Folklore* 65: 341–51.

———. 1957. " 'Mary Hamilton' and the Anglo-American Ballad as an Art Form." *Journal of American Folklore* 70: 208–14.

———. 1963. *The British Traditional Ballad in North America.* Rev. ed. Philadelphia: American Folklore Society.

———. 1977. *The British Traditional Ballad in North America.* Rev. ed. With a *Supplement* by Roger deV. Renwick. Austin: University of Texas Press.

———. 1985. "A Method of Indexing the Texts of the Anglo-American Love Lyric." In Edwards and Manley 1985: 60–70.

Cohen, Anne B. 1973. *Poor Pearl, Poor Girl!* Austin: University of Texas Press.

Cohen, Norm. 1981. *Long Steel Rail: The Railroad in American Folksong.* Urbana: University of Illinois Press.

Combs, Josiah H. 1967. *Folk-Songs of the Southern United States.* Ed. D. K. Wilgus. Austin: University of Texas Press.

Copper, Bob. 1971. *A Song for Every Season.* London: Heinemann.

Cormack, Effie. 1949. "The Rambling Man (Gallows Tree)." *Archive of California and Western Folklore,* UCLA. Audiotape 64–26.

Coster-Wijsman, Lina Maria. 1929. *Uilespiegel-Verhalenin Indonesië.* Santpoort, Netherlands: C. A. Mees.

Cox, Harry. 1947. "Newlyn Town." Sound recording. BBC 21482; Vaughan Williams Memorial Library, London, Audio Collection, no. 790.

———. 1964. "The Crab-Fish." Audiocassette. Folktrax 034.

Cox, John Harrington. [1925] 1967. *Folk-Songs of the South.* New York: Dover Publications.

Cray, Ed. 1959. "Some Rarities from Arkansas." *Midwest Folklore* 9: 21–30.

———. 1969. *The Erotic Muse.* New York: Oak Publications.

———. 1992. *The Erotic Muse: American Bawdy Songs.* 2nd. ed. Urbana: University of Illinois Press.

Creighton, Helen. 1962. *Maritime Folk Songs.* Toronto: Ryerson Press.

Dance, Daryl C. 1985. *Folklore from Contemporary Jamaicans.* Knoxville: University of Tennessee Press.

Darling, Charles W. 1983. *The New American Songster.* Lanham, Md.: University Press of America.

Davis, Arthur Kyle, Jr. 1949. *Folk-Songs of Virginia: A Descriptive Index and Classification.* Durham: Duke University Press.

Diggins, John Patrick. [1973] 1992. *The Rise and Fall of the American Left.* New York: W. W. Norton & Company.

Doerflinger, William Main. 1951. *Shantymen and Shantyboys.* New York: MacMillan.

Doyle, Charles Clay, and Charles Greg Kelley. 1991. "Moses Platt and the Regeneration of 'Barbara Allen.' " *Western Folklore* 50: 151–69.

Dugaw, Dianne. 1989. *Warrior Women and Popular Balladry, 1650–1850.* Cambridge: University of Cambridge Press.

Dundes, Alan. 1971. "The Sherente Retellings of Genesis." In *Structural Analysis of Oral Tradition,* ed. Pierre Maranda and Elli Köngäs Maranda. Philadelphia: University of Pennsylvania Press, pp. 295–8.

Dunstan, Ralph. [1933] 1972. *Cornish Dialect and Folk Song.* Padstow: Lodenek Press.

Edwards, Carole L., and Kathleen E. B. Manley. 1985. *Narrative Folksong: New Directions.* Boulder: Westview Press.

Elwin, Verrier. 1947. *The Muria and Their Ghotul.* Bombay: Oxford University Press.

An English Folk Music Anthology. 1981. Recorded by Sam Richards and Tish Stubbs. Ethnic Folkways Records FE38553.

Fielding, Henry. [1751] 1988. *An Enquiry into the Causes of the Late Increase of Robbers and Related Writings.* Ed. Malvin R. Zinker. Middleton, Mass.: Wesleyan University Press.

Fine, Gary Alan. 1987. "Welcome to the World of AIDS: Fantasies of Female Revenge." *Western Folklore* 46: 192–7.

Fischer, David Hackett. 1989. *Albion's Seed: Four British Folkways in America.* New York: Oxford University Press.

Foley, John Miles. 1991. *Immanent Art: From Structure to Meaning in Traditional Oral Epic.* Bloomington: Indiana University Press.

———. 1995. *The Singer of Tales in Performance.* Bloomington: Indiana University Press.

Fowke, Edith. 1965. *Traditional Singers and Songs from Ontario.* Hatboro, Pa.: Folklore Associates.

———. 1970. *Lumbering Songs from the Northern Woods.* Austin: University of Texas Press.

Fowler, David. 1968. *A Literary History of the Popular Ballad.* Durham: Duke University Press.

Furnivall, Frederick J. 1868. *Bishop Percy's Folio Manuscript: Loose and Humorous Songs.* London: Printed by and for the editor.

Fuson, Harvey H. 1931. *Ballads of the Kentucky Highlands.* London: Mitre Press.

Gardner, Emelyn Elizabeth, and Geraldine Jencks Chickering. [1939] 1967. *Ballads and Songs of Southern Michigan.* Hatboro, Pa.: Folklore Associates.

Gerould, Gordon Hall. [1932] 1950. *The Ballad of Tradition.* New York: Oxford University Press.

Gilchrist, Anne G. 1940. Review of *Folk-Songs of the Roanoke and the Albemarle,* by Louis W. Chappell. *Folk-Lore* 51: 155–7.

Gordon, Robert. 1924. "Old Songs That Men Have Sung." *Adventure Magazine,* Apr. 20.

Green, Archie. 1993. *Songs About Work.* Bloomington: Indiana University Press.

Green, Thomas A. 1997. *Folklore: An Encyclopedia of Beliefs, Customs, Tales, Music, and Art.* 2 vols. Santa Barbara, Calif.: ABC-CLIO.

Greenhill, Pauline. 1995. " 'Neither a Man nor a Maid': Sexualities and Gendered Meanings in Cross-Dressing Ballads." *Journal of American Folklore* 108: 156–77.

———. 1997. " 'Who's Gonna Kiss Your Ruby Red Lips?': Sexual Scripts in Floating Verses." In Cheesman and Rieuwerts 1997: 225–35.

Greig, Gavin. 1963. *Folk Song of the North-East.* Hatboro, Pa.: Folklore Associates.

Gulzow, Monte, and Carol Mitchell. 1980. " 'Vagina Dentata' and 'Incurable Venereal Disease' Legends from the Viet Nam War." *Western Folklore* 39: 306–16.

Gummere, Francis B. [1909] 1959. *The Popular Ballad.* New York: Dover Publications.

Gundry, Inglis. 1966. *Canow Kernow: Songs and Dances from Cornwall.* N.p.: Federation of Old Cornwall Societies.

Gutwirth, Marcel. 1993. *Laughing Matter: An Essay on the Comic.* Ithaca, N.Y.: Cornell University Press.

Hall, Gordon. 1994. ["The Wild and Wicked Youth."] Transcription from tape of a radio broadcast.

Hall, Jacqueline Dowd, et al. 1987. *Like a Family: The Making of a Southern Cotton Mill World.* Chapel Hill: University of North Carolina Press.

Hamer, Fred. 1967. *Garners Gay.* London: EFDS Publications.

Hammontree, Corrie. 1927. "Ramblry Roy." *Western Kentucky Folklore Archive; Archive of California and Western Folklore.* UCLA.

Hand, Wayland D., Anna Casetta, and Sandra B. Thiederman. 1981. *Popular Beliefs and Superstitions: A Compilation of American Folklore.* 3 vols. Boston: G.K. Hall.

Harker, David. 1985. *Fakesong: The Manufacture of British "Folksong" 1700 to the Present Day.* Milton Keynes, England: Open University Press.

Healy, James N. 1967. *The Mercier Book of Old Irish Street Ballads.* Vol. 1. Cork, Ireland: Mercier Press.

Helm, Alex. 1980. *The English Mummers' Play.* Totowa, N.J.: Rowman & Littlefield.

Henry, Mellinger Edward. 1934. *Songs Sung in the Southern Appalachians.* London: Mitre Press.

———. 1938. *Folk-Songs from the Southern Highlands.* New York: J. J. Augustin.

Hodne, Ørnulf. 1984. *The Types of the Norwegian Folktale.* Oslo: Universitetsforlaget.

Holm, John A. 1988. *Pidgins and Creoles.* Vol. 1: *Theory and Structure.* Cambridge: Cambridge University Press.

Hubbard, Lester A. 1961. *Ballads and Songs from Utah.* Salt Lake City: University of Utah Press.

Hudson, Arthur Palmer. 1926. "Ballads and Songs from Mississippi." *Journal of American Folklore* 39: 93–194.

Huntington, E. G. 1958. *Folksongs from Martha's Vineyard.* Phonodisc. Folkways FA2032.

———. 1990. *Sam Henry's "Songs of the People."* Rev. by Lani Herrmann. Athens: University of Georgia Press.

Hyman, Stanley Edgar. 1957. "The Child Ballad in America: Some Aesthetic Criteria." *Journal of American Folklore* 70: 236–9.

"The Isle of Cloy." Broadside in Cambridge University's Madden Collection, vol. 8, sheet no. 1194; Vaughan Williams Memorial Library Microfilm Collection, reel no. 75.

Janelli, Roger. 1997. Personal communication, July 13.

Jekyll, Walter. [1907] 1966. *Jamaican Song and Story.* New York: Dover Publications.

Journal of the English Folk Dance & Song Society (1932–65).

Journal of the Folk-Song Society. (1899–1931).

Karpeles, Maud. 1967. *Cecil Sharp: His Life and Work.* London: Routledge & Kegan Paul.

———. 1974. *Cecil Sharp's Collection of English Folk Songs.* 2 vols. London: Oxford University Press.

Kennedy, Peter. 1975. *Folksongs of Britain and Ireland.* London: Cassell.

Kidson, Frank, and Alfred Moffat, eds. 1926. *A Garland of English Folk-Song.* London: Ascherberg, Hopwood & Crew.

Krauss, Friedrich S. 1904. *Anthropophyteía.* Vol. 1. Leipzig: Verlag-Aktien-Gesellschaft.

Lamb, Derek. 1958. *She Was Poor but She Was Honest.* Phonodisc. Folkways FW8707.

Laws, G. Malcolm, Jr. 1957. *American Balladry from British Broadsides.* Philadelphia: American Folklore Society.

———. [1964] 1975. *Native American Balladry.* Austin: University of Texas Press.

Leach, MacEdward. 1963. "What Shall We Do with 'Little Matty Groves'?" *Journal of American Folklore* 76: 189–94.

———. 1965. *Folk Ballads and Songs of the Lower Labrador Coast.* Ottawa: National Museum of Canada.

Leach, Maria. 1949–50. *Funk & Wagnalls Standard Dictionary of Folklore, Mythology and Legend.* 2 vols. New York: Funk & Wagnalls.

Legman, Gershon. 1968. *Rationale of the Dirty Joke: An Analysis of Sexual Humor.* First series. New York: Grove Press.

———. 1975. *Rationale of the Dirty Joke: An Analysis of Sexual Humor.* Second series. New York: Bell Publishing.

Ling, Percy, and Geoff Ling. 1977. *The Ling Family: Singing Traditions of a Suffolk Family.* Phonodisc. Topic 12TS292.

Lloyd, A.L. 1967. *Folk Song in England.* London: Lawrence & Wishart.

Lodge, David. 1984. *Small World.* New York: MacMillan.

Logsdon, Guy. 1989. *"The Whorehouse Bells Were Ringing" and Other Songs Cowboys Sing.* Urbana: University of Illinois Press.

Lomax, Alan. 1960. *The Folksongs of North America.* New York: MacMillan.

Lomax, John A. 1910. *Cowboy Songs and Other Frontier Ballads.* New York: MacMillan.

Lomax, John A., and Alan Lomax. [1934] 1994. *American Ballads and Folk Songs.* New York: Dover.

Lomax (John Avery) Family Papers. Center for American History, University of Texas at Austin.

Long, Eleanor R. 1971. *"The Maid" and "The Hangman."* Berkeley and Los Angeles: University of California Press.

———. 1973. "Ballad Singers, Ballad Makers, and Ballad Etiology." *Western Folklore* 32: 225–36.

MacColl, Ewan, and Peggy Seeger. 1977. *Travellers' Songs from England and Scotland.* Knoxville: University of Tennessee Press.

Madden Collection, Cambridge University, from copies in the Vaughan Williams Memorial Library Microfilm Collection, London.

McCarthy, William Bernard. 1990. *The Ballad Matrix: Personality, Milieu, and the Oral Tradition.* Bloomington: Indiana University Press.

McLynn, Frank. 1989. *Crime and Punishment in Eighteenth-Century England.* New York: Routledge.

Meade, Guthrie T., Jr., Collection. Research notes held in University of North Carolina, Chapel Hill, Special Collections.

Meade, Guthrie T., Jr. 1958. "The Sea Crab." *Midwest Folklore* 8: 91–100.

Merricks, Linda. 1988. "Re-Thinking Popular Culture." *History Workshop* 25: 178–82.

Minton, John. 1993. " 'The Waterman Train Wreck': Tracking a Folksong in Deep East Texas." In Green 1993: 37–76.

———. 1995. "That Amazing Texas Version of Child 84, 'Boberick Allen.' " In Porter 1995: 61–75.

Moeran, E. J. 1932. *Six Suffolk Folk-Songs.* London: J. Curwen & Sons.

Moore, Ethel, and Chauncey O. Moore. 1964. *Ballads and Folk Songs of the Southwest.* Norman: University of Oklahoma Press.

Moreira, James. 1997. "Ballad." In Green 1997: 1: 81–4.

Morton, Robin. 1970. *Folksongs Sung in Ulster.* Cork: Mercier Press.

National Library of Ireland Broadside Collection, Dublin.

Newell, William Wells. [1903] 1963. *Games and Songs of American Children.* Second ed. New York: Dover Publications.

Nygard, Holof Olger. 1958. *The Ballad of Heer Halewijn, Its Forms and Variations in Western Europe.* Knoxville: University of Tennessee Press.

O'Lochlainn, Colm. 1965. *More Irish Street Ballads.* Dublin: Three Candles.

Owens, William A. 1976. *Texas Folk Songs.* Second ed. Dallas: Southern Methodist University Press.

Palmer, Roy. 1981. *Everyman's Book of British Ballads.* London: J. M. Dent & Sons.

———. 1983. *Folk Songs Collected by Ralph Vaughan Williams.* London: J. M. Dent & Sons.

———. 1996. " 'Veritable Dunghills': Professor Child and the Ballad." *Folk Music Journal* 7: 155–66.

Parsons, Elsie Clews. 1918. *Folk-Tales of Andros Island, Bahamas.* Memoirs of the American Folk-Lore Society Vol. 13. Lancaster, Pa.: American Folk-Lore Society.

Peacock, Kenneth, ed. 1965. *Songs of the Newfoundland Outports.* 3 vols. Ottawa: National Museum of Canada.

Pettitt, Thomas. 1997. "The Ballad of Tradition: In Pursuit of a Vernacular Aesthetic." In Cheesman and Rieuwerts 1997: 111–23.

Poggiali, Gaetano D., ed. 1815. *Novelle de Franco Sacchetti.* Vol. 22 of *Raccolta de novellieri Italiani.* Milan: Giovanni Silvestri.

Porter, Enid. 1969. *Cambridgeshire Customs and Folklore.* New York: Barnes & Noble.

Porter, James. 1991. "Muddying the Crystal Spring." In *Comparative Musicology and Anthropology of Music.* Ed. Bruno Nettl and Philip V. Bohanon. Chicago: University of Chicago Press, pp. 113–30.

———. 1993. "Convergence, Divergence, and Dialectic in Folksong Paradigms: Critical Directions for Transatlantic Scholarship." *Journal of American Folklore* 106: 61–98.

———. 1996. *Ballads and Boundaries.* Los Angeles: Department of Ethnomusicology and Systematic Musicology, UCLA.

Preston, Cathy Lynn. 1992. " 'Tying the Garter': Representation of the Female Rural Laborer in Seventeenth-, Eighteenth-, and Nineteenth-Century Bawdy Songs." *Journal of American Folklore* 105: 315–41.

———. N.d. *A "Working" KWIC Concordance to Francis James Child's* The English and Scottish Popular Ballads *(1882–1898).* On-line electronic database. <http://www.colorado.edu/ArtsSciences/CCRH/Ballads/ballads.html>

Purslow, Frank. 1972. *The Constant Lovers.* London: EFDS Publications.

Ramsey, Obray. 1958. *Obray Ramsey Sings Folksongs from the Three Laurels.* Phonodisc. Prestige-International 13020.

Randolph, Vance. 1946–50. *Ozark Folksongs.* 4 vols. Columbia: State Historical Society of Missouri.

———. 1992. *Roll Me in Your Arms: "Unprintable" Ozark Folksongs and Folklore.* Vol. 1. Ed. G. Legman. Fayetteville: University of Arkansas Press.

Reeves, James, ed. 1960. *The Everlasting Circle.* London: Heinemann.

Renwick, Roger deV. 1980. *English Folk Poetry: Structure and Meaning.* Philadelphia: University of Pennsylvania Press.

———. 1992. "Folksong Scholarship Today: A Rich Palimpsest." *Journal of Folksong Research* 29: 73–81.

———. 1996. "Folksong." In Brunvand 1996: 292–4.

———. 1997. "Folksong, Lyric." In Green 1997: 2: 343–7.

Richards, Sam. 1982. "Bill Hingston—A Biography in Song." *Oral History* 10: 24–46.

———. 1992. *Sonic Harvest: Towards Musical Democracy.* Charlbury, Oxford: Amber Lane Press.

Ritchie, Jean. 1962. *Precious Memories.* Phonodisc. Folkways FA2427.

———. 1997. *Folk Songs of the Southern Appalachians.* Second ed. Lexington: University Press of Kentucky.

Roberts, Helen H. 1925. "A Study of Folk Song Variants Based on Field Work in Jamaica." *Journal of American Folk-Lore* 38: 149–216.

Roberts, Leonard. 1974. *Sang Branch Settlers: Folksongs and Tales of a Kentucky Mountain Family.* Austin: University of Texas Press.

Rosenberg, Bruce A. 1969. *The Folksongs of Virginia: A Checklist of WPA Holdings at the Alderman Library, University of Virginia.* Charlottesville: University Press of Virginia.

Roud, Steve. 1994a–present. *Broadside Index.* Electronic database. Maresfield, Sussex: Steve Roud.

———. 1994b–present. *Folksong Index.* Electronic database. Maresfield, Sussex: Steve Roud.

Russell, Ian, ed. 1986. *Singer, Song, and Scholar.* Sheffield: Sheffield Academic Press.

Scarborough, Dorothy. [1925] 1963. *On the Trail of Negro Folk-Songs.* Hatboro: Folklore Associates.

———. 1937. *A Songcatcher in Southern Mountains.* New York: Columbia University Press.

Schinan, Jan P. 1957. *The Frank C. Brown Collection of North Carolina Folklore.* Vol. 4: *The Music of the Ballads.* Durham: Duke University Press.

Seeger, Peggy, and Ewan MacColl. 1960. *The Singing Island.* London: Mills Music.

Sharp, Cecil J. 1904–9. *Folk Songs from Somerset.* 5 parts (parts 1–3 with Charles L. Marson). London: Simpkin.

———. 1920. *English Folk Songs.* Selected ed. London: Novello.

———. 1932. *English Folk Songs from the Southern Appalachians.* 2 vols. Ed. Maud Karpeles. London: Oxford University Press.

Sharp, Cecil, Autograph Field Notebook Collection: Folk Words. Vaughan Williams Memorial Library Microfilm Collection, reel 1, London.

Sharp, Cecil, Collection: Folk Words. Vaughan Williams Memorial Library, London.

Sharp, Cecil, File: Informant Database. Vaughan Williams Memorial Library, London.

Shepard, Leslie. 1962. *The Broadside Ballad.* London: Herbert Jenkins.

Shields, Hugh. 1988. *Old Dublin Songs.* Dublin: Folk Music Society of Ireland.

Shuldham-Shaw, Patrick, et al. 1981–97. *The Greig-Duncan Folk Song Collection.* 7 vols. Aberdeen: Aberdeen University Press/Mercat Press.

Thompson, Flora. 1954. *Lark Rise to Candleford.* London: Oxford University Press.

Thompson, Stith. 1966. *Motif-Index of Folk-Literature.* 6 vols. Rev. ed. Bloomington: Indiana University Press.

———. 1964. *The Types of the Folktale.* Second rev. ed. FF Communications no. 184. Helsinki: Suomalainen Tiedeakatemia.

Tocqueville, Alexis, de. 1969. *Democracy in America.* 2 vols. Garden City: Anchor Books, Doubleday & Company.

Toelken, Barre. 1995. *Morning Dew and Roses: Nuance, Metaphor, and Meaning in Folksongs.* Urbana: University of Illinois Press.

Tolman, Albert H. 1916. "Some Songs Traditional in the United States." *Journal of American Folklore* 29:155–97.

UCLA Special Collections, Los Angeles.

University of Virginia Special Collections, Charlottesville.

Vaughan Williams Memorial Library Microfilm Collection, London.

Vaughan Williams, Ralph, and A. L. Lloyd, eds. 1959. *The Penguin Book of English Folk Songs.* Harmondsworth, Middlesex: Penguin Books.

Waltz, Robert B. ("Bob"), and David G. Engle. N.d.–present. *The Traditional Ballad Index: An Annotated Bibliography of the Folk Songs of the English-Speaking World.* On-line electronic database. <http://www.csufresno.edu/folklore/BalladIndexTOC.html>

Warde, R. C. 1852. "Shropshire Ballad." *Notes and Queries.* First series, 6: 118–9.

Warner, Anne. 1984. *Traditional American Folk Songs from the Anne and Frank Warner Collection.* Syracuse: Syracuse University Press.

Webb, Jeff A. 1992. "Cultural Intervention: Helen Creighton's Folksong Broadcasts, 1938–1939." *Canadian Folklore canadien* 14, no. 2: 159–70.

Wesselski, Albert. 1911. *Der Hodscha Nasreddin.* Weimar: Alexander Duncter.

Wilgus, D. K. 1958. "Shooting Fish in a Barrel: The Child Ballad in America." *Journal of American Folklore* 71: 161–4.

———. 1959. *Anglo-American Folksong Scholarship Since 1898.* New Brunswick, N.J.: Rutgers University Press.

———. 1960. "Arch and Gordon." *Kentucky Folklore Record* 6: 51–6.

———. 1964. "The Rationalistic Approach." In Tristram P. Coffin et al., *Folksong and Folksong Scholarship.* Dallas: Southern Methodist University Press, pp. 29–39.

———. 1970. "A Type-Index of Anglo-American Traditional Narrative Songs." *Journal of the Folklore Institute* 7: 161–77.

Wilgus, D. K., and Eleanor Long. 1985. "The 'Blues Ballad' and the Genesis of Style in Traditional Narrative Song." In Carole L. Edwards and Kathleen E. B. Manley 1985: 437–82.

Wilgus, D. K., and Lynwood Montell. 1968. "Clure and Joe Williams: Legend and the Blues Ballad." *Journal of American Folklore* 81: 295–315.

Woods, Frederick. 1983. *The Oxford Book of English Traditional Verse.* Oxford: Oxford University Press.

Yates, Michael. 1980. "Daniel Wyatt Tate: Singer from Fancy Gap." *Folk Music Journal* 4: 3–24.

Young, Katharine, and Barbara A. Babcock. 1994. "Bodylore." *Journal of American Folklore* 107, no. 423.

GENERAL INDEX

Abrahams, Roger D., 4–5, 8, 17–8, 21–3
AIDS, in folktale, 131
American Folklore Society, xvi
Andersen, Flemming G., x, 59
"Anglo-American" and "Anglo/Ameri-
 can," usage of, 153 n 1
Atkinson, David, xi

ballad: blues (genre), 25–6, 31, 33–6;
 broadside (genre), x, 27, 30, 39; Child
 (genre), ix, 19, 21–2, 27, 69, 71–2, 74,
 85, 93; emotional core in, 8, 105, 110;
 as genre, 10, 59, 60–3, 71–2, 76, 78, 83,
 87; incremental repetition in, 64–9. *See
 also* folksong
Baring-Gould, Rev. Sabine, 48, 53
Barnouw, Jeffrey, 125
Barrett, W. A., 158 n 19
Barry, Phillips, 7
Beckwith, Martha Warren, 11, 22
Belden, Henry M., 97, 108
Bell, Mary Lou, 113
Bickerstaff, T. A., 95
bodylore, 137–9
Boswell, James, 125
Bow Street Runners, 27, 43
Broadwood, Lucy E., 7
Bronson, Bertrand Harris, ix, 21
Brunvand, Jan Harold, 59
Buchan, David, x, 15, 59
Bunting, Edward, 154 n 5
Burns, Tom, 8
Burton, Thomas G., 95, 97
Byrne, Moyra, 137

castration, in folklore, 131
Child, Francis James, 59, 72, 91, 93
Churchill, Charles, 119–21, 125–6, 128,
 132, 134–5, 137
"climax of relatives," 6
Coffin, Tristram Potter, ix, 8
Combs, Josiah, 157 n 10
Cox, John Harrington, 97
Cray, Ed, 126
Creolization, 6–25, 153 n 1, 153 n 6. *See
 also* hybridity

Davis, Arthur Kyle, Jr., 104
débat, 74

Elwin, Verrier, 126

Fielding, Henry, 27, 31, 158 n 22
Fielding, Sir John, 27, 31
flyting, 73–4
Folk Music Journal, xi
folklore, as scholarly field, xi–xii, 3, 24
folksong: animal songs, 76; atomism in,
 83–5; boundedness in, 76–8; catalogue
 songs, 60–9; contexts of, 4–5, 49–57;
 cumulation in, 72–3, 82, 89, 90–1;
 determinacy in, 85–6; dialogue in,
 73–6, 89–91; enumeration in, 67, 70,
 73–4, 82, 85, 88, 91; as genre, 49, 59;
 good company, songs of, 89; incrementation in, 64, 69, 71–2; iteration in,
 67–9, 73–5, 81–2, 87–8, 90–1; local
 songs, 65, 83; lying songs, 67, 81, 85;
 lyric songs, 60–2, 72, 76, 78, 83, 85,
 153 n 3; moniker songs, 65; names in,

SINGER INDEX

SONG INDEX